T0320116

The Political Economy of Status

For Eleni

The Political Economy of Status

Superstars, Markets and Culture Change

Theodore Koutsobinas

University of Patras, Greece

Edward Elgar

Cheltenham, UK • Northampton, MA, USA

© Theodore Koutsobinas 2014

All rights reserved. No part of this publication may be reproduced, stored in a retrieval system or transmitted in any form or by any means, electronic, mechanical or photocopying, recording, or otherwise without the prior permission of the publisher.

Published by
Edward Elgar Publishing Limited
The Lypiatts
15 Lansdown Road
Cheltenham
Glos GL50 2JA
UK

Edward Elgar Publishing, Inc.
William Pratt House
9 Dewey Court
Northampton
Massachusetts 01060
USA

A catalogue record for this book
is available from the British Library

Library of Congress Control Number: 2014941549

This book is available electronically in the ElgarOnline.com Economics Subject Collection, E-ISBN 978 1 78347 745 6

ISBN 978 1 78347 744 9

Typeset by Columns Design XML Ltd, Reading
Printed and bound in Great Britain by T.J. International Ltd, Padstow

Contents

Preface   vi
Acknowledgements   ix

1. Introduction: status, superstars and markets   1
2. The economics of status and superstar markets   14
3. The fundamental forces: technology, tastes and values   45
4. Psychology and behavioural forces   58
5. The anthropology of popular culture and identity formation   87
6. The sociology of distinction, superiority and deprivation   106
7. Contentment, politics and the philosophy of superiority   125
8. Alternative policies for positional activities   144
9. The political economy of status and culture change policy   168

Appendix: table and figures   187
Notes   192
References   209
Index   239

Preface

The period of Great Moderation, roughly from the early 1980s until the financial crisis of 2007–2008, was a defining moment of history, in which self-interest, business and consumer optimism thrived in a commercialized era of contentment. The media, the financial world, the stock market with companies, mainly from the information technology sector, were glamourized and media superstars and celebrities like Donald Trump and Madonna were widely seen as symbols of this period. In the midst of financial and housing bubbles, uncertainty was considered impossible constraining well-informed analysis to mere what-if questions. 'Can it happen again?' Hyman Minsky asked thirty years ago regarding the prospect of a severe economic crisis, which eventually materialized with the Great Recession.

The glamourized world of contentment was certainly not a new phenomenon. John Kenneth Galbraith warned in his influential books, *The Affluent Society* and *The Culture of Contentment*, that contentment relates closely to affluence and its attitudes cherishing the earlier ideas of Thornstein Veblen on the behaviour of the leisure class. More than a century ago in his masterpiece *The Theory of Leisure Class*, Thornstein Veblen utilized the notion of *conspicuous consumption* to analyse the preoccupation of the rich with conspicuous consumption as a display of status and superiority.

However, contentment is not confined only to the superrich as middle-class individuals, even those from its lower social groups, have indulged in consumption excesses for expensive goods and services relative to their underlying incomes. In addition, they have become eager to pursue occupation choices, which are highly competitive in order to become rich instantly. During the Great Moderation, social and cultural norms were strikingly different from the turbulent 1960s and 1970s, when concerns for social equity and social change were popular. But in the subsequent years of glamourized contentment, calls for social and cultural change to address urgent issues of income inequality and social injustice had little influence. People have been caught in the seductive world of commercialism fuelled by the explosion of media, popular culture trends and the lives of media superstars. Many individuals experienced an enormous saturation of images and symbols in diverse aspects of their social life rendering them powerless.

The phrase: 'sell the *sizzle, not the steak*', which became popular in the 1980s, was the epitome of modern sales, marketing and advertisement. Economic change is not only a matter of mechanical markets. The sustainability of free-market economies depends also on the human condition and its psychological tendencies to seek the sizzle of the glamourized world of contentment through exposure to status goods and superstar opportunities. On the basis of this condition, the present volume develops an alternative behavioural companion to a burgeoning literature on economic issues such as inequality and unemployment. This happens because although status matters more to the privileged, poorer latecomers are hurt more from being involved in the excesses of superstar markets.

Fortunately, the explosion of financial markets during the last three decades allowed economists to grasp the importance of principles of human psychology and how they relate to economic realities. The new field of behavioural economics has grown immensely challenging the dominance of traditional wisdom in different areas. In this creative milieu, novel ideas were cultivated and tested empirically. One such idea was Sherwin Rosen's *superstar hypothesis*, upon which a great literature was developed. Subsequently, Robert Frank focused on the impact of professional superstars and the social cost of luxury consumption, and proposed the idea of a progressive consumption tax on status goods and services to facilitate an adjustment towards equality without impairing economic prosperity. This proposal has been opposed fiercely by the neoliberal establishment.

While this form of policy faces obstacles, a supplementary and more practical option is to develop distributive policies for those groups of individuals, who are more exposed to the costs of overconsumption of status goods and services and of their overexposure to the tournament characteristics of superstar markets. This strategy is especially effective within a framework of culture change policies, which are already implemented in the European Union in sectors such as health, education and the environment.

The title of this book describes the process of addressing political economy concerns on status and superstars and relating them with policies of culture change. My approach is pluralist and interdisciplinary, drawing insights from diverse social disciplines and schools of thought. The rich microeconomic evidence from behavioural economics is enhanced by human psychology research and relates to ideas from sociology, anthropology and philosophy, which offer valuable insights into social issues and their political dynamics. Thus the book offers an

The political economy of status

added impetus to the expansive behavioural dimension of mainstream economics by pursuing behavioural economics more generally into other disciplines including sociology. In this vein, the 'return to Veblen' serves as a very appropriate line for taking the broadening of the behavioural approach forward.

This pluralist approach is advantageous because it unveils overlooked dynamics and enriches the analysis concerning the interplay between markets and its incentives, human psychology, visual symbols, social costs and inequality towards a direction that standard economics with its technical orientations has not managed to produce. Nevertheless, the message is an optimistic one: properly fine-tuned culture change policies can effectively address the social costs of status and superstar markets and circumvent policy inertia regarding the implementation of a progressive consumption tax. In doing so, these interventions can empower people to become socially conscious, to realize the sizzle of authentic lifestyles and to develop successfully their talents.

Acknowledgements

My work on the project began in the late 1990s. I returned to the United States to conduct post-doctoral research under a NATO fellowship at Cornell University. The late Robert Heilbroner, who was one of my mentors during my doctoral studies at the New School for Social Research in New York, was aware of my interest on issues of contemporary social and culture change from various doctoral workshops and encouraged me to examine the idea of positional markets and the intellectual contribution of Robert Frank. Over the years and as my research was expanding, I presented my work in conferences and workshops. I benefited from comments offered by participants at the International Conference on Humanities in Rhodes, Greece and the SCEME Workshop on Culture and Economic Policy, which took place in the University of Stirling, UK and I developed working papers for possible publication.

One special debt of gratitude is to Matt Pittman and Katy Roper, of Edward Elgar Publishing, who have provided me with support and guidance to complete this book. I am especially grateful to Wilfred Dolfsma, for valuable comments on several drafts of a working paper, which was part of an earlier manuscript. I am also grateful to Sheila Dow for comments and encouragement on a working paper, which was part of an earlier draft and to Malcolm Sawyer for his encouragement on my book proposal. I am greatly indebted also to an anonymous referee of the nearly completed manuscript in 2013. Overall, suggestions helped me to improve and clarify my presentation, for which I remain solely responsible, including any errors and omissions.

My pluralist approach to cultural political economy and/or to post-Keynesian openness to behavioural economics has been benefited by communication and discussions with Clas Wihlborg, Sheila Dow, John King, Philip Arestis, Gary Dymski, Matthias Klaes, Tony Lawson, Steven Pressman, Gary Mongiovi, Korkut Erturk, John Davis, and earlier, with John Eatwell, Edward Nell and Tom Palley. The usual disclaimers apply. I am grateful also to Nancy Remoundou, Fotini Papantoniou, Nancy Boubouli and Katerina Deiveki for administrative assistance during earlier stages of this project.

My wife Eleni Bellou has made interesting and valuable observations on realities and paradoxes of consumer markets. I would like to thank her especially for her encouragement and patience during periods of intensive writing. Finally, my very special thanks go to my mother, Eleni, and my father, Thomas, who as a philomath impressed upon me the significance of historical, cultural and psychological experiences since antiquity in understanding the nature of economic and political processes.

1. Introduction: status, superstars and markets

THE CONSUMPTION OF STATUS GOODS AND THE GROWTH OF TOP EARNERS

One important aspect of modern life is that middle-class individuals participate in Veblenian consumption excesses for status goods and have become more willing to be involved in occupational markets, which are monetarily rewarding but risky. These markets are characterized by tournament dynamics, which exhibit greater failure rates and produce highly rewarded and visible professionals or superstars. Consumption excesses were in the past common only among members of the upper class but today they are evident in the behaviour of individuals from the middle class and even from the working class.

Overconsumption does not result only in greater levels of aggregate demand but causes higher sales for highly priced goods and services. After all, today there is an abundance of expensive consumption goods and services to choose from. Expensive watches, summer vacations to Ibiza, Florida, the Caribbean islands and other exotic destinations, brand clothing such as Abercrombie and Fitch or Benetton, gourmet dinners at fancy restaurants are all examples of expensive goods and services, which contribute to a different lifestyle from the average main-street or neighbourhood outlet experience. Such indulgences have now become an indispensable part of life for many. In addition, it is evident that buying expensive cars or SUVs (sports utility vehicles), bigger or new houses in the suburbs and often a summer house or a holiday home are not just dreams for the distant future. Such considerable household expenses for durable goods are quite common for middle-class individuals and families today. Thus the emergence of lifestyle consumption as an important aspect of contemporary life cannot be easily ignored.

The middle class follows a variety of consumption patterns that are influenced by new lifestyle preferences. However, the origin of those preferences is not arbitrary. On many occasions, these preferences are similar to the trends followed by the superrich in various forms of their consumption such as for prime housing locations or luxury cars. Excessive lifestyle consumption for the middle class relates to what has been labelled in the past as *conspicuous consumption*. This term, which was introduced by Thornstein Veblen at the turn of the nineteenth to the twentieth century, was not confined only to the excesses of the superrich at that time. Veblen was aware that excess consumption in general relates to the self-worth of the consumers. He argued that feelings of inferiority and dishonour are generally associated with the failure to consume.[1]

The strength of conspicuous consumption nowadays is caused by objective factors such as the liberalization of the credit system and the growth in earnings. This form of consumption is enjoyed not only by individuals who already belong to the upper classes, but also by the growing numbers of professionals in different occupations such as, dentists, lawyers, actors, media personalities, consultants, sports players and others. In addition, the growth in earnings for the middle class has surely contributed to conspicuous consumption. A considerable share of the excessive consumption not only of the elite but also of the middle class, is directed towards positional or status goods. These goods are valued better the more advantageously they compare with the items consumed by others.[2]

Various terms have been attributed at different times to describe the goods and services that are influenced by these behavioural patterns and forces. The most common definitions are status or positional goods and the segments of the markets in which they are traded are called status or positional markets, which are characterized by relative comparison concerns. Status goods and services appear in homogeneous markets when people's preference for buying them increases as a direct function of their price. The underlying motivation for such a preference is often the desire of individuals to acquire distinction. In heterogeneous markets, status goods and services are different from standard items because they are valued not according to their absolute properties, but according to how they compare with the goods or services consumed by others.

The high growth in earnings materializes also because the market today attributes a higher value on the services of highly visible top performers, the superstars in those occupations. However, the markets that produce famous highly paid performers, the markets of superstars are different than traditional markets. High visibility is a quality that makes top performers realize earnings that are much greater than the compensation expected from their absolute performance or contribution at work. The number of highly paid workers has increased rapidly even as the average white-collar job has been barely keeping up with inflation. In 2002, the size of the annual earnings in the USA, which corresponded to the top 1 per cent of the population in terms of income was about US$286 000. By 2011, according to the US Internal Revenue Service, the size of the annual earnings to make it into the top 1 per cent of the population in terms of income skyrocketed to around US$506 000. Obviously, those professionals were members of a special elite social group, which mainly included doctors, lawyers, executives and managers, sales supervisors and representatives, accountants, consultants as well as arts and entertainment professionals including writers, actors, musicians, artists and athletes.

This phenomenon has received considerable attention during the past three decades following the seminal work of Rosen on superstars.[3] Subsequently, Frank and Cook introduced in the context of labour markets the concept of 'winner-take-all' markets, which are one of the outcomes associated with the advent of the super high earnings for top performers. Frank and Cook's research utilizes a microeconomic analysis, which emphasizes the rewards received by those top professionals for their relative advantage in performance. This view contradicts the traditional economic wisdom, in which rewards are the result of absolute performance of workers. In addition, this framework differs considerably from the traditional static economic analysis because it uses findings from behavioural approaches such as social psychology in a way that compares to rational behaviour. Later on, the examination of the superstar phenomenon in labour markers was enhanced by Frank's analysis of luxury consumption. In this analysis, three important distortions that motivate individuals to be involved in positional consumption are identified: advertising, adaptation and the attractiveness of luxury per se.

However, in the mainly mainstream approaches on status and superstars, positional consumption is dealt with largely within a framework that is highly compatible with rational behaviour and policies are confined to general horizontal public programmes, which raise welfare for all. The design of social policies that provide greater value to the underprivileged is absent. Subsequent attempts to introduce inequality in the analysis are highly constrained by the fact that the proposition of horizontal social policy measures is maintained.[4] Instead, a focus on a behavioural framework could explain better the nature of distortion in the endogenous formation of preferences in status markets and help design appropriate social policies with respect to status and superstar markets, which address better the issue of inequality. These policies respond to the fact that although the rich have stronger incentives to be involved in activities of superstar markets, it is the poorer that experience greater financial losses relative to their incomes and substantial human distress from their participation in status tournaments.

SUPERSTARS, MARKETS AND BEHAVIOURAL FORCES

The consumption of status goods and services reflects lifestyle preferences that to a great extent involve discriminatory judgement. Besides objective factors such as the increase in earnings, conspicuous consumption is attributed also to behavioural forces that influence preferences. Specific consumption preferences and lifestyle practices reflect different occupations and class fractions. In these consumption practices, the object of purchasing is to appropriate distinction, that is, to gain status through signalling the high exchange value of the purchased consumption goods or services. Lifestyle preferences and tastes are critical for understanding whether a product can be classified to the special group of commodities that reflect status. In modern times, the formation of lifestyle preferences is determined to a great extent by behavioural forces through the market for culture, especially popular culture. This market includes books, magazines, movies, concerts, sporting events and television programmes. The value of these media arises from the fact that they help shape lifestyle tastes and determine which items are the status goods. The formation of preferences takes place through an individual internalization process, which involves the validation of needs such as self-perception and self-worth. Other psychological forces that are associated with economic activity such as the motive to protect one's own territory are also responsible for the contemporary intensification of the struggle to 'keep up with the Joneses', the phenomenon of relative social competition.

There are evidently behavioural forces, which are inconsistent with rational choice and influence activities that take place in status or positional markets. Those markets are heavily shaped by the activities of an elite group of people. This elite group may include superstars, who are famous and are often viewed as role models, command high fees for their services and offer high-quality services in their profession, and celebrities, who are visible people in the media. The term of superstar markets will be used interchangeably with positional or status markets to emphasize the impact of media visibility attributed to superstars in their occupations and to celebrities, who are famous individuals but are not necessarily successful. Status markets are facilitated by a portion of superstar markets and interface with them, resulting in augmented conspicuous consumption, wrong occupational choices and career inertia.

The trends established by superstars are emulated usually by top-tier consumers, that is, rich consumers. This creates status benchmarks for the following tiers of consumers including the lower middle class. Thus status markets exhibit a meaning, which is much broader than the one associated with the purchase of status goods and services alone. This expansion happens because they fully incorporate the impact of behavioural forces and media visibility across superstars, top-tier consumers and the lower social strata in the society. The enhancement provides a social dimension to the analysis of status markets.

For this reason also, the analysis is extended beyond the impact of immediate social comparison at work or in the neighbourhood. Although real-world proximity is an important consideration (that is, to neighbours, co-workers, past classmates and so on), the variability of social identity across individuals is so broad that positional concerns are often expressed in diverse and creative ways that contradict narrow ranking calculations. Superstar markets are generated in segments of consumption and labour markets, in which individual behaviour is influenced endogenously not only by the mere behaviour of other members of the social group in which they belong, such as neighbours and colleagues at work, but also by the strategic processes of identification with the most prominent agents across different occupations, the superstars. These processes are strategic because individuals choose from a large number of superstars to identify with in order to develop a particular sense of social identity. These processes have an impact on individual consumption and occupational choices since the goods or the services associated with the superstars exhibit the highest status or positionality. Thus superstar markets emerge not only because people respond to objective economic motives, but also because they simply hold inflated expectations due to the impact of behavioural processes. The individual propensity to develop an exaggerated social identity beyond one's own resources relates to the utilization as a strategic benchmark of the lifestyles of the most visible and prominent agents, the superstars. Thus the superstars constitute a strategic dominant group in social networks that conveys top status so that positional decision-making of the vast majority of consumers is socially influenced by their signals. This refines the theory of positional markets from a theory of relative concerns to a broader theory of social distinction and discrimination.

Even before capitalism existed, human history was full of economic and social events that arose by the desire to validate an advantage in relative social competition. Today, in remote agricultural villages some form of relative social competition exists by means of material possessions. But what constitutes a remarkable difference from the past is the almost epic advent of the lifestyles of superstars in our mundane everyday life with the aid of new media technologies and the sensational experiences that the latter produce not only for the top-tier but also for the bottom-tier consumers. The analysis of these markets not in narrow economic terms but more broadly in psychological, anthropological or even philosophical terms illustrates that the strongest motive to participate in these markets is not merely relative comparison but the possibility to touch the sunshine or to want the moon as Keynes once claimed observing the individual expectations of financial investors.[5] By analogy to Greek mythology, whereas by becoming heroes people tried to reach the status of gods, the strategic contemporary individual psychological propensity in superstar markets is to emulate some of the status qualities of superstars. Thus the human environment is dominated by new technology and the media visibility that it offers to the most successful professionals, the superstars. The individual internalization of this phenomenon produces the strongest psychological incentive to those willing to participate in markets characterized by tournament forces and relative comparisons. People compare themselves with the 'Joneses' today more than in the past because they are more exposed to what constitutes the ultimate benchmark of relative social competition, the lifestyles and the privileges of the superstars, the virtual Joneses. From a social economy perspective, a valuable area of study is how members of the top class (in terms of income) become first comers in adopting trends from superstars and celebrities. The presence of this top-tier group of consumers of positional goods and services explains the social link between superstars and next-comers in the queue, the Joneses. In such a framework, it is possible to discuss status markets in terms of social groups.

Without a thorough understanding of this mechanism the successful assessment of this phenomenon and the design of appropriate policies can eventually prove ineffective. This phenomenon has become pervasive not only because people seek to match their positional standings to relatives, colleagues, neighbours or friends. Superstars and celebrities are in many ways more useful objects in processes of social competition than people such as neighbours or friends. Since the superstars and celebrities are very well-known and information about them is easier to find and be shared, superstars are like neighbours.[6] Thus people have developed high expectations of not wanting to be left behind or deprived by what constitutes the ultimate standards as set by superstars' performances and attitudes.

To sum up, in essence the phenomenon of status and superstar markets is expressed through conspicuous consumption, relative social competition and participation in highly rewarding labour markets characterized by risky tournament processes. On the demand side, the relative social competition is associated with the consumption by households of distinctive goods and services. On the supply side, these markets are associated with the willingness of households to compete in occupations, which exhibit tournament processes and produce highly visible top earners. Thus visibility is a common denominator in the operation of these markets and relative social competition.

The impact of positional activities is damaging not only because it reduces welfare but also because it produces inequality and relative deprivation. There is in fact a greater burden for lower middle-class individuals and families. When they participate in positional activities the less financially comfortable end up in a worse position. For example, they face greater income losses relative to the privileged, higher levels of financial obligations relative to their income, poorer access to information relative to the contented and take greater risks when it comes to important occupational and investment decisions.

ALTERNATIVE POLICIES AND STATUS MARKETS

These effects constitute ultimately a high social cost, which can be mitigated through the development of specific policies. In connection to policy formulation, Frank proposes a form of a progressive consumption tax that can potentially support the finance of several horizontal social programmes. These include, for example, better quality standards, better pay for teachers and community workers, and better maintenance of infrastructure. However, the issue of distribution of welfare benefits across different income groups is not addressed in this approach. Thus a substantive area for policy intervention remains open especially if one considers that the distribution impact from government spending has been effective.

The analysis that supports the proposal of the progressive consumption tax stands in between traditional economic analysis, which emphasizes the effectiveness of free markets and alternative progressive approaches, which support state intervention. The first traditional strand includes advocates of orthodox economic theory while the progressive group consists of Keynesians, who support the European social model and post-Keynesians, institutionalists in Veblen's and Galbraith's tradition, Marxists and other radical thinkers. Frank's framework is based on Rosen's seminal work on micro-foundations such as his tournament theory.[7] Therefore, it stands on the margin of neoclassical equilibrium analysis and non-neoclassical approaches and their presumptions. For example, according to the Austrian school agents, entrepreneurs do have indefinite preferences while in the post-Keynesian approach portfolio investors face unexpected opportunities.[8] Still, those non-neoclassical approaches provide certain interesting insights. For example, in post-Keynesian economics, theorists have sought an alternative to neoclassical choice theory by turning to Maslow's hierarchy of needs.[9] Furthermore, the social theory of Bourdieu has been proposed as an alternative to Maslow's approach, providing the basis for a social critique of consumerism and an alternative evolutionary theory of consumption.[10] This is essentially a class-based approach in which particular importance is attributed to the role of cultural capital. For those at the bottom of the social hierarchy, culture has a powerful influence over individual expenditure patterns. However, those with higher cultural capital temper their consumption of luxury goods in pursuit of greater status. Thus lifestyles and motives can be better identified across the social hierarchy through instrumental concepts such as, for example, Bourdieu's *habitus* and through the separation between the cultural and economic capital held by individuals.[11]

SOCIO-ECONOMICS AND THE POLITICAL ECONOMY OF CULTURE CHANGE

The interest in conspicuous consumption and status markets is not confined only to alternative approaches within the field of pure economics. There is also a large and mainly sociological literature in culture studies that spans from American pragmatism to approaches of French radical sociologists such as Baudrillard, Lyotard and Bourdieu. In the USA, one of the most representative radical sociologists on this issue is Jameson. These thinkers approach the phenomenon of excess consumption and status markets on the basis of the notion of post-modernism. According to this approach, the post-modern era is characterized by an expansion of culture throughout the social domain, to the point at which everything becomes cultural. Those accounts are predominantly of a Marxist orientation and exhibit the same tendency towards emphasizing the inflation of culture. However, they provide a useful link, ignored largely in economic analysis, between culture, media, and the symbols embedded in positional goods of technology and media that provide an 'ecstasy of communication'. This causes the phenomenon of hyperreality where it is no longer possible to distinguish the imaginary from the real. The everyday experience is full of signs, distinctive poses and symbolic meaning. The culture of symbols is expressed by lifestyle preferences and consumption choices that show our own discriminatory judgements of taste to others. In this respect, the symbolism is present not only in the design of the production and marketing processes but also in the demand for goods and services. According to this type of analysis, the symbolic associations of goods can be utilized to emphasize differences in life-style, which demarcate social as well as class relationships. Thus the phenomenon of superstar markets does not entail solely economic forces such as the impact of earnings growth and technology but also behavioural considerations including the impact of endogenous preferences or meta-preferences in today's virtual world. The analysis that focuses on sociological patterns and philosophical principles makes, as we will see in the following chapters, a convincing case for the role of social discrimination and conflict in status markets, a factor that is overlooked in the economics of 'winner-take-all' society. However, the analysis of European sociological tradition on post-modernism lacks the wealth of economic and psychological empirical evidence associated with the analysis of status markets from an economic viewpoint. As a consequence, it has not yet produced a framework for the formation of concrete policy measures beyond concerns of solidarity and partisanship. The purpose of the present volume therefore is to develop a comprehensive political economy of status markets, in which superstars act as powerful facilitators and to relate it to policies of culture change, which integrates the conclusions from the sociological examination of post-modernism regarding the cultural aspects of social discrimination and conflict with the economic evidence on positional activities.

The method that is followed here is socio-economic in character.[12] Socio-economics is a method that was supported more notably by worldly philosophers such as Weber, Schumpeter and Lowe in the past.[13] Since the 1960s, this approach was endorsed by thinkers such as Etzioni, Sen, Simon, Heilbroner and Kahneman. Socio-economics involves the fulfilment of certain conditions such as the pluralism in approaching economic problems and the open interface between economics and other social sciences.[14] There is an emphasis also on dealing with substantive issues associated with the importance of culture and the complexity of human behaviour, drawing similarities to behavioural economics. Although the term socio-economics in its revival is a relatively new term, there is a rapidly growing number of scholars especially in the USA, who consider themselves socio-economists and who contribute to a growing literature in new journals and books that challenge traditional economic thought.

If it was only a matter of pure economics, superstar markets could be explained by factors such as the impact of new technologies that make possible massive economies of scale and the forces of supply and demand. Actually, most economic explanations of the superstar hypothesis, including those of Rosen, Adler and Pesendorfer, focus on the effects of supply-side forces. In this book, the emphasis is on research evidence, which restores the balance because it analyses demand-side effects. Behavioural analysis is especially valuable in this connection because it explains demand-side processes.

The extension of pure economic notions into the realm of society or culture such as the idea of cultural capital and the impact of behavioural forces, allows the consideration of rich evidence from social sciences for the study of superstar markets that is broader than what is defined by traditional economic boundaries. For example, psychological analysis explains meta-preferences while sociological inquiry highlights the role of relative deprivation across different groups of people. Through anthropology, lifestyles and poses of distinction are comprehended as part of individual cultural capital. Political analysis explains effectively the relation between signalling, power and distribution. Philosophical discourse is essential for understanding better the individual need for distinction across different classes. To sum up, the rich evidence from social sciences enriches the economic analysis of positional concerns at a microeconomic level.

THE DESIGN OF NEW POLICIES AND CULTURE CHANGE IN A POLITICAL ECONOMY FRAMEWORK

The integration of diverse social disciplines leads to insights, conclusions and policy measures that differ from those proposed within the boundaries of standard economics. For example, one important conclusion of the present study is that policy measures should not be confined to the support of social programmes through horizontal measures but should deliver value to those who are at greater disadvantage because of the impact of positional concerns. Therefore, the approach followed here is a cultural political economy framework, which proposes a correction in the form of a redistribution policy. This form of intervention aims at the reduction of economic and social imbalances, which are caused by status markets.

For example, policies can have alternative forms and objectives. They can be designed to support individual motivation, culture change, regulation, monetary rewards and so on. These alternative forms of policies are supported by different analytical concerns. Policies which focus on individual motivation do exhibit a psychological dimension. Monetary and fiscal policies are economic in nature, regulation policies are influenced heavily by political factors and culture change policies relate mostly to sociological, anthropological and philosophical considerations. Thus the design of suitable policies mirrors the socio-economic nature of the analysis.

Moreover, as it will be shown in the last chapter of the book, quite often there is interdependence between different categories of economic policies such as taxation, redistribution, regulation and culture change policy. For example, cultural intervention in the form of cultural capital development influences individual behaviour through public programmes that emphasize creativity, productivity and real-life focus at the expense of positional activities and can be financed by the proceeds obtained by the imposition of a progressive consumption tax. Furthermore, culture change policies rely on the political commitment to relate positional waste with redistributive policies, moral leadership and the acknowledgement that culture change and institutional measures can indeed improve social welfare.

CULTURE CHANGE AND CULTURAL POLITICAL ECONOMY

The political economy of status, superstars and culture change is situated within a broader culture economy, or cultural political economy framework. These accounts provide an interdisciplinary area, which focuses on interactive themes of conventional disciplines and combines approaches to produce enhanced accounts to aid the better understanding of the complexities of the real world. As a result, it helps overcome the constraints imposed by the methods utilized in separate disciplines as is the case, for example, with rational models in economics, in which the application of the principle of complete information is pervasive. In contrast, the framework of culture economy or cultural political economy is pluralist because it is open to all disciplines. More precisely, with regard to the study of status and superstars, I develop an extensive analysis utilizing the rich evidence produced by eclectic economic and mainly behavioural analysis and compelling insights from other disciplines such as psychology, sociology and anthropology to produce open, innovative and pragmatic accounts on this issue. A key feature of this socio-economic expansion is that it highlights the political economy dimensions of positional activities and the role of distribution among different social groups, which belong in different social classes.

There is a divergence of opinions about the precise identity of culture economy, or cultural political economy. The political economy of status relates to a broader literature, which includes several alternative attempts to bring forth the importance of culture in economic analysis. These alternative approaches investigate substantive areas that include, non-exhaustively, cultural dimensions of economy, cultural production, cultural anthropology aspects of economy, political economy of culture, culturalization of the economy, cultural aspects of everyday life, cultural theory and policy, cultural norms, economics of habits and conventions, and mainly Marxist accounts of cultural political economy.[15] There are also evidently other research projects, which highlight the relation between economics and culture.

As I mentioned above, the distributive shares and the underlying conflicts of social groups play an important role and, therefore, the analysis in the present book uses a political economy methodology. However, this account differs from cultural political economy approaches, which adopt Marxism as offering a totalizing perspective on social relations, although it is pluralist and draws important insights from several sources of Marxist origin. More specifically, I envisage cultural political economy in a broader sense to include not only class or social conflict but also other types of conflict of cultural origin such as those embedded in economic, social, cultural and religious systems and their underlying social norms. Thus, the political economy approach followed here is situated within a broader spectrum of conflict theories because it implicitly acknowledges that market economies and liberal or social democracies have succeeded relative to Marxist-related planned modes of social systems and the Soviet experience with regard to wealth creation, improved economic and social conditions, liberal institutions and freedom of expression.

CONCLUDING REMARKS

Overall, the book develops a political economy theory of status, superstars and culture change. Through its political economy approach, the book enhances in a contemporary context the institutional tradition of Galbraith and Veblen by analysing new evidence from socio-economic (interdisciplinary) research. This approach introduces a new term, status and superstar markets, which refers to segments of consumption and labour markets. In these segments, individual behaviour is influenced endogenously through the media by relative comparisons, strategic considerations and processes of identification with the most prominent and visible agents in positional markets. Visibility and media play an important role because they provide their own context, which feeds behavioural (as opposed to rational) aspirations. Technologies extend beyond immediate comparisons such as catching-up with the Joneses. The methodology is based on evidence from behavioural economics, which uses psychological insights rather than rational choice. Behavioural analysis describes specific psychological processes, which show how expectations and aspirations are determined endogenously (short termism, anchoring, cognitive biases, affective and automatic identification, behavioural polarization, deprivation processes, envy and so on) so that rational choice is severely bounded. Psychological analysis explains complex strategic dynamics of emulation in terms of predominantly top-down emulation. Top-tier and bottom-tier consumers in status and superstar markets are associated with social classes bringing to the surface the dynamics of polarization in positional markets and relating it to social inequality and to political economy. The middle class experiences relative deprivation both financially and psychologically in reference to the top social groups when it participates in positional markets. I conclude with effective social policy measures and institutional interventions, situated within a culture change policy, which alleviates social inequalities. While the analysis favours Frank's progressive consumption tax, it develops a cultural capital specificity approach which combines culture change, regulation and taxation.

In the last chapter of the book, the present analysis concludes with social policies for policy-makers that extend beyond the analysis of traditional monetary rewards and costs. Specific policies are identified which correspond to factor-specific cultural capital profiles. Unlike approaches that focus on horizontal programmes, I propose a redistributive culture change policy for different specificities such as the urban community, the youth, the family, the workplace and so on.

To sum up, this book explains how behind the growth of media lies the spread of status and superstar markets, a conceptual framework in which status signals of superstars amplify positional concerns for all, distort the aspirations of the middle class and cause relative deprivation. Building on themes first identified in the institutional tradition by Veblen and Galbraith and supported by modern-day institutionalists, post-Keynesians and political economists, I analyse extensively evidence from behavioural economics and essential modern interdisciplinary research, which contributes constructively to a new genre of economic analysis. The political economy of status and the proposals for culture change compel us to consider seriously effective redistributive public policy proposals targeted to assist the underprivileged and to review the cultural rules for our society.

2. The economics of status and superstar markets

INTRODUCTION

The intensification of competition and the impact of status markets constitute now a global phenomenon, which is influenced by complex forces. The orthodox thought in economic analysis does not provide the analytical tools for an adequate understanding of this process. There are various factors and complex interlinkages to be considered, which involve the emergence of new services, the influence of information technology, television, social media, globalization and culture change. Therefore, the analysis of status markets can be enriched with assumptions that are not viewed as fundamental in traditional economic thought. For example, the marginal approach which views technological progress, tastes or preferences and institutions as given must be superseded by an analysis that allows for the impact of changes in these forces. In addition, since status markets are highly influenced by rapid changes in technological progress, preference shifts and institutional reform, it is necessary to expand the area of study. This involves the examination of various subjective and institutional factors and the overturn of standard concepts in traditional economic analysis such as, for example, the assumption of diminishing returns to scale. Therefore, from an economist's perspective, an essential task is to examine status markets through an eclectic approach, which facilitates the integration of different forces and perspectives.

What follows is the development of an economic framework that meets these criteria. More precisely, the framework developed in this chapter allows for the influence of both objective and subjective factors. On the one hand, the first group emphasizes the role of visible economic forces such as relative monetary rewards, technology, earnings and wealth in producing superstars in various occupations. On the other hand, I take into account subjective factors such as the emergence of endogenous preferences due to psychological propensities including the validation of self-esteem, which is influenced by forces such as media, advertisement and popular culture. This explains positional competition strategies by

14

individual agents, in which the superstars, that is, highly visible and successful professionals, are envisaged as a measure of comparison and emulation. The positional behaviour is influenced heavily by the role of culture and its capacity to confer distinction and to signal competence and supremacy to economic agents. Yet as we will see in this chapter, this process produces ineffective economic outcomes. The role of distribution between different social groups or classes turns out to be an essential component of the analysis. This important factor will help us understand the various aspects of economic decision-making related to status and the activities of superstars.

I   ECONOMIC FORCES, SUPERSTARS AND SYMBOLIC ANALYSTS

Relative Rewards and Mass Markets

The conventional economic theory cannot be easily applied in superstar market economies. This happens because a fundamental characteristic of the tournament operation of the superstar system is the process of rewarding participants by means of their relative performance instead of compensating their absolute performance.[1] This constitutes the essence of the *superstar* hypothesis. For Rosen, superstars are relatively small numbers of people, who earn enormous amounts of money and dominate the activities in which they engage. In essence, what is rewarded is the difference in performance, or the value added in performance of a worker relative to another. Relative differences are important not only in labour markets but in commodities and services as well. Positional goods and services are different because their value depends on their rankings in conferring advantage when they are compared to substitutes. Therefore, positionality represents the degree to which value depends on the relative position of goods and services.[2] What matters is not the absolute use-value of a good or a service but the distinction it signifies to the buyer relative to others. Most people think of compensation as a reward of absolute performance with respect to a duty, function or time. In addition, economists conventionally assume that reward depends only on absolute performance. Yet what we experience in superstar markets is that a small variation in talent or effort causes frequently substantial differences in success in mass markets and, eventually, in incomes.[3] Many analysts have recognized now the fact that in superstar markets a small number of people take the vast majority of rewards.

The rising importance of the relative-performance premium of super-star markets is evident when we consider the influence of relative performance on careers. There is a 'path dependency' in the careers of many individuals in different occupations. Graduates of the best colleges are more likely to study in the best graduate programmes than others who lack only marginally in talent or skills.[4] Afterwards, some of the best graduate schools such as Harvard or Stanford generate the numbers of MBA executives, the lawyers and the doctors who have much better chances than their peers to obtain high-profile positions in their profession.[5] This is also true for other careers such as those of Ph.D. researchers and academics.

Supply and Economies of Scale

The effect of relative performance in mass markets is not of course the only cause of superstar markets. On many occasions, the phenomenon of superstar markets is associated with the distribution of the products and services. For example, the services of the best professionals today are frequently reproduced at low additional cost with the aid of media and new information technology. This supply-side effect here is a fundamental force that underlies the presence of superstar markets.

Today people witness the elimination of the obstacles that once prevented the best professionals from accessing wider markets. For example, in the music industry the most important force was the appearance of popular recorded music, but it was the advances in technologies with regard to physical production that were critical for the development of this market. Similar improvements have been made also in other sectors with the support of developments in media and information technology. In this environment, there are substantial economies of scale in the production or distribution of services. Many producers and merchants view this aspect of the market as being highly profitable and are motivated to capture further these opportunities. Yet in the very end, only a few products, services, or professionals tend to dominate the markets. This reflects the tournament quality of superstar markets.

In this environment, a single act or decision involves a greater burden of responsibility. Besides the impact of technology and media, this factor explains why superstar markets are associated with big corporations. The decisions of the executives of those institutions are most likely to influence a great number of people. When a key executive makes a mistake, this is at the cost of all workers, consumers and investors that are involved. The top-notch executive who is responsible for an important decision carries a deep responsibility. The burden of responsibility is immense in professions, in which uncertainty is greater.[6] This variation is reflected in the executive's compensation because a small differentiation in a single decision can cause a substantially different outcome. This factor leads to massive differences in monetary rewards and exceptionally high salaries for the executives.

Earnings Growth and Wealth

Superstar markets cause a solid change in the categories of incomes that are observed today in the economic process. Yet an important demand-led source of superstar markets relates to the concentration of great wealth in the hands of a few individuals. The trends with regard to income distribution and their implications for wealth accumulation since the 1970s are remarkable. In the USA, in 1988 more than 1.3 million people reported incomes that were over one million dollars, up US$180 000 from 1972.[7] Moreover, in 1998, the top 1 per cent started at US$230 000.[8] From 1970 to 1998 the growth of the top 1 per cent wage share increased sharply from 5 per cent to 1 per cent.[9] The explosion of incomes at the top continued through the 2000s to reach US$717 000 in 2012. In 1970, the average top 0.01 per cent was 50 times the average income; by 2002, it reached 300 times the average income. By 2012, it was 500 times the average income. This growth in incomes is attributed heavily to earnings growth despite cyclical losses in the stock market between 2000 and 2002 and again during the international financial crisis 2007–2008 and the Great Recession. It must be noted that the empirical evidence shows that there are important similarities between the American, French and British experiences despite the fact that the explosion of top incomes is less prevalent in France.[10] This trend has been intensified further by financialization and the rise of financial rewards for those who are involved in the financial services sector such as traders and investment bankers.

Moreover, rich people commit substantive financial resources to achieve their private and personal goals. This development spreads the base of superstar markets through network effects. The creation of wealth leads to an unprecedented rise in the prices of the services that are offered to affluent individuals. This link explains the increase in highly priced lawyers, consultants, financiers, doctors, personal assistants and others. This phenomenon exemplifies simply the fact that when the reputation and interests of rich clients are at stake they will pay high prices for the services of the best professionals.[11]

Earnings, Income Inequality and Superstar Markets

Yet superstar markets are linked also with inequality. In the past twenty years, people have experienced the persistent growth of earnings inequality in the USA as well as the rise in unemployment in Europe. To a certain extent, this inequality in earnings may be attributed to technological progress. This has been the case in earlier historical moments when new technology was applied. For example, early industrial technology was not only labour saving but also capital using. There is a broad agreement among economists that the same phenomenon is happening to developed economies. Today, the rewards of technological change are directed not to the owners of industrial capital but to the highly skilled. As a result, lawyers make much more compared with state clerks than they did twenty years ago. The best paid lawyers also make much more when compared with the average lawyer as was the case twenty years ago.

In this vein, while people of the middle class have barely managed to keep up their standards of living, the rich have become undeniably richer. The greater gap of incomes and the lack of growth in the incomes of the middle class are now evident to such an extent that they appear as natural symptoms of free-market economy.[12] The growing gap in wages and benefits between top paid professionals and the rest of the workforce leads to the emergence of a deeply polarized society. As time passes, the presence of a small cosmopolitan elite of affluent professionals who are secluded becomes more obvious. On the contrary, the number of impoverished workers and unemployed individuals increases every day.

Besides technological progress, several other explanations have been proposed as contributing to these trends in earnings polarization. One reason refers to the process that relates to the decline of trade unions, the drop of employment in manufacturing and the spread of the neoliberal growth model. This framework supported the break-up of the link between wages and productivity growth, regimes of low inflation and interest rates, and financial bubbles to make up for a weak aggregate demand.[13] This has resulted in a more or less permanent loss of steady blue-collar jobs, which traditionally were the source of relatively high compensation and supported the standards of living of the middle class. In contrast, in standard economic theory the polarization of earnings appears still as a puzzle. A great deal of research has been conducted to explain the part of earnings, which remains after observable determinants of workers' compensation, such as education, occupation and demographic characteristics, are taken into account. Yet this line of research does not take into consideration the concerns that exist for the gains of the financial sector and CEOs' compensation, which relate not to performance but often to luck and rent transfers.[14]

The earnings growth creates spillover wealth effects. First, it is accompanied by the phenomenon of financialization in global markets, that is, the spectacular rise of the financial services sector all over the world and the rise of profits of financial investors or rentiers. The increase in earnings both from technology and financialization over time raises further the level of wealth, which in turn has a sizeable effect on ownership of real estate. In the recent past, a higher propensity to consume from housing rather than from financial assets motivated not only the rich, but even average-income households to concentrate their wealth in real estate.[15] In fact, with booms in real estate prices the propensity for conspicuous consumption from real estate wealth becomes considerable. As recent evidence shows, during booms the marginal propensity to consume from housing is higher than that from financial wealth.[16]

Apart from wealth and distribution effects, the explosion of earnings for the highly skilled can be partially explained by the incentives and rewards in careers characterized by tournament processes, a phenomenon that is evident in today's superstar markets. The technological effect on distribution is related to the superstar hypothesis.[17] Furthermore, the growth in earnings inequality in favour of successful professionals indicates that the market places an excessively high premium on the services of the top performers. The superstar characteristics of contemporary markets come in contrast with the traditional standard analysis regarding the causes of high earnings of top producers today. For example, according to human capital theory differences in incomes can be explained simply by factors such as education, training, experience, intelligence, motivation and other human characteristics that influence productivity.

Yet according to the superstar hypothesis there are causes other than the personal characteristics of the workers that are at play. One such factor is the nature of workers' positions. In organizations, there are different levels of responsibility depending on the nature of each position that are eventually reflected in the presence of organizational hierarchy as well as in compensation. From this perspective, the high monetary rewards that are paid to people who hold top positions are directed towards the *ex post* compensation of the high burden of responsibility that those professionals carry within the scopes of the organization.

As a result, on many occasions it is more cost effective to hire the best available person in the market place with an outrageously high salary than two professionals with relatively mediocre track records. This kind of consideration is irrational from a labour theory perspective that uses physical capital as a measure. Yet in terms of human capital analysis, it provides a reasonable explanation. One talented or highly skilled professional is in many cases a greater bargain than two average lawyers, executives, singers or basketball players.[18]

Besides these factors, the growth of media and new information technology today also leads to the spread of this phenomenon.[19] One superstar can attract millions of people through a television show or website while a club singer will be contained to a small audience of a few hundred people. From this perspective, television produces high financial rewards for its superstar actors like Marcia Cross and Jerry Seinfield.[20]

In addition, information technology applications such as the Internet and social media provide an absolutely new and effective medium for the easy expansion of services of numerous highly visible professionals. As a result, wages will be highly influenced by the tournament or lottery quality of superstar markets.[21] The very first professionals, chosen sometimes on the basis of seemingly irrelevant criteria, will receive enormous compensation packages, while those who are in terms of competition slightly less fortunate will wait to receive little or relatively nothing. Judging from recent experience we should expect the growth in technology to give rise to an ever-growing premium on skill and talent. For this reason, earnings distribution becomes an important determinant for personal investments in skill enhancement and specialized education. Equivalently, self-corrective measures in the markets for superstars are not always effective.[22]

Polarization, the Decline of Middle Class and the New Rich

The wide earnings dispersion relates also to the phenomenon of polarization and the difficulties that middle-class individuals experience. In many cases, there is evidence of a new demographic category that is called the declining middle. This situation appeared first in the 1980s when more than 1.5 million mid-level management jobs were eliminated. The trend continued in the 1990s to make space for upper-level management executives. In addition, the managerial class has begun to feel like participating in auction processes, a situation that reminds us of the tournament quality of the market for superstars. In this new environment, it becomes increasingly difficult for many executives who lose their jobs to find an equivalent position with similar benefits. The extent of the decline of the middle class has been reduced however because more women enter the workforce. The percentage of dual-earner couples has increased sharply since the 1970s. The observed rise in this percentage is from just over one-third of married couples (35.9 per cent in 1970) to nearly three in five married couples (59.5 per cent in 1997) and four in five couples in 2008 and although the pace has slowed down since then the percentage is now greater.[23]

With respect to the structure that relates superstar professionals with other groups of the workforce, it must be noted that below the super wealthy there is a larger rich group that accounts for 5 per cent of the workers of the USA. This group consists largely of the new professionals, who are predominantly highly trained knowledge workers or symbolic analysts. These individuals stand on the leading edge of their professions in the new information technology and media dominated economy. Their strength manifests clearly in their relative position with respect to earnings and benefits. Although they account for 5 per cent of the workforce, they earn as much as the entire bottom half of American wage earners. This coincides with the process of accumulation since the early 1970s.[24] These trends influenced the attitudes of high-income individuals. For example, the level of risk aversion assumed by the contented in their consumption of luxury goods is eventually less than the observed average.[25]

Many of the talented superstars are knowledge workers, who constitute a diverse group united by their use of state-of-the-art information technology to identify, process and solve problems. They create and manage a substantive part of the information in the post-industrial, service-led global economy. Their ranks include: research scientists, design engineers, civil engineers, software analysts, biotechnology researchers, public relations specialists, lawyers, investment bankers, fund managers, management consultants, new services entrepreneurs, architects, strategic planners, marketing specialists, film producers and editors, art directors, publishers, writers, editors and journalists. The top performers in superstar markets lead a separate life from the rest of the population through their global linkages, good schools, comfortable lifestyles and excellent health care.

However, the rise of superstar markets coincides with the reduction in the number of service jobs that traditionally were sought and executed by blue-collar workers, since these jobs have been replaced by information technology. As a result, this process contributes to a growing and mainly unemployed urban underclass in poor townships and urban enclaves. A policy issue in the new economy is to prevent a form of class conflict between knowledge workers and manual workers. In certain circumstances where there is a lack of information, social segmentation may seem useful to some since it operates as a substitute for signalling.[26] This social segmentation weakens the motive for individuals to be involved in conspicuous consumption. Yet with the growth of technology, information is enhanced and becomes pervasive so that society becomes less segmented. Thus it becomes possible for people with very different economic backgrounds to compete for the same social rewards. The final outcome seems to depend on the nature of the economic relation between consumption and status. When pure consumption and status are good substitutes, the relative importance of status-seeking will decrease with prosperity.[27] Although in poor societies there is evidence of status-seeking, its expansion in richer societies is enormous. Thus the rise of positional markets links with the fact that pure consumption and status are in essence imperfect substitutes and matter more to rich.

Technology, Skill Enhancement and Economic Incentives

According to traditional economic analysis, the terms technology or technological change mean a specific relationship between input and output. This technocratic conception of technology differs from the notion of applied science, which is predominantly the mainstream usage in everyday life. Therefore, when economists refer to technological change they speak broadly about any kind of change and do not confine their discussion to applied science change. From this perspective, it is obvious that since the 1980s skilled workers have led technological change. This kind of change is so widespread that is not confined only to the performance of symbolic analysts. In practice today there is a beneficial environment for skilled workers such as home health aides, human services workers, personal and home care aides, computer engineers and scientists, system analysts, physical and corrective therapy assistants and aides, physical therapists, paralegals, teachers and special education workers. This bias towards skilled workers is related of course to the sharp developments in the technology of the economy. The excessive rise in the relative earnings and benefits of skilled workers would have been a visible and immediate motive for businesspeople to prefer less skilled workers. Yet we observe that the opposite case takes place with the employers consistently paying a premium in their attempt to raise the skill standards of their workers.

However, the analysis of superstar markets cannot be confined solely to the role of new technologies and symbolic analysts because, as mentioned earlier, there is a tournament quality, which allows only few high rewards. This quality accounts for the pattern of earnings that is observed in the entertainment industry. As in this industry, this pattern has provided in several other service sectors substantive incentives to a great number of people. These incentives motivate them to withdraw from other productive options in order to be able to go after the alternatives that offer the highest rewards.

In the end, this decision often proves to be counterproductive for the majority of individuals and produces less than expected results. In superstar markets, the top rewards attract too many contestants but the opportunities are few. This trend causes considerable waste as there is a deviation from the optimal situation.[28] In this context, it is evident that national income would be higher if there was a better allocation of effort. This adjustment could take place if a smaller number of professionals chose to compete in superstar markets and opted for other careers. The role of market incentives is therefore important because superstar markets induce too many candidates to participate in them while relatively few turn into alternative professions.

Often, the decision to compete in a superstar market is similar to buying a lottery ticket.[29] In the case of a positive outcome, the earnings that are realized are many times more than those achieved in a profession not characterized by the lottery quality of superstar markets. Yet the participation in a superstar system tournament is risky because in the case that there is a negative outcome, the realized earnings can prove to be much less than in an alternative non-risky career. It becomes apparent therefore that the rise of superstar markets is associated with the presence of overconfidence of market participants.[30]

On the upside, when more people attempt to become highly skilled professionals, it is more likely that their employers will observe quality work. In contrast, if there are only as many contenders as needed to fill the available positions, a substantial incentive will be missed and the quality of work will be expected to decline. Yet this does not take into account the effect of overall satisfaction on the quality of work. A higher relative wage does not necessarily increase satisfaction for workers with long-term prospects, although this is not the case for workers more concerned with short-term rewards.[31]

II THE BEHAVIOURAL MICRO-FOUNDATIONS OF POSITIONAL MARKETS

Social Intrinsic Motivation, Leisure and Attitudes towards Consumption

Status seekers care not only about their relative income but also about other variables that confer status as, for example, their relative consumption, their relative wealth, their relative ranking at work and their relative leisure time and activities.[32] Depending on the variable, this situation generates alternative behavioural paths. For example, if there is a strong motive for building relative wealth, then poor individuals would be willing to sacrifice consumption in the early stage of their life to build up wealth and eventually catch up with the rich.[33]

Yet this situation can become quite complicated when leisure and the intrinsic rewards from experiences in leisure activities are considered. For example, price-related behaviours, whether to spend low, spend high, or attempt to maximize value, do not depend only on income or consumption but also on leisure. In the presence of leisure activities, there are many alternative strategies that offer a variety of consumer lifestyles. One can categorize certain attitudes and discern certain alternative personas in today's market place, which include the Value Seeker type, who is tight with money and materialistic; the Big Spender, who is loose with money and materialistic; the Non-Spender, who is tight with money and not materialistic; and, the Experiencer, who is loose with money and non-materialistic because they prefer to be involved in leisure activities.[34] Thus the existence of all those profiles manifests that intrinsic motivation emerges as a key to well-being.

Social Networking, Gift-Giving and Perception

An additional complication arises when seemingly leisure activities interface with other processes such as social networking and the rewards that are usually associated with them. Sometimes, the intrinsic motivations, such as those associated with the willingness to participate in social networking are indispensably associated with economic rewards. An example is the case of expensive positional activities such as lavish wedding celebrations in relation to underlying incomes. This phenomenon is pervasive in developing countries such as India.[35] For example, in rural India households spend considerable sums of money to build social networks and to generate tangible rewards such as lower prices on food and higher social status that leads to more invitations for free meals and better access to available services.[36] This process is not limited to social networking only. For example, it extends to gift-giving, which is associated with the gradual development of cooperative behaviour in the form of special occasion signalling or gift-giving.[37] There are also implications for the corporate world since employers engaged in long-term working relations with their employees may want to develop positive worker sentiments by offering unanticipated rewards and bonuses. These rewards may take the form of gift-giving since the desire to maximize the gift recipient's gain may motivate the employer to surprise the receiver either through the choice of the right time or gift.[38]

Strategies such as gift-giving or social networking through special occasion expenditures involve at times some form of deception. Thus it comes as no accident that deception is present in positional markets. Some apparent strategies involve the consumption of counterfeit versions of prestigious brand-name goods, which is perhaps the most frequently used individual strategy in both developed and developing countries. In this case, the status-signalling costs are lower because deception is involved.[39] This situation manifests that deception, positional goods and activities and social welfare are often related. There can be negative consequences especially in developing countries. If the less rich follow the rich establishment in buying expensive original brand-name goods to prevent a status loss, valuable resources are drawn away from non-conspicuous consumption, which might produce over time a decline in their nutritional, health and education standards.[40]

Uncertainty and the State of Confidence in the Global Economy

Another factor that contributes to the rise of superstar markets is complexity in current affairs and uncertainty about the outcome of certain decisions. This situation forces executives to seek familiar methods and patterns of performance. Managers tend to hire only the best to protect themselves from the criticism they would face in adverse conditions. Moreover, the labour segments of superstar markets such as professional sports and other activities represent a combination of market and productive uncertainty. There is a motive therefore for the producers to take action to reduce the high levels of uncertainty. For example, in sectors such as the entertainment industry, consumers' choices will most certainly continue to be shaped in significant ways by excess financial resources for extravagant marketing campaigns in order to reduce product uncertainty.[41]

Thus uncertainty and risk-taking are influenced by the higher stakes of the contested issues that prevail today. In practice, the decisions of managers and consumers are influenced by the changes in risk and uncertainty. First, those changes imply the universal spread of risk and uncertainty because of new possibilities such as global catastrophes from nuclear power or ecological destruction, new public health hazards and security deterioration from population movements jeopardizing opportunities for every citizen irrespective of class, ethnicity or other subjective position. Second, risk and uncertainty are systemic and enormous in certain occasions. The risky environment affects large groups of the population through financial markets crises that produce worldwide runs, political instability, military conflicts, price increases of energy commodities and other similar crises. Furthermore, the institutional dimension of risk cannot be ignored as many growing industries such as investment markets or stock exchanges, gambling sports and insurance regard risk as the core of their operations. Not only this, but people are susceptible to the reflexiveness of risk. This quality seems to produce in many occasions unintended and sometimes very intense side-effects or boomerang effects, which include ecological dangers that result from industrialization, crime and negligence as results of unregulated social interactions, and new cultural problems produced by contemporary work patterns or lifestyles.

There are supplementary factors that make the experience of risk and uncertainty more acute. In our times, people are more sensitive to threats and dangers. This sensitivity is associated with the disappearance of magical and religious defences and rationalizations that were so common in the past. In addition, there is a more common awareness of threats. This takes place through the rising level of education and the growing recognition that expertise in fact is limited. This is no surprise as people frequently observe faults in the operation of the system. These realities highlight the influence of uncertainty and the degree of confidence upon which people can ground their decisions. The role of uncertainty was stressed by famous economists in the past such as Fisher and Keynes.[42] According to Keynes, the willingness to invest in assets depends on the weight of argument or evidence upon which we can base our estimates. Keynes described the weight of evidence as a measure of the amount of relevant evidence and of the completeness of the information upon which probability is based.[43] Thus there is a discernible relation between uncertainty, completeness and size of relevant evidence in uncertainty, weight of evidence and state of confidence.[44] With the growing complexity of everyday life and the emergence of an ever-changing environment, in which information is always incomplete, it is no wonder why people today face a serious confidence crisis about their future and psychological propensities become influential. An antidote to this type of crisis seems to be provided by the rise of superstar markets. In this fragile environment, the presence of superstar experts in various professions becomes useful. With their relative performance advantage, superstar professionals are sought by people to provide visible and, therefore, credible solutions. In the presence of superstars, information is perceived to be more complete and the stress associated with the lack of confidence is reduced.

Subjective Premia and Superstar Markets

The introduction of subjective characteristics such as the role of uncertainty in the analysis is valuable because positional and superstar markets can be examined through a *premium-specificity* approach. This implies that the degree of security or rewards attached to goods or services by individuals vary with respect to several factors and in the very end can explain the great value attached to the services of top performers as well as to positional goods. For example, in pure Keynesian financial analysis, the security of assets implies that liquidity premia vary among other factors, which include term to maturity or marketability with respect to subjective forces such as the state of confidence. This framework can be extended to the study of status markets. We can assume that there are many goods and services with premia, which depend on various specificities. In this vein, the demand for assets, goods and services is determined with respect to its underlying premium-specificity.[45]

This abstract framework translates simply to the fact that the demand of positional goods and services differentiates with respect to the rewards and the security they offer. Different groups of economic, political, psychological or cultural factors, which are studied by separate disciplines of social sciences, determine those rewards and securities. Thus there is a link between the premium-specificity analysis of positional markets and the approach of the political economy of culture change that encourages an interdisciplinary integration of variables. For example, one group of factors relates to pure economic factors such as relative performance, wealth and the rise of uncertainty in a global economy. Yet another group includes sociological factors such as the influence of television, advertisement, popular culture fragmented lifestyles and the cultural production of symbols. A supplementary group involves psychological considerations that support the growth of superstar markets and relative position competition. As we will see later on, these psychological factors consist of the ability to signal competitive strength to fellow players, the perception of positive self-worth and the capacity to avoid frustration. In addition, political considerations constitute obviously an important issue. For example, there are political economy effects when individuals attempt to signal social demarcation and discrimination in order to have better access to wealth resources and opportunities.

Consider now the case in which goods differentiate with respect to the subjective psychological rewards they offer and the greater psychological need among consumers to signal competitive ability. This subjective factor leads to a higher demand for positional goods as well as to higher prices for them. An analogous assumption can be made to represent differences in rewards as a result of the influence of anthropological and sociological variables. This analysis implies a system of demand prices of a set of goods and services, which are determined according to their premium-specificity that relates to economic, sociological, psychological, political or anthropological premia. For example, positional goods embody higher uncertainty premia because people feel more secure with their purchase.

Advertisement and the Endorsements of Superstars

Besides uncertainty and the premia attached to superstar markets, advertisement acts as another powerful force and has gained momentum with the boom of consumerism and individualism. The view according to which advertisement is critical for taste formation does not belong entirely to one school of thought. In fact, there is a similarity between Mandel's Marxist 'late capitalism' concept, which emphasizes the role of the consumer, and other lines of thought in economics such as the institutional approach advocated by Galbraith on the society of contentment. The analysis of Galbraith emphasizes that a critical turn for capitalism was when industrialists realized that in order to increase sales they had to make people want things they had never previously desired. Therefore, they had to rely on 'the dissatisfied consumer'. This process could be facilitated through advertisement. Therefore, the new goal of business was to 'create the wants it seeks to satisfy' through advertisements. This mission was engineered during the first decades of the twentieth century, when most people were producing many goods, such as soap or clothes, at home. Initially, advertisement was used to degrade homemade goods and to emphasize the superior store-bought and factory-made quality of many commodities.

Today advertisement and endorsements are designed to capture also the inclination of younger generations for novelty and fashion leadership. This activity leads to campaigns that attempt to plant a feeling of shame against peers for wearing or using old-fashioned products. Thus advertisement campaigns seek to exploit the distinction between being modern and old-fashioned. Since the 1980s, we observe workers in the USA and Europe behaving as status-conscious consumers, who in many instances seek distinction through the purchase of positional goods. This trend was initially the outcome of high labour-productivity increases that led to higher wages for specialized labour. Therefore, money wages are an important issue for workers and entrepreneurs alike. For this reason, Ford claimed that workers should be paid enough otherwise they would be unable to purchase the goods that industries were producing.

The rise of superstar markets today motivate millions of middle-class professionals to social pre-eminence competitions that take place through positional goods consumption and occupational tournaments. Earlier on, with respect to the second class, Keynes noticed that there is a class of needs which is the result of competition contests to keep ahead of their peers. These needs may prove to be insatiable following self-fulfilling tendencies. Therefore, a direct link exists between production and excessive consumer practices. This link is made possible through the advertisement agencies, marketing and the superstars. The desires or needs that are created through advertisement are incompatible with the idea of independently created wants. This is because an important objective of advertisement is in fact the creation of new desires, that is, bringing to life desires that were previously absent.[46]

This line of thought that emphasizes the role of advertisement as a creator of new desires can be extended further to take into account the fact that advertisement disturbs often the balance of preferences between public and private goods. According to traditional forms of analysis, individuals decide what share of their private income they prefer to forego in order to be able to enjoy certain public services that either they are in need of, or that the private sector does not substitute at low prices. In a sense, the consumer acts as a voter and makes an independent choice between public and private goods. Thus in the traditional framework, there is balance regarding the relative preference for private and public goods. Yet this view depends on the idea that consumer preferences are independently determined, an idea that is in sharp contrast with the type of analysis that emphasizes the role of advertisement. Since its role is the creation or the deepening of new desires and needs, it is absurd to maintain that the condition of balance existing in free choice between private and public goods is maintained.

Relative Consumerism and Social Comparisons

The idea that people are concerned about their relative position has been increasingly acceptable in economics. Dating back to classical and institutional economists such as Smith and Veblen respectively, there has definitely been an awareness of the importance of social status in decision-making and individual welfare.[47] More recently, economic research has emphasized the role of interpersonal comparisons and status-seeking. Still, one particular difficulty with traditional economic wisdom is that individuals do not agree on the benchmark that determines one's relative position in society. Economic studies of social status have typically focused on individuals engaging in relative comparisons based on certain characteristics such as consumption and wealth without considering why these characteristics are deemed 'status worthy'.[48] Yet research in psychology has demonstrated that the factors people use to compare themselves change in systematic ways. This implies that there are several indicators to be taken into consideration and that eventually the role of psychology is important. There is now a growing literature that extends economic theory to recognize that people may also be motivated not only by economic behaviour on the basis of self-interest but also by factors such as the psychological propensity or aversion driven by fairness rules.[49] It is evident therefore that economic motivations such as economic security are not the only class of variables in terms of what individual decision-making takes place. Decisions are often linked with pure psychological motives such as self-esteem.[50]

Thus economic decision-making depends also on indirect social and psychological mechanisms that change the way individuals evaluate their social positions. Understanding the process of psychological adaptation and how it feeds back on economic variables is pivotal because it helps design better policies in positional markets, especially with respect to individuals coming from lower classes. The social and psychological conditions accompanying those living in the lower levels of the economic pyramid, and in many instances in poverty, can create discomfort. This leads members of the lower classes to follow alternative paths to enjoy the 'sunshine' provided by the exposure to status markets and superstar occupations. This may increase the level of discomfort and inertia felt by people, who belong to low-income groups and, as a consequence, encourage them to abandon mainstream norms and work ethics that are useful to them.[51]

Individuals choose in principle a status-earning characteristic in order to reduce mental discomfort (dissonance). Usually, those individuals with the highest marginal utility from income are often the first to misconstrue or abandon these incentives in favour of alternate forms of seeking status.[52] The concern for the maintenance of self-esteem may also lead people to engage in seemingly irrational behaviour. The latter involves strategies such as avoiding information, creating obstacles to their own performance, adopting snob or other contrarian behaviour and allowing self-deception through mental-specific capacities such as selective memory, limited awareness and related forms of belief manipulation. Moreover, in interactive situations, conflicting interests will generally imply that self-confidence matters. Thus the role of self-confidence as a motivator for other tasks is fundamental. This psychological approach provides an explanation to why and how much people care about their self-image. Self-confidence acts as supplementary variable to 'the working of fundamental preferences, technological constraints and the structure of incentives'.[53]

Furthermore, an alternative motive advanced by psychologists for the maintenance of self-esteem involves purely affective rather than cognitive considerations; people just like to think of themselves as good, able, generous and attractive so that they have good feelings when they act. Self-image is an additional variable that contributes to personal utility or satisfaction. This mechanism potentially allows people to care about a broader set of self-attributes. Yet from an economist's point of view, this process has an impact only on utility. Motives and attributes may exhibit strong interconnections. The process of savings offers a good example of the possibility of the interdependence of motives. The process of social stratification can be confused if an alternative framework is followed, that is, using a hierarchical approach. At the bottom of the hierarchy we find more concrete motivations, such as saving for a better house, a new car or a holiday, which represent the objectives of individual independence and autonomy. This motivation may be contrasted with other concrete incentives such as the availability of money, for precautionary purposes related to old age, illness and retirement. In this context, three general motives towards the goal of saving are easily recognizable. The first one is associated with avoiding debt and of achieving a certain security in life, the second relates to the desire for self-gratification, and the last one relates to reaching old age with self-esteem. Yet it is obvious that there is interdependence among these three goals. Thus the fact that security, self-esteem and self-gratification are reciprocally connected manifests how motives are essentially interdependent.[54]

III CULTURE AND CULTURAL CAPITAL

Status Markets and Cultural Goods

As mentioned earlier, advertising campaigns and endorsements by superstars and celebrities play an important role in the formation of the image of goods and services. To the extent that this image is projected to the consumers and influences their view of identity, their values and way of life, the possession of positional goods and services today manifests a cultural quality. This situation explains why with the purchase of real goods individuals buy essentially cultural symbolic goods.

One could view positional or status goods and services as circulating not in the main market of traditional real industrial goods but in a parallel market, the cultural market. In this market, it is ideas, identities and distinctions rather than wealth that are exchanged. One important difference with traditional industrial commodities is that in the domain of cultural markets the consumer preference between similar goods is not based on the comparison of similar use-values. Although in the industrial era there was a visible pattern to standardize goods and services, today the choice for various goods with a cultural quality depends on cultural values. The preference of one particular good over substitutes is for the consumer a matter of own meanings, identities and distinctions rather than of standardized general entities.

In this framework, there is an interdependent relation between these seemingly separate markets, the financial and the cultural. When in the traditional markets a good, service or programme is produced, the producers sell it to distributors as a simple material commodity. Yet the rise of media and new information technology allow a change of direction since the cultural quality of many goods, services and programmes can produce audiences that are marketed afterwards by advertising or public relations.

An example of this type of interdependence between the traditional market and the cultural market is provided by television programmes and sitcoms. Film producers create programmes and sell them for distribution to television channels such as CBS, ITV or Canal Plus. The television channels conduct the marketing of sizes of audience to companies such as Coca-Cola, Opel or Renault, which sponsor the programmes. Often, the shows rate respectably but not impressively. Television channels could, if they wished, modify the format and content of the series to increase the size of the audience. The attempt to increase the audience size may alter the targeted mix of the audience with respect to its socio-economic qualities. Naturally, from a marketing viewpoint, some large companies like Pepsico or Chrysler may not be interested in sponsoring a modified programme with a different targeted mix of the audience. Therefore, we observe programmes with relatively moderate show rates surviving longer than expected.

This is not the case with cultural commodities and services. As stressed earlier, they are not merely agents of standardized meanings and identities. In many instances, they provide an opportunity to the consumer to reveal their own meanings and distinctions. Therefore, cultural commodities and services can be viewed in a sense as being uniquely produced by the consumer and as serving solely personal objectives. These demand characteristics are often more important than the supply-side effects associated with the low cost of reproduction of products or services. This happens because a greater number of consumers use these products or services in ways that make them more valuable.

Traditionally, cultural goods do not have an obviously described use-value. Yet for Marx, the production of aesthetic pleasure was a use-value. Certainly, there are differences between the use-value of a work of art and that of a machine or a bottle of wine, although it is difficult to provide a precise account. However, the exchange value of cultural commodities can be identified more easily. Cultural goods exhibit common qualities with the services of top performers as they have relatively high initial production costs and very low reproduction costs. Therefore, the distribution of cultural goods provides a safer yield on investment rather than their production.

The process involved in the circulation of cultural goods and services differs from the mass distribution of popular culture and popular identities. The failure rate of mass distribution is sometimes high. For some analysts, the high failure rates that exist for products and services that can be reproduced by media and new information technology is an important motive for the production of repertoires of products.[55] Since the prediction rates of the success of cultural commodities and services are very low, in many cases it is more prudent to produce repertoires of products and let the audiences to find their own identities and distinctions.

Today popular culture becomes an endless source for fantasy of social or personal identities to the extent that it is difficult sometimes to tell the difference between the real and the virtual. This world of escapism is viewed often as a sign of weakness coming from the incapacity to come to terms with reality. The daydreaming allows the consumers of popular culture to achieve their desires in a way they are never capable of in the real world.[56] Therefore, 'fantasy' functions as a psychological compensatory process that makes up for the weaknesses of poor people in reality. One could argue that daydreaming through popular culture is a feel-good quality, for which a whole industry has been developed since it allows people to achieve the desires that are difficult to attain in the real world.

There are two contradictory forces at work with respect to the supply of cultural goods, homogenization and diversification. This dual process takes place because of the conflict of interest between the producers of cultural goods and the versatile groups of people who consume them. For example, with respect to television, on the one hand there are economic forces that exploit the oligopolistic nature of traditional television with few licences going to big channels and attempts to market homogeneous popular cultural programmes. On the other hand, these programmes allow viewers to create their own fantastic identities and new technology supports the multiplicity of channels that target specific audiences. Therefore, television can become a decentred and diverse medium. As time passes, we could expect to see television as a source of pluralism and diversity, especially with the aid of changes in information technology such as the Internet and social media.[57] As a result, this development may provoke a diversity of personal and social reactions to attempts of homogenization.

Status Markets and Cultural Capital: Emulation and Snobbery

The introduction of cultural goods can be expanded towards other theoretical directions like the analysis of class conflict. Thus not only high culture, but lifestyle culture as well, constitutes the domain for the contemporary war between social groups belonging in dominant and bottom-tier classes in modern societies.[58] The consumption of culture becomes 'predisposed, consciously and deliberately or not, to fulfil a social function of legitimating social differences'.[59] Therefore, culture is viewed as an instrument of social groups of the upper class to reproduce social norms that validate its social ruling role. In this framework, what is important is not merely the differences in the forms of contemporary culture but the importance of cultural distinctions, through the purchase of cultural goods, to legitimate power positions and privileges associated to a great extent with market position and income inequalities. Evidence from survey data shows that higher individual and household incomes raise both self-rated power and welfare.[60] To the extent that cultural goods are used for this form of legitimacy, the purchase of cultural commodities is regarded as cultural capital through which the social reproduction of distinction is acquired. This is an important quality in the strategic process of individual attitudes of emulation and snobbery. This cultural capital can also be envisaged as yielding both a profit in distinction, which is proportionate to the scarcity of financial means required to appropriate cultural material and a profit in legitimacy, which represents the self-righteous experience of being justified in one's own decisions and attitudes. Therefore, the notion of cultural capital is important because it is associated not merely with competence, skills, talent or knowledge but with social distinction. One can argue that there is a motive to accumulate cultural capital because this ensures the continuous legitimacy of social distinction. Since the access to cultural capital takes place through the capacity to purchase, then it is an unequally distributed capital. In a classless society, there is no need for considering the acquisition of cultural goods as a vehicle to legitimize social distinction.

One valuable source for cultural capital is the system of education that includes traditional institutions as well as more informal forms of education.[61] The role of the education system is important because in many circumstances it is used to legitimize privileges, which are at work already. For example, there is a tendency to overvalue the education forms associated with prestigious business schools that in many instances validate the cultural preferences of individuals of the upper class who sponsor them. This takes place simultaneously with the devaluation of the needs or preferences of individuals in the lower classes for free university education or greater levels of financial assistance. In this manner, the hierarchy is reproduced and the education system reproduces, rather than helps eliminate social inequalities. The education system makes social hierarchies look natural rather than a product of cultural conceptions.

Ideological concerns function as a process of legitimacy of social privileges that pretend that the latter are eventually a gift of nature or talent. In this vein, in status markets there is often an attempt to legitimize social distinction in a manner that is similar to the aristocracy's blood or right of birth. The projection of this idea, that is, the projection of culture as a gift of nature requires the representation of culture as a distinct domain from the economic world. As a consequence, although distinction is purchased, it is not realized in the economic field but in the field of culture. Access to power and privileges are viewed as the outcome of access to cultural distinction. This merit is presented as a natural quality rather than as a property secured by economic capacity.

Homogenization, Diversification and Cultural Capital

From a socio-economic viewpoint, any social phenomenon can be explained in reference to different fields: economic, educational, cultural and so on. Individuals can invest in one or more relatively autonomous fields in order to reap personal rewards. These rewards are not immediately monetary since the objective of this investment is the accumulation of symbolic capital, in the form of prestige, distinction or access to power. As a result, involvement in these fields takes into account strategies of different groups of the upper classes to secure exclusivity and to maintain the expression of status and distinction, usually associated with the lifestyles of the very top performers in economic life.

Despite assertions to the contrary, cultural capital is not exactly similar to economic capital. The members of the audience of a television programme that expresses aspects of contemporary popular culture consider it a familiar medium rather than a totally foreign or hostile instrument of the upper or upper middle classes. This is because those individuals are able to identify with different role models. In the case of popular culture, it is very difficult to say whether there is a process of ideological domination. Today people live in a world where they receive messages from different ideological sources. In some instances, there are alternative ideologies that serve those social groups who do not fit perfectly into the picture of the current status quo. Therefore, what ideology does is to help individuals who belong in those groups to get a sense of intelligibility of their social position. People acquire a capacity to experience a representation of their social identities. This opportunity stands in conflict with traditional accounts of domination. Yet the path for such a social representation, popular culture, is not always the right choice because in many situations it projects not real but elusive imaginative identities. In such a case, the representation is simply a path for escapism from real identities and the difficulties of real life.

IV DISTRIBUTION

Inequality, Distribution and Positional Markets

The division of cultural capital across classes raises the issue of distribution and its relation with positional markets. It is broadly acknowledged that the best policy in order to overcome poverty is the redistribution of income from wealthier members of society to the poorer ones. This is also the case with positional markets. Thus even in terms of traditional economic analysis, correction of the observed market failures of status and superstar markets can take place through cultural capital redistribution from the rich to the poor that can be financed by the implementation of tax policies on positional goods and services.[62]

In status markets, the position of individuals can be described by their rank with respect to certain factors such as the distribution of consumption of positional goods. In this case, there is a strategic consideration in individual decision-making. The satisfaction of one individual depends on the consumption patterns of other people in alternative strategic processes of emulation and snobbery. The result in the context of this strategic game is that each individual spends inefficiently more money on positional activities. In a rich but unequal society, almost all individuals spend variably more on positional consumption so that individual utility is reduced at each income level.[63] In less wealthy societies, or in situations in which financial constraints appear at some stage sooner or later, the poor are worse off.

A particular case is when we explicitly consider the motives of individuals from different social groups. For example, upper-class individuals seem to care more about the preservation of their high social position because they are afraid that they may lose their competitive edge. However, individuals who belong in the lower-class social groups care less about preserving their low social context through positional signalling. If the maintenance of the initial social position is the only variable in the explanation of persistent inequality across generations, then lower-class individuals have a weak incentive to change habits of low effort and to target activity levels associated with upward mobility.[64] It comes as a surprise therefore that people from bottom-tier social groups are justified to exert little effort in this context. They do not care much about social position since they cannot change much. Although it may sound counterintuitive, welfare improving policies should eventually have as their objective to assist people from the lower classes to reduce their effort even further since some individuals from the lower classes are unresponsive to financial incentives to conform to a process of upward mobility.

Undoubtedly, this analysis points out to some extreme possibilities. For example, there is an incentive for the rich to adapt to judicious choices so that they can reveal their social position with smaller expenditures. Moreover, since conspicuous consumption has an impact on social segmentation, that is, on the partition of the society into discernible social groups, then signalling a competitive advantage seems to be the natural choice in order to benefit from social interactions within a social group.[65] In this case, measures such as the taxation of positional goods can improve welfare. This happens because taxation reduces the waste associated with positional lifestyles. These options may appear ineffective since rich people have the financial capacity to accommodate their choices with respect to their signalling needs. For example, even in the presence of distribution taxes, many individuals may still prefer to continue with their positional consumption. This tendency survives because they want to signal their social standing through expenditures related to positional consumption goods and services at higher prices (because of the transfer of the cost of the distributive tax). Yet this tax can be used as a financial transfer to the poor and can improve social welfare.[66]

Distribution, Behaviour and Ideology

In addition, if self-fulfilling beliefs involve the internalization of discrimination and/or imperfect rational learning, then redistribution should take place to influence the beliefs produced by the processes necessary to implement the positional concerns of those belonging to the upper classes.[67] Thus the redistributive policy should not only increase the monetary receipts of the poor but should also manage to minimize the psychological discomfort and the relative deprivation of the less comfortable so that they are less likely to adopt extreme behaviour. Most economic analysis that stands against redistribution places an emphasis on the potential side-effects that may strengthen the opposite incentives. Yet if there is a choice between attempting to catch up with a positional lifestyle and trying harder to develop one's own skills, redistribution can strengthen the incentive of the poor to exert effort and to withdraw from pursuing to adjust to positional norms.[68]

Psychological research has indicated that the social environment plays an important role in the process that determines the extent in terms of which people may feel distanced from other groups of the society.[69] For example, policies to promote individualism and, as a consequence, produce negative images of behaviour associated with low class may in fact influence the size of this group. In the long term, the interaction of special forms of individuality and negativity constitutes in essence the 'moral environment of the poor'.[70] The outcome is influenced also by other factors such as the frequency of interactions among members of the same group of poor people (neighbourhood effects), the exposure of individuals of this social group with mainstream values and social mentoring by those individuals who act as public workers and have access to the group.

As previously mentioned, the effect of redistribution varies with respect to the variable through which individuals choose to signal social status (that is, income, wealth, consumption and so on). When this measure is income alone, the poorer individuals enjoying the highest satisfaction from their income at that time have the strongest incentive to reduce cognitive dissonance in the presence of positional lifestyle in favour of trying to achieve positional advantage even through alternative activities such as leisure activities. In this case, an increase in the desire for positional activities increases in principle the consumption tax rates.[71]

An important consideration in this context is whether individual actions take place in the process of social competition with respect to a reference level or whether they are eventually influenced by social discrimination.[72] Another question is whether individuals, who belong in lower-income classes are expected to be less successful because they lose less in social recognition for not being successful or in fact because they are discouraged. The analysis that incorporates the role of inequality and distribution highlights the fact that the impact of status markets is different across people from various economic and social strata and depends also on psychological considerations. Possibly, both discouraging references and discriminating behaviour that distorts upward mobility takes place. Thus although people from the lowest social groups do not have incentives for upward mobility through a behaviour change with respect to positional norms, this is not the case for individuals who come from the low segments of middle class. People from these social groups are psychologically more responsive to superstars' lifestyles because they expect that they can achieve upward mobility. In their case, the objectives of welfare-improving policies should be to support their aspirations through human capital improvement rather than by allowing them to participate uninformed in wasteful adjustment towards high positional norms.[73]

Status, Fashion Leaders and Class

While agents often think actively about the reference group in which their local status is determined, we never really know exactly who is in the reference group people care about.[74] Although proximity is an important consideration (that is, to neighbours, co-workers, past classmates and so on), the variability of social identity across individuals is so broad that positional concerns are often expressed in diverse and creative ways that contradict narrow ranking calculations. In this context, the process of image projection and the impact of visibility become decisive because people utilize media information about superstars, who are perceived to act as 'fashion leaders', a notion which is used in standard economics to describe leaders in establishing trends in different areas of life.

Television provides inexpensive and effortless artificial relationality that, despite lacking any direct relational content, is commonly and increasingly used as a substitute for actual interpersonal relationships.[75] Phenomena such as speculative bubbles in financial markets are characterized by excessive reporting in the media, which dominates social discussions between neighbours or within the workplace.[76] People often imitate an external source as a strategy to impress others in their internal status game. Moreover, highly visible media superstars such as Warren Buffet (for finance) and Bono of U2 (for community causes) are leaders who are well-respected in the general community and they are connected to many other agents in other networks. Overall, media visibility appears a substantive force in positional and superstar emulation.

Studies of superstar and celebrity endorsements are consistent with experimental evidence showing that media superstars and celebrities enhance product recall and enhance the consumer perception of product value.[77] In this context, superstar and celebrity endorsements are a fixed cost and they are chosen for products that have large potential customer pools. They also provide large coordination returns to consumers for products for which peer or aspiration effects are apparently large. Given the fixed cost, the payoffs for superstar and celebrity endorsements are excessive and this strengthens the formation of a cascade towards the consumption of the endorsed product.

Furthermore, visibility, which is a characteristic of superstars, is viewed as a particular aspect of leadership. In a network of several neighbours or co-workers deciding between luxury cars, the most well-informed is a 'fashion leader'. Social psychologists report that people imitate the actions of those who appear to have expertise. This process underlies the success of product endorsements in which athletes are seen to use a particular brand of athletic shoes or tennis racket. Thus there is a 'fashion leader' version of the cascades model in which the less precise free-ride informationally on the more precise.[78] This happens because the dominant agents have greater absolute benefit from acquiring precise information or because there are scale economies in information acquisition. The 'fashion leader' model provides a rational approximation of herding and the domination of certain groups of agents such as experts, opinion leaders and media superstars. In addition, the cascades framework is different from approaches that stress the impact of microeconomic benefits.[79] Fashion cycles are explained through a cost–benefit approach according to which the benefits realized from introducing fashionable items compete with the costs of developing and marketing new products. Consumers appear to be manipulated to buy the new fashion because that is their only way of obtaining status. The phenomenon of superstars is also explained by the learning process of consumption and the accumulation of expertise or information. In this type of analysis, each category of activities constitutes a market with its own stars and the sophisticated (knowledgeable) consumer may have a large and diverse set of stars. Thus even in a rational context, there are forces that make it possible for the status-minded consumer to overcome narrow ranking considerations.

However, behavioural accounts enhance our understanding better because a crucial aspect is that behavioural processes are influenced by cues associated with purely cognitive and social psychology forces. The impact of cues on the preferences and aspirations of agents appears more noticeable in domains such as the media and advertisement, in which highly visible and prestigious agents are prevalent. Imitation of individuals with high prestige may be based on a belief that the prestigious are good decision-makers. In situations in which people are uncertain about the wisdom of modelled courses of action, they must rely on cues such as general appearances, speech, style, age, symbols of socio-economic success and signs of expertise as indicators of past successes.[80]

In terms of behavioural game theory, numerical beauty contests highlight the severe cognitive demands required so that decisions about what constitutes a conventional average outcome stabilize very quickly.[81] While cognitive demands may not lead to the most dominant state, it allows for the effectiveness of highly visible cues that comfort those demands. For example, players care about their own payoffs, and they dislike others having more than them.[82]

An alternative way that explains the emergence of dominant agents in the consumption of positional goods and services beyond the process of imitation is evidence from the dynamic discrete-choice model of consumption in which peer, distinction and aspiration effects on the corresponding group shares of agents are central.[83] This framework is based on evolutionary economics and evolutionary game theory. In practice, the consumer seeks to associate with those who are close in the 'status' spectrum, to distinguish themselves from those who are below, and to emulate the consumption behaviour of those above them in terms of a scalar representation.

The difference between distinction and aspiration seekers can also be examined through the behaviour of snobs and followers.[84] Snobs value exclusivity, and consequently the utility derived from a product depends not only on its base value, but also on the expected number of people who will buy the product. The greater this number is, the stronger incentive for the snobs to seek distinction by buying an alternative product giving rise to substantive variations in utility. Among other forces, innovation is a process that is utilized in attempts to resist the monopoly of status. People imagine that they live closer to their idols. Thus in expressing who they are or who they want to be, they resist or attempt to overcome the dominant status process.[85] Finally, an important aspect of the process that results in the emergence of dominant agents in positional activities is associated with the role of diffusion and social influence.[86] For example, if the fraction of adopters in a personal network is higher than a threshold, the agent feels social influence, otherwise they do not.

Overall, all theoretical approaches in mainstream economics support the significance of the impact of the signals of the top class of agents. In this respect, the superstar hypothesis is enhanced to take place through a variety of forces (that is, rational, behavioural and evolutionary) as a 'fashion-leader' account, either universally or in terms of a localized strategic superstar process in positional markets. This evidence relates to the emergence of strategic processes, which although they come to surface as a result of instrumental considerations, acquire a life of their own because visibility and the institutions that promote it such as the media act as a substitute for actual interpersonal relationships. The activities of 'fashion leaders' or strategic superstars dominate the social networks of agents in status markets, a phenomenon which implies that consumption is not just an instrumental activity.[87] The sociocultural signification of commodities associated with assumed or projected social and cultural identity of the consumer is also an important aspect of this process. This stands in contrast with the representation of positional markets solely as a result of narrow relative concerns. Moreover, the evidence from marketing studies of endorsements shows that the evidential weight and the implicit value that the most dominant agents convey in their signals, as well as the realization of privilege in terms of access to visibility, constitute the most important forces that influence agents of lower positionality to follow their lead. To put it in real-world terms, people seek in the lifestyles or in the commercial preferences (endorsements) of the stars cues in terms of which they can substitute their own missing information. This deficiency motivates them also to override social psychology forces associated with their lack of confidence and of self-esteem so that they are able to implement effectively strategies of emulation and snobbery.

There is also strong evidence in mainstream economics of stratification in status emulation across social groups and of social domination by the 'fashion-leader' group. This evidence is associated with visibility and the institutions that promote it. For example, the media act as a substitute for actual interpersonal relationships. Fashion leaders such as superstars, celebrities and top-tier consumers dominate the social networks of agents in status markets. The media as a facilitator of visibility is an institution through which images are borrowed or appropriated for the expression of an identity. People choose images (and identities) to express sociocultural values which are not justified by their own financial and social situation. In positional markets, those choices are influenced by the interplay of social, psychological and strategic considerations so that meta-identities are formed and second-order sociocultural values are expressed. Images are generated in the media (and social media) world of superstars and in the celebrated lifestyles of the top social group, the Veblenian leisure-class or the Galbraithian affluent-class which, most likely, acts as a first comer to fashions and positionality. In this way, the psychological process of formation and expression of own identity is related to the social discourse. First comers and latecomers, or alternatively, top-tier and bottom-tier consumers are associated with social classes bringing to the surface the dynamics of polarization in positional markets and the impact of social inequality.[88] Thus it is useful to analyse consumption in status markets in terms of social groups and of their relation to the class structure.

CONCLUDING REMARKS

In the new age of technological progress and globalization, competition has become more intense in the domain of production. What matters is relative performance rather than absolute performance dictated by traditional economics. Small advantages in relative performance materialize into huge differences in compensation, which has caused the emergence of professional superstars and the expansion of superstar markets. Specific aspects of technological progress such as in information technology and advances in media technology create greater masses of prospective clients and substantial economies of scale for the producers and distributors of products and services. Bigger institutions, a fiercer competitive environment and uncertainty that are caused by the fast pace of economic and social changes increase immensely the weight of responsibility on the part of suppliers of products and services and the burden of the right decision on the part of consumers. These economic factors explain why the compensation of top performers skyrockets. Technological progress, global markets and greater accountability of the market players in an era of intense competition and uncertainty lead to the creation of the phenomenon of superstar markets. This segment of the labour market is accompanied not only by new wealth but also by income inequality. One specific observation is that the phenomenon of superstar markets encompasses any sphere of economic activity but it is more predominant in the area of services. Moreover, the rise of the new rich attracts millions of competitors in the sectors of the labour markets that produce superstar professionals. Since the huge rewards are destined for the few, many contestants commit serious occupational mistakes.

New wealth intensifies excessive consumption especially for positional or status goods. This phenomenon is primarily explained by a signal effect, namely, by the need of the rich to signal that they are competitive and that their services must be preferred. Yet besides the best performers and rich top-tier consumers, large masses of the middle class are involved also in this social contest. This occurs even when they cannot afford it or through less expensive positional goods, services or activities. These individuals attempt to transcend their immediate social environment because they want to signal that they are able to keep up with the better players, the top-tier consumers. This strategic process operates on the basis of psychological motives and supports the rise of status and superstar markets. Thus individuals care about both relative income and relative consumption. Concerns over relative consumption include items such as expenditures for holidays and housing, which are typically viewed as non-positional goods.[89] This process is facilitated by the huge influence of the media and advertisement and endorsements of superstars and celebrities that establish stereotypes and intensify and diversify the demand for positional goods, services or activities. The repercussion of the media and advertisement has a cultural impact because it changes the set of values and preferences of decision-makers from traditional utility choices to status ones. Since positional concerns help establish the signalling identity of economic agents within the strategic processes of emulation and snobbery, positional goods and services serve in essence as a cultural medium or capital to legitimize distinction, privilege and discrimination against the less competitive.

Finally, from an economic viewpoint, all these considerations manifest that the rise of status and superstar markets is better explained by an eclectic framework that involves alternative approaches such as behavioural, evolutionary, institutional, post-Keynesian and even neo-Marxist ideas rather than the traditional standard economic assumptions. The context of the inquiry is broad because various subjective, institutional and sociological questions cannot be answered adequately solely on the basis of pure economic analysis. Thus it remains to be discussed in the following chapters in what manner social disciplines other than economics can enhance our understanding of status and superstar markets.

3. The fundamental forces: technology, tastes and values

INTRODUCTION

Positional activities do not take place in a static economic, social and cultural environment. By contrast, there are rapid and fundamental changes in various frontiers. Some of them such as the progress in information technology have massively influenced our lives. Situating the analysis of status markets in the context of important changes, which take place in the economic, the social and cultural environment becomes useful for two reasons. First, it allows the study of these markets on a firmer footing. The second reason is that it facilitates the analysis because it highlights important trends, which are linked with changes in everyday life. The influence of fundamental forces such as technology, preferences and wealth are usually considered as a fixed datum in traditional economic analysis but are allowed to vary within a socio-economic perspective. Thus the impact of advanced technological possibilities, inflated consumer choices and new wealth must be also taken into account. Another issue is the role of modern finance in supporting various categories of expenditures, which relate to consumption and investment preferences. These choices reflect to a smaller or a larger extent different sets of values or cultural beliefs. An essential question is how global trends in technological advancement, preference formation, wealth creation and financialization alter the economic, social or cultural structures, in which individuals live and act today.

For example, a fundamental development during the last decades is the emergence of a post-modern identity that is self-centred and egocentric. This personality is influenced by popular culture and media, is relativist both in perceptions and in the formation of beliefs, open to new experiences, emotional and reactive with respect to social changes and uncertainty. Thus it would be useful to sketch the contemporary human environment, in which post-modern individuals live beyond the impact of forces such as media visibility and technological innovation, which have already been identified as being relevant for the development of status markets.

NEW TRENDS IN GLOBALIZATION

The changes that take place today in technology, society, culture and markets are fast and often dramatic.[1] Some of these forces such as the economic rise of new regions such as South East Asia and Latin America, the emergence of ethnic lifestyles and cultural nationalism, the renaissance in the arts and the explosion of popular culture, the new age of communication and the expansion of science have been quite visible during the last decades. Yet there are other more controversial trends, which include the globalization of the economy and financialization, the contraction of the welfare state, the worldwide spread of the westernized lifestyle and the environmental crisis. With respect to individual lifestyles, since the 1980s there has been a shift towards a materialistic life as well as towards adopting conservative values. In addition, commercialism has embraced everything to such an extent that social solidarity has lost considerable ground relative to private sector interventions such as the corporate sponsoring of social events. Overall, there is a movement away from public finance of social care to a situation where corporations form alliances to help meet business goals and support social causes. These activities coincide often with contradictory reports of a middle class that has either died, or has moved to the upper classes.[2] Thus, besides the expansion of the private influence in various spheres of life, another characteristic of the contemporary era is the growing inequality in society.

There are several repercussions in the global economy where no individual country can survive alone with a sufficient economy. The relative efficiency of free-market economies has made them better equipped to adapt to a world economy. Moreover, the developments in information technology support immensely the emergence of the global economy. Through the 'home-centred' society that was predicted during the 1980s, people have become able to exploit opportunities around the globe.[3]

Of course, not everything is quite new as there are areas where the traditional industrial forces still operate. For example, the traditional industrial work-ethic is still present while in certain sectors a great part of service work remains 'Taylorized'.[4] In these sectors, the office is industrialized as the white-collar work is subjected in many instances to routines that remind us of practices in blue-collar work.[5] In this environment, the belief in substantive and rapid changes, like the spread of a new principle of work or a new ethic of professionalism, do not appear to gain momentum, pointing to a situation in which industrial and post-industrial culture co-exist. However, in attempting to resolve this type of ambivalence, one must take into consideration that the current state of free-market economy is, after all, capitalist. It is driven as before by the power of accumulation. The restructuring at work, which is related with technological development, late capitalism and the information society, is intended to provide a new boost to free-market dynamics.

ENTREPRENEURIALISM, COMMERCIALISM AND POPULAR CULTURE

An important force in the development of positional preferences and high-profile careers is that the post-modern individual is more self-interested and egocentric relative to the past. In this individualistic context, the marketplace today provides an environment, in which entrepreneurialism and commercialism thrive. These propensities do not appear in a vacuum since there is support from technological advancements. For example, for three decades now the central symbol and analytical engine of society has been the computer and its information technology and communication capacity.[6] It is around this technological advancement that information society is structured. One outcome of the information technology revolution is the movement to an entrepreneurial service society and the rapid growth of professional and technical jobs. These developments are supported by the determination of business entrepreneurs and managers to steer productivity and increase profits and by the growth of individualism and consumerism. Moreover, leisure time has become important in our everyday lives in a manner that fuels excessive consumption. The concern for acquisition and consumption of goods receives quite often a symbolic connotation. The modern culture of shopping promotes conspicuous consumption and is an activity that provides positive emotions independently of the question whether there is a real need for the purchase of a good.

Beyond repercussions of entrepreneurialism and commercialism, there are certainly changes in individual values. The first change is the diminishing importance of traditional beliefs and values and their replacement by ideas and conventions, which are validated by popular culture events and beliefs. This tendency strengthens steadily despite being at variance with the value system associated with the growing role of science and the expansion of knowledge, which is used in technological, productive or social processes. In addition, despite the democratization of formal education, the influence of popular culture is massive. In fact, the widespread adoption of education coincides with the manifestations of mass culture, which frequently undermine education norms. This happens because aesthetic, literary and artistic products of popular culture are in essence market commodities, which target rather primitive or unrefined preferences of the public. Finally, in another spectrum of social everyday life, people are experiencing a remarkable escalation of work-related obligations, which increasingly distances them from family life.[7] Thus there is an intensification of individualism, which is often mixed with greater exposure to uncertainties related to professional and family obligations.

This economic system of individualism, entrepreneurialism and consumerism reshapes the structure of the society and existing hierarchies. The rise of status markets takes place therefore in an environment where monetary ownership and market position become fundamental factors of social status (often replacing age, ethnicity, gender, religion and other traditional determinants). When ownership and market position become so important, the large parts of the population who fail to adjust become poorer and end up marginalized.

THE IMPACT OF TECHNOLOGICAL PROGRESS AND COMPLEXITY

Contemporary technology forms such as information technology constitute revolutionary forces, which facilitate commercialism and globalization. As it has been said, the use of technology is neither good nor bad, nor is it neutral. It is more of a force, probably stronger than ever before with the speed of contemporary technological progress.[8] By way of analogy, computer technology is to the information age what mechanization was to the industrial revolution.[9] The emergence of information technology helps the increase in knowledge to be qualitative, not just quantitative.[10] The traditional mass media sent standardized information to uniform mass audiences. The new media of Internet communication, the social media, permits the segmentation of both senders and receivers into separate units. Information fits the most specialized and the most individualized constraints.[11]

Despite the enormous opportunities that emerge from contemporary technology, the social terrain is evidently more complex for the post-modern individual. Technological growth takes place not only in terms of information communication.[12] For example, the rise of biotechnology has become massive. This example shows how pervasive technological innovations embrace not only material life, but also various spheres of social life as well. In the near future it is possible that we could eliminate various illnesses or almost any affliction we choose and our decision-making span will certainly widen. However, in this totally new environment individuals will not be sure whether their choices are wise or morally correct. The achievements in biotechnology do not come without moral dilemmas. Also, what is at issue is the accelerating tempo in the spread and deepening of the genetic revolution. In retrospect, the visible and dramatic progress of technological forms such as that of biotechnology, adds an element of complexity-thinking for the post-modern individual. This complexity-related way of thought is required as a method for understanding diversity, rather than using a technology-based meta-theory that explains contemporary phenomena in terms of the impact of technological change only.[13] Thus understanding the new complexities such as the saturation of signals generated in positional activities becomes more pressing for people today.

THE DECLINE IN MANUFACTURING, THE RISE OF SERVICES AND UNCERTAINTY

Another important trend is the reduction of traditional manufacturing jobs in western developed economies. Since the 1980s, there has been a decline in the number and importance of the blue-collar working class, which is the basis of labour unions. Many individuals resort to part-time jobs, a phenomenon which was viewed as quite unacceptable in the past. Labour markets and income expectations have become less stable for the post-modern individual. In this unstable environment, individuals may experience a confidence deficit and may be more willing to participate in other fields such as services. Such sectors are often characterized by tournament processes with more flexible labour conditions. Nevertheless, the decline in manufacturing jobs coincides with the rise of both producer services and social services. In the first group, the emphasis is on business services while in the second group health services seem to take a visible lead.[14]

Other trends include the diversification of sources of service jobs, the growth in professional and technical jobs, and the steady emergence of a new white-collar poor that take clerical, freelance and sales positions.[15] The increase in the size of the upper and lower ends in the structure of employment contributes to the appearance of a wider gap in income distribution. However, a relative improvement of the occupational structure over time is witnessed also. There is an increasing share of the occupations that require higher skills and advanced education. This increase is proportionally higher than the increase of the lower-level categories.

According to several studies, an occupational change has taken place since the 1990s. More than 60 per cent of the work force in the USA is related now to the information economy. Similar figures exist for other industrial countries; for example the estimate for the UK amounts to 65 per cent of the working population. Many social scientists argue that information technology will have in essence the character of an infrastructure. Therefore, knowledge capital, which is an important feature of post-industrial activities, will start to predominate over material capital in the structure of the economy leading to the strengthening of the creative class of symbolic analysts. In this vein, as industrial society replaced agrarian society, the information society replaces industrial society.[16]

This categorical description of societal transition tends to overlook in many cases the cultural and institutional diversity of advanced societies, as well as the interdependence that exists in a global economy.[17] In practice, the transition to an information society moves along different paths in different countries.[18] These paths are specific to the economic and social processes that take place in each country.[19] Thus there are interlinkages that are specific to the 'service economy model', represented by the USA and the UK.[20] This paradigm is characterized by a rapid decline in manufacturing employment after 1970s, and an acceleration of the adoption of new information technologies. However, the developments in Japan and in Germany show that the share of manufacturing employment remains at a relatively high level, despite the adoption of new information technologies. An intermediate situation takes place in countries such as Sweden and France that develop fast service economies and new information technologies, but support a relatively strong manufacturing base that interfaces with both producer and social services.[21] These differences imply that the relative weight of status markets may in fact differ from country to country because they account for different patterns of transition from the industrial society to a service-driven and information technology society.

TASTES, SATURATION AND THE RISE OF THE POST-MODERN INDIVIDUAL

The sharp changes that take place in the various spheres of the contemporary world have also changed people's personalities. The post-modern individual is increasingly ready for new experiences and more open to changes than people were in past societies. Furthermore, post-modern individuals feel more able to form opinions regarding a large variety of issues, to value positively the diversity of opinions and to use emotions as an evaluative instrument. The affective and complex cognitive behaviour of the post-modern individual associated with self-esteem and identity formation is important for preference formation. As it will be discussed in terms of psychological analysis later on in this book, this behaviour relates to individual reactions in relative social competition and in status markets. Today individuals are more aggressive because of their orientation towards the present and the future rather than the past. Self-confidence and self-esteem have become important to the contemporary individual's capacity to organize their life and to overcome everyday difficulties. Nevertheless, these obstacles also involve a greater sense of uncertainty. Planning, that is, anticipating future activities towards assumed goals is frequently disrupted and trust in the predictability of social life is usually undermined.

In the new social environment, the conflict between popular culture, which pervades middle-class lifestyles, and high culture disappears. The artistic lifestyle has now an attractive romantic ambience for those who live or are attracted to inner-city areas. However, individuals from the middle class and lower middle class increasingly value the role of culture in their lifestyles. As a result, people have an increasingly open attitude towards consumer culture. They show willingness to interface with popular cultural intermediaries. Thus the democratization of culture has become an important aspect of contemporary society. However, although this democratization is a positive development, it takes place within the broader social process, in which certain aspects of status markets such as social discrimination remain.

The analysis has to take also into account the decisive role of cultural or symbolic analysts, who are often superstar professionals in their own fields and visible agents of lifestyle culture. Symbolic analysts have an interest in promoting a sort of pedagogy for the new type of markets, society and life that people face today. These analysts seek to reject traditional forms of culture. In order to gain a competitive edge in the area of status markets, one of their strategies is to create a synthesis of cultural niches that undermine the traditional definition of aesthetics that expresses itself. Thus high culture is replaced by novel forms of music, fashion and movies. Plastic surgery has become an aesthetic or artistic experience with symbolic connotation and everyday professional or private activities are dressed in artistic forms to signal effectively.

POST-MODERN CULTURE AND DIVERSITY

The rise of post-modern culture in the new information society has become also a force of complexity.[22] In the information society, cultural services and information have acquired value; value was once thought of as something that could only be attached to material goods. In such a context, the defence of one's own culture against the logic of markets becomes a pressing question for many individuals with diverse social backgrounds. Thus the important question becomes how, in a world characterized by both globalization and fragmentation, the analysis can combine new technologies, historical roots, science and different communication cultures.[23] These processes influence organizational change and employment conditions.[24]

This interdependent framework emphasizes contemporary lifestyle as the domain where different cultures manifest themselves and interact. The options for an individual today appear numerous. For example, there is an observable approach to life, which is characterized by an insatiable quest for both security and adventure. This leads to enormous fragmentation and to a realization of an urgent need to overcome it. One analytical route to overcome fragmentation effectively is to introduce other dimensions. For example, the introduction of time into the social space can be one dimension for distinguishing styles from lifestyles. Taking a longer view helps individuals recover their sense of distinction and values.

THE FRAGMENTATION OF UNIVERSAL BELIEFS IN POST-MODERN VIRTUAL SOCIETY

In today's culturally fragmented environment, people no longer live in a world that operates through universal beliefs as was the case with traditional beliefs in the past. The analysis cannot explain consumer culture in terms of a fundamental all-pervasive ethic or take this code for granted. Thus under certain circumstances we are unable to judge and analyse new symbolic and intellectual goods and services in terms of frameworks that assume universal beliefs. The major theories, the meta-narratives of western modernity, for example science, humanism and socialism, exhibit facets that are in fact problematic.[25] Since these basic ideological narratives are undermined, people do not possess the confidence in their own judgement and in their own ability to mould society in terms of themselves and to overcome their own relativism. Thus a more convenient role for the post-modern individual has been to undertake the role of spectator or commentator who codifies the various aspects of cultural phenomena without the intention of judging them.

This holds not only for ideological and moral narratives but also for the legitimacy of forces such as the technology and the market economy sectors that are based on it. In the light of everyday experience, this may seem as a paradox but the post-modern individual is aware that technological progress and the inherent scientific knowledge are not independent. While science seems to be accepted more than any other narrative, it is nevertheless condemned as being more or less a narrative, in terms of which a meta-narrative is legitimized. Despite enormous progress, science is not considered to be universally valuable because of the uncertainties it creates with respect to individual freedom and individual knowledge. With this loss of confidence in the universal belief of the social role of science comes the decline in the belief that the current market paradigm has effective regulatory power. There seems to be no way in the contemporary market economy environment to effectively regulate science in the name of a universal belief. The competition for economic and financial power is a process that poses difficulties to the possibility of such regulation. Yet the demise of traditional universal beliefs in the contemporary cultural and social environment leads also to a gradual loss of an understanding of the social role of classes. This contemporary tendency makes it difficult to communicate a framework for the evaluation of individuals such as famous professionals from the perspective of a universal belief system regarding social classes.

THE DECLINE OF INTEREST IN POLITICS AND THE MULTICULTURAL SOCIETY

Before the international financial crisis of 2007–2008 and the Great Recession there had been for quite a long time a decline in interest and in participating in political movements of social change. The western liberal democracy is associated with a modern confidence to be self-assertive and a willingness to centre individual hopes on the future. This modern confidence has produced the reformist politics and the social engineering that have led to tolerance, a free press, universal education, social care, parliament and the rest of the institutions of liberal democracy. However, one may argue that this progress depends on the primacy of the universal principle of the pursuit of increased tolerance and decreased suffering.

With the decline of the importance of universal concepts such as socialism, political programmes have been losing over a long period much of their legitimacy. Since there is no universal social subject as labour was for Marxism, there are only diverse subjects for different social groups and various cultures that depend on beliefs that may be inconsistent with each other.

Thus the phenomenon of status markets cannot be approached only in terms of the welfare cost that it produces for the whole of the society. One issue that must be addressed is whether there are greater relative costs for certain groups of the society that are at a more disadvantaged position. In this case, pragmatism and humanistic resistance to any sort of exploitation meet each other because people at a disadvantage can be mobilized to pursue the 'pragmatist utopia' of improving their own social conditions.[26]

THE ROLE OF FINANCIALIZATION

These objectives must materialize in an environment of growing globalization. An important phenomenon that relates closely to globalization is financialization. Financialization facilitates and benefits from globalization, which is characterized by the elimination of controls in trade, capital markets and labour markets through sourcing. The development of financialization is caused by the growing importance of financial markets and global financial institutions such as Citibank and HSBC in contemporary globalized economies. Financialization signifies mainly the fact that capital markets surmount the activities of bank-based credit markets. A fundamental feature of financialization is that all forms of tangible and intangible value with different specificities such as, for example, time, material of asset and ownership, are expressed into financial instruments and their derivatives. This facility expands transactions for industrialists, traders, workers and others. For example, workers can purchase houses through standardized financial instruments such as mortgages by discounting their expected money wages. Private and public debt expands and becomes available to all economic actors.[27]

A critical aspect of financialization is that financial instruments are structured on the basis of complete information, the absence of strong uncertainty and the omission of the impact of financial crises. This premise is supported by conventional economic theory with its reliance on rationality and efficient markets. According to orthodox presumptions, the expansion of financial markets supports economic efficiency, speculation is a stabilizing force towards returning to fundamental values and equity replaces industrial capital.[28] In addition, the Modigliani–Miller theorem under perfect information has equated debt-finance to equity-finance, providing a rationalization of the outburst of appetite for debt instruments. Other arguments of the conventional economic theory justify the explosion in top management compensation in the form of salaries, bonuses and stock options. Overall, financial markets relax prudential practices and corporate balance sheet constraints through management, and often manipulation of collateral values and credit availability. The incompatibility between the foundation of complete information and the existence of strong uncertainty and psychological reactions of investors is the main reason, which explains why financialization creates severe financial crises and unstable business cycles with dramatic effects on employment. The financialized business cycle depends on financial boom, asset price inflation, increasing debt and cheap imports.

One particular feature of financialization is the unresponsiveness of financial executive pay to crisis, although the global financial institutions and banks survived the international financial crisis 2007–2008 with the help of government support, which creates a culture of privilege and contentment.[29] An explanation for the existence of high rewards is individual performance so that top workers cannot easily leave for another firm that would reward them more. Another explanation is deciding bonuses on the basis of the value of workers to their companies. Yet this value may depend on intrinsic motives, which pervade relations of trust in conducting risky and often devious business. Overall, financialization raises concerns about the sustainability of status markets and superstar occupations as it represents a fragile mechanism in the process of globalization and in the sustainability of the new rich. Issues of equitable development and support of labour markets towards full employment through government intervention are also parts of an evolving agenda that relates to financialization.

CONCLUDING REMARKS

The various trends that underlie the economic, social and cultural environment, in which we live today provide a fertile ground for boosting feel-good and want-it-all aspirations. Despite the frictions that exist in the transition from the industrial centrally administered world to the decentralized information-technology era, technological progress facilitates the liberalization, financialization and globalization of markets and leads to a surge of entrepreneurialism, commercialism and contentment. In this environment, individuals' actions exhibit more self-centred and dynamic personalities and feel encouraged to form ambitious expectations.

The transition from the industrial era to the information technology world results in liberalized labour markets, flexible labour relations, deeper inequality and augmented uncertainty that questions people's own confidence. Then again, the technological progress, whether informational, industrial or biogenetic, and its effects on markets, lead to new wealth opportunities, supports the creation of the new rich and adds considerable complexity to today's life. The human environment facilitates the development of higher individual expectations despite unfavourable odds produced by greater uncertainty and complexity. Since people today live in a world of rapid changes, in which fast adaptation is very important even in situations of limited information, it is not a surprise that we observe excesses in occupational decisions and consumerism.

Furthermore, the changes in the marketplace and the workplace give rise to new social trends in education, health and other areas of everyday life, and alter the margins between the public and the private, the individual and the collective, the contented and the disadvantaged. Certain channels of technological progress such as communications, information technology or digital television technology make the transmission of different categories of information to different users possible so that information is now fragmented.

This situation in turn creates fragmented social and cultural subspaces, in which individuals operate and communicate, and this leads to the co-existence of different and sometimes contradictory beliefs. As a result, we observe the demise of universal beliefs that act as a reference for the mobilization of support for social changes in traditional mixed economies. This new social condition implies that citizens could have difficulty in assessing the dramatic changes in the social environment and so enthusiastically support interventionist policies on the basis of traditional politics. Alternative policies require a change in political thinking to identify and to eventually overcome the fragmentation of social identities. A special force is the influence of television, which facilitates the visualization of certain attitudes, norms or stereotypes. Television helps bring down several walls, such as the difference between high culture and popular culture, and allows individuals to visualize a rich lifestyle that could not be internalized in the experience of real everyday life. Imaginary or hyperreal individualism in modern times is a personal attitude that motivates people to compete harder for the riches and privileges that the new society allows to the few superstars. Overall, in today's economic, social and cultural environment people observe not only fundamental and rapid changes but also a diversity of forces that alter the way they think and behave. In order to analyse the complex changes in individual behaviour in a concrete manner and to develop a coherent framework to design proper policies, it is necessary to examine the phenomenon of status markets from alternative angles including sociological, anthropological, psychological and political perspectives.

4. Psychology and behavioural forces

INTRODUCTION

Since preferences and motives play an important role in status markets, explaining positional activities solely on the basis of economic principles constrains the analysis. A fundamental question that usually arises is why preferences change towards specific goods, services or activities. While one cause is the influence of economic environment, there are several subjective factors that require closer examination. For example, certain changes in preferences towards positional goods, services or activities may be attributed to a sort of subjective bias or to our perceptions of self-worth. These are forces that are dealt better within the field of social psychology rather than within the domain of economics. It is obvious therefore that we have to expand the range of analytical tools, which are suitable for the study of status markets so that we include the influence of psychological considerations. This will help identify cases, in which status is important because of behavioural factors such as the quest for approval or recognition by other people rather than financial rewards. Another task is to examine the cognitive limitations of human beings, which surface in certain situations and shape the manner in which preferences are expressed. In addition, we need to examine how in the context of subjective analysis interpersonal considerations arise and what role they play with regard to the distortions of status markets. Supplementary psychological processes may include the impact of psychological internalization due to the overexposure of positional activities through advertisement and the phenomenon of subjective deprivation due to the impact of social discrimination. The theory and practice of social psychology is better suited to provide satisfactory answers on these matters.

THE QUEST FOR STATUS GOODS AND SERVICES

In superstar markets, status or prestige are considered as being important qualities. One example is that most top executives in well-known corporations usually come from elite universities. Often, these executives are hired more on the basis of the prestige that their university carries relative to other less-known institutions rather than their own academic competence or their own talent and professional expertise. This mis-representation relates to behavioural or psychological factors because prestige is often perceived by people as signifying more closely com-petency, excellence, credibility and potential for success.

A tendency that relates to prestige is that people value on the basis of relative rather than absolute factors. How people, services or goods are compared to others is an important issue, which did not remain unnoticed by economists in the past. Thus Hirsch labelled those status or relative comparison goods as 'positional goods'.[1] The psychological quest for positional goods, services, activities and occupations is not confined only to the joy that comes with the realization of one's own status. Obtaining a superior relative position is also important because even when indi-viduals do not have a specific interest for their own status they care about how their possession of positional goods compares with that of others.[2] One fundamental explanation of this tendency is that positional goods represent an opportunity to show our ability to others.

Signifying ability through relative position advantage can take alter-native forms for different groups of people. For prosperous professionals, expensive possessions such as SLK Mercedes cars, houses in exclusive suburbs and costly leisure activities such as exotic trips and cosmopolitan getaways demonstrate to others a better social standing. At lower levels of income, this attitude is facilitated by credit support and is directed towards similar but less expensive goods or services. Among other items, these include stylish cars, bigger houses in better suburbs and long holiday packages abroad. Besides individual ability, the quest for fame and its desirability is another strong incentive. Fame is a desirable quality which drives artists, athletes, television personalities and, more broadly, successful professionals such as investment bankers, lawyers, doctors and others. Being famous contributes definitely to a relative position advan-tage and multiplies monetary rewards. Winning in a visible market that is covered by television, radio or magazines and being famous appears often more important than winning in a less visible market because it provides psychological rewards and can materialize to superior financial gains.

The psychological rewards that are provoked by the approval or recognition of other people are mainly affective. Positional superiority in the form of enjoying status or prestige is fascinating not only because of the financial rewards that often come with them but because they are basic determinants of positive affect and personal satisfaction. Successful people seem very happy because they are exposed to expressions of appreciation by their clients, collaborators and public in their daily routines. This attribute fuels the desire to achieve a superior relative position even if sometimes there is no immediate supplementary financial reward. Many individuals would treasure a warm applause in a professional, artistic or athletic event or a medal from a competition.

THE PSYCHOLOGICAL IMPORTANCE OF STATUS AND PRESTIGE

Signalling competitiveness may not mean only potential for success but also the ability of an individual to protect what they consider to be their territory. For example, credibility of opinion is necessary when somebody decides to protect their rights or to bargain some of them. This is achieved by using an ultimatum that communicates the boundaries of non-negotiable rights. The more the individual appears competitive and is approved of by their fellows, the more that individual's opinion will be perceived as credible and they will be more successful in attaining their goals. In addition, competition for context-dependent activities is important because it enhances cognitive capacity and carries information that can be helpful in future decisions. The context of relative position competition varies with respect to different contingencies. Sometimes, intense competitions matter more within a group rather than outside the group that they belong to. Individuals within their professional or social group seem to seek references which then help them to evaluate potential relative position changes. Yet the tendency to signal competitiveness through status-seeking is not only emotionally fulfilling, it is fun, motivational or informative for future activities. It can be primarily translated into financial rewards or professional success. A professional who drives a Porsche Cayenne or enters the office dressed in a Versace suit with the latest model of Bulgari watch on their wrist signals that they are already successful in the market and that their abilities or talents are unquestionable. This appears to be so even in situations in which a professional is not fully competent. However, the professional's status image will induce any prospective clients or partners to assume erroneously that the professional is somebody, who will support their interests successfully.

Besides simple everyday observation and evidence from occupational psychological tests or surveys, there is a strong interest in neuroscience research that links behavioural with neurological or biological conditions. There is robust evidence that relates perceptions of relative position to a concentration of the neurotransmitter serotonin that regulates moods.[3] In addition, in tests with human subjects there is strong evidence that connects the presence of more testosterone in the body with the experience of a better relative position.[4]

LACK OF PREDICTION, VISIBILITY AND EXPOSURE

Overall, biological advantages, territorial protection, positive feelings from social approval and referential information for future changes, are important factors that induce people to prefer positional goods or services. Yet some of these factors are actually associated with the feeling of insecurity and the incapacity of individuals to predict how their satisfaction or good feelings from the consumption of a commodity will change over time. Thus possessions such as villas and holiday homes, expensive cars and yachts may provide variable satisfaction over time, since after the initial high thrill satisfaction gradually falls to lower levels. Then again, although many other leisure activities like swimming at the beach, walking by the lake or participating in a community concert do not provide the context for relative position competition they produce a long-lasting feeling of satisfaction.

This example shows that the individuals who prefer positional goods do not allocate their tastes in accordance with enduring levels of satisfaction because they concentrate on the initial high thrill. In essence, the concern for positional superiority makes these people unable to foresee their satisfaction for goods in the future.[5] This weakness can prove harmful because the benefits from some non-positional activities such as athletics or education are realized only with the passage of time.[6]

In addition, visibility is a fundamental consideration since some people prefer positional goods and services over non-positional ones because they are more visible. For example, the houses and the cars of neighbours are more visible than their leisure or cultural activities. This process can also explain why more and more people seek to participate in context-related activities in the contemporary world, which are often dominated by the visibility provided by the media. To sum up, the misallocation of resources that takes place in status markets may be attributed to the fact that in our post-modern media world, some goods, services or activities are made more visible than others and, therefore, some people are more induced to seek context-based activities.

Even in a rational-choice context, exposure to visible consumption trends alters the form of tastes and may create undesired preferences. People may prefer to act upon the will they have (that is, what is usually called first-order preferences) rather than the will they desire to have (that is, the so-called second-order preferences).[7] An analysis of the transformation of preferences for social status must include the study of different tiers of transformation with regard to persuasion. For example, one such obvious tier is the purposeful effort of parents to socialize their children to their own vision about different lifestyles.[8] The prevalence of undesired preferences is in essence a consequence of complex repercussions. The mechanism that strips people from their own will generates both positive and negative spillovers and suboptimal choices and creates tastes, which have become 'polluted' with regard to persuasion.

COGNITIVE LIMITATIONS

Yet another factor that stimulates our preferences for positional goods stems from our mental capacity limitations. For example, according to the hypothesis of rationality that is fundamental in traditional economics, people know the system that dictates their real-life experiences and can predict most of the times correctly. This stands in contrast with situations, in which there is a lack of information and, sometimes, lack of visibility. Contrary to rationality, our decisions are affected by our mental capacity to foresee the future. The relative position advantage is sought in many instances by seemingly irrational people, who have a limited mental capacity or interest about the distant future. Often it is hard to predict the capacity of adaptation to future experiences, as novelty is usually an important aspect of positional goods. Even when people are able to predict and adapt relatively well, the adaptation may be difficult because of unexpected effects associated with novel features of positional goods or activities. Thus in seeking to be involved with positional activities people prefer to act 'irrationally' on the basis of cognitive and affective forces.

These observations raise altogether the issue of cognitive limitations that exist when individuals act as consumers or as producers in contemporary saturated markets. According to psychological tests, people seem to feel difficulties when their consumption includes a number of goods that exceeds a list of ten items.[9] This evidence applies also in a broader context in the sense that buyers are in fact unable to keep track of a list of competing products or services that resemble each other. Thus people prefer to relate their consumption or other activities with a smaller number of items in order to save time and cognitive capacity. There is strong evidence that suggests that people are able to hold satisfactory conversations because they share 'heroes' in their activities.[10] Thus in various social settings, from neighbourhoods and the workplace to family and friends' gatherings, conversations evolve around a few famous or well-known names with information from television, the Internet or magazines. The fact that people do not seem to have sufficient 'self-space' obliges them to circle their conversations around well-known names. In principle, the higher the prominence of these well-known names, the greater the length of conversation about them or the excitement involved.

FURTHER EVIDENCE ON COGNITIVE BIAS

Thus cognitive bias induces people to centre their attention on a few famous products, services or people. For example, even institutions such as firms cannot be rational in their decision-making because they do not possess complete information about their business environment. In this vein, they are unable to maximize their profits and they opt better to achieve a certain level of profit or market share. Thus managers, like normal people, cannot act rationally in complex situations because they cannot within realistic computational limits generate all the admissible alternatives and compare their respective merits.[11] In addition, we cannot recognize the best alternative, even if we are fortunate enough to generate it early, until we have seen all of them. For this way, we 'satisfice' for alternatives in such a way that we can generally find an acceptable option after only moderate searching.

This process is highly influenced by limitations of short-term memory.[12] An individual can process only a few symbols at a time. In addition, the symbols that are processed must be held in special, limited memory structures, whose content can be changed rapidly.[13] There is a difficulty in applying efficient strategies because of the very small capacity of the short-term memory structure and the relatively long time (approximately five seconds) required to transfer a chunk of information from the short-term to the long-term memory.

The importance of cognitive limitations has been stressed also by a group of cognitive psychologists, who formulated the prospect theory.[14] These psychologists study the cognitive biases that arise from our ability to assign probabilities in real-life decision-making. Some biases are relevant to the visibility effects of superstar markets. First, according to empirical evidence, there is the heuristic of availability of information, in which individuals attribute higher evaluations to a category or a frequency of events that they can recall easily than to other types that are more difficult to remember or think about. The second systematic cognitive bias is the heuristic of representation, according to which, people seem to assign the same probabilities to events or causes that appear similar. This is a poor judgement because in many situations there is no reason for similarity and frequency to match.

The third cognitive type of bias relates to anchoring and adjustment. Often, individuals find a starting point of reference or an anchor as a convenient benchmark to estimate a magnitude.[15] The choice of an anchor may be the result of a learning adjustment process. Yet the movement from the initial anchor may be too slow or towards a false direction. It seems that people attribute a higher probability of success to a lottery number they picked themselves rather than to one given to them, even when there are monetary incentives to act more rationally.[16] Overall, the presence of systematic cognitive biases indicates the tendency of people to fixate their attention on a limited number of anchors. This inclination provides an additional explanation of why visible positional goods, services or activities and well-known names easily become the centre of attention.

For many social scientists, a fundamental question is how the cognitive biases can be minimized or corrected. It seems however that there is not an adequate alternative to decision-making under cognitive bias. Since cognitive capacity is a scarce resource, the information-gathering and calculations that are assumed to take place consume time and energy to such an extent that in many cases they are not worthy to be undertaken.[17] Thus given the cognitive limitations, decision-making on the basis of common sense, habits or other non-rational rules frequently appears the most reasonable choice even when we know that the variety of decisions available are inferior to those of a hypothetical fully informed rational individual.

There have been extensive attempts to analyse non-rational rules of thumb as it is demanding to describe some representative rules of thumb.[18] In addition, there is some difficulty to prove the validity of the rules of thumb or to connect them clearly with a logical explanation that is associated with rational behaviour. In any case, the utilization of rules of thumb is frequently observed in our economic and social milieu. They help overcome the cognitive biases experienced by the post-modern individual, which induce them to desire positional goods or services and to be more attentive to the activities of highly visible persons.

SELF-WORTH AND THE INTEREST FOR RELATIVE POSITION

Another psychological consideration involves the role of self-esteem. There is a small, reinforcing and significant positive relationship between socio-economic status and self-esteem in the sense that happy people make more money, which in turn makes them happier.[19] This situation may change when people are involved in relative position comparisons. This happens because a behavioural force that strengthens our interest for context and relative position is in fact our perception of self-worth. When the perception is negative we tend to compare ourselves with others more than usual. Studies of differences between compulsive spenders and average consumers with respect to their self-esteem and to their attitudes towards money based on the scales of self-esteem and beliefs, imply that compulsive spenders have relatively lower self-esteem than 'normal' consumers. In addition, compulsive spenders have beliefs about money which reflect its symbolic ability to enhance self-esteem.[20] Thus the quest for self-esteem is a compelling cause along with other motives for obtaining power, prestige and security.

In this environment, lifestyle possibilities materialize with respect to attitudes towards spending for material goods and, as a consequence, towards adopting a positional behaviour. Accordingly, as it has been mentioned in the previous chapter, there are various strategies regarding a wide range of consumer lifestyles that fulfil material wants, leisure activities and individual values.[21] These strategies may reflect different combinations of spending attitudes and variable preferences towards material properties and leisure activities.[22] These possibilities highlight the contradiction of the pleasure derived from material spending with the satisfaction that is experienced by participating in leisure activities. In recreational activities, the satisfaction increases naturally with time. In contrast, it becomes more difficult for people to enhance their satisfaction by increasing the activity that is associated with material or positional goods. Yet despite this implicit cost many individuals prefer to be involved in a context-dependent activity because they are concerned with their relative position. As it has been mentioned, the preference for context-dependent activities or positional goods has an evolutionary significance since survival depends more on the availability of material resources rather than on leisure activities. Material resources and leisure activities are both desirable but when it comes to survival there is clearly a preference for material resources. Nonetheless, if the context-dependent activity is very stressful because of intense competition or if there is uncomfortable congestion, then the desire for access to positional goods and for preferential use of material resources runs into serious problems because of the costs that it incurs. In this state, there is a greater propensity to be involved in leisure activities.

SELF-WORTH AND COGNITIVE DISSONANCE

It is important to mention that self-worth is also associated with cognitive processes. According to cognitive dissonance theory, the presence of inconsistent ideas in the mind produces an aversive drive state that is minimized when individuals distort their own beliefs to reduce the psychological inconsistency.[23] This state gives rise to an emotionally unpleasant situation that resembles guilt. The psychological inconsistency is more present when aspects of our self are related to cognitions. This means that when unflattering cognitions about ourselves or about our character or image surface, we feel more uncomfortable and anxious and we are more willing to distort our views.[24] In addition, people distort their beliefs when they see themselves behaving as incompetent, unjustifiable or immoral.[25] Overall, there are three aspects of actions that carry implications for ourselves: (i) the degree to which we have control of them (have a choice about them); (ii) the degree to which our actions are justified; and, (iii) the magnitude of the consequences of our actions.

Yet in psychological experiments, individuals exhibited dissonance in cases in which they did something foolish but certainly not immoral. This evidence indicates that what is at stake is something more general than the sense of morality, perhaps, self-worth.[26] More precisely, individuals distort their beliefs or views when their behaviour influences negatively their sense of self-worth, whether morality or competence is involved. Hence many individuals choose to undertake context-dependent activities and prefer positional goods and services in order to demonstrate competence, affirm self-worth and avoid unpleasant dissonance. These individuals who affirm their values do not exhibit dissonance, while those who are not able to affirm their values, display dissonance. Affirming a worthy self makes it less important to deny that one had lied. Nevertheless, feeling like a hypocrite produces dissonant states of mind even in cases in which there is no serious objective pain to oneself or to others.

According to attribution analysis, there are several biases when people reason about behaviour. People seem to believe that their own actions are externally caused while believing that other people's behaviour is internally caused. The most important attributional mistake is to accept behaviour as being really indicative of somebody's qualities, even when there are reasons to believe that under different circumstances this person would act differently.[27] Another finding is that people usually assume that other people behave in the same way or evaluate things in the same way as they do.[28] Thus there is an inner tendency to participate in relative position competition. This egocentric attitude can be worse in cases in which people seem to make external attributions for their mistakes but internal attributions for their achievements.[29]

Furthermore, attributions are crucial because people are often more interested in knowing who is responsible for something, than they are in simply knowing who caused it. Another reason is because we draw inferences from a person's behaviour to the traits that account for that behaviour.[30] Finally, according to inference theory, our suppositions about the causes of human behaviour become gradually uncertain as we find out that people may have more reasons or interests for acting the way they do. In contrast, the urge for context and positional signalling causes a feeling of certainty. In recent years, psychologists have attempted to expand their analysis of cognitive biases by developing the framework of cognitive schemata which helps to control our attention, integrate our information and guide our memory.

STATUS DIFFERENTIATION AND COGNITIVE DISSONANCE

Psychology therefore helps us understand the impact of cognitive biases and points out the idea that individuals who fail to earn status experience dissonance. As it has been noted above, this is a feeling generally described as psychological discomfort. In the original theory of cognitive dissonance, individuals holding inconsistent beliefs, or acting in a manner contrary to their beliefs, experience dissonance. The elimination of this dissonance is a motive for behavioural and cognitive modification.[31] The latter involves primarily considerations of self-esteem and the motive to justify one's own actions. For example, dissonance and dissonance reduction operate when beliefs are in conflict with the individual's desire to be considered competent, morally good or an intelligent person.[32] The incompatibility between the individual's desire for prestige and the lack of social esteem results in dissonance. People facing this situation can either allocate more effort to increase private consumption to attain status or to modify their own attitudes regarding what they view to be status worthy.[33]

However, since different individuals utilize variable strategies of a leisure status game versus a consumption status game, there is the possibility of smoothing the scarcity of social rank so that eventually social welfare improves. This happens because the choice of leisure activities in a strategic context helps improve an individual's self-confidence. As a result, there are status characteristics in leisure activities that are different from traditional economic variables, such as wealth and consumption, and these will help reduce individual dissonance.

Furthermore, people care about the maintenance of their own self-image which can lead them to engage in seemingly irrational behaviour. This irrational behaviour can include the avoidance of information and own-deception processes via elaborate strategies of selective memory, limited awareness and belief manipulation. In strategic decision-making however, conflicting interests generally imply that self-confidence matters even when people are fully time-consistent.[34]

Thus self-confidence serves as an important motivation in individual practices. The value of self-confidence arises endogenously from fundamental preferences, technological constraints, uncertainty and the structure of incentives. Finally, an alternative motive considered in social psychology for self-esteem maintenance involves affective (rather than purely cognitive) concerns: people just like to think of themselves as good, able, generous, attractive and so on.[35] As a result, memory management and similar forms of self-deception which link with the maintenance of self-esteem, may be ultimately detrimental while, conversely, the adoption of personal rules that help the classification and processing of unfavourable information, can prove valuable.

OVEREXPOSURE AND COGNITIVE EVALUATION

Often, context-dependent activities and relative position considerations arise because of a psychological or behavioural reaction to overexposure to positional goods and services, and the activities of superstars and celebrities. In principle, exposure to a stimulus seems to influence our reaction to it. Individuals can exhibit various attitudes through time, which include a continuous positive reaction to a stimulus, an initially negative reaction that becomes positive later on, a continuous negative reaction and a positive reaction that turns negative at a later stage. Subjects that were initially evaluated negatively, but subsequently were viewed positively, create a great deal of attraction for that subject.[36] Hence positional goods or services involve novelty and may cause frustration in the beginning, but they can become very attractive once they are evaluated positively. Furthermore, once there is an established pattern, positive evaluations can be continuously reinforcing. People seem to like anything they are exposed to over and over, better and better.[37] This is a simple manifestation of the overexposure effect.[38] In this sense, overexposure to positional activities in today's television and information technology world drives people to pursue them more. Positive evaluations are also caused by the expression of competency and the reaction to genuine appreciation. For example, competent people are generally better liked than incompetent people. Superstars today represent competency and this feature is a fundamental reason that explains why they are liked especially when they look natural and humble like common people. Today's television world is in essence a field in which superstars are represented as highly exceptional and friendly. This process in turn makes them look attractive and persuasive. It is no accident therefore that people choose passionately to emulate overexposed role models from the media world.[39] The information that is made available in television programmes, however trivial, is used as a means of reference for social conduct and communication. Thus the next-day gossip at the shopping mall, the gym or even in the executive room that follows the episode of a television programme shown the night before is highly enjoyable, sometimes more than watching the television show itself. Oral communication about television programmes has been elevated to such an extent that it represents clearly a cultural terrain that must be studied more closely. To assume simply that there is only a social use in oral communication such as in television or business information is not enough. Actually, there is a process of interactivity to the extent that oral communication itself constitutes a culture, which is significant in constructing not only social relations but also our sense of social identity. People live in communities and organizations of every sort. In these social organizations they talk about the information and the superstars promoted by the mass media in a way that accomplishes much of the cultural aspect of television shows, the representation of a pleasurable social experience. This is important because it helps us come in touch with different aspects of our social identity. These facets do not develop directly from the cultural commodities of television. They are rather the product of synthesis between the television information and the conventions that exist in the oral communication in the communities or organizations in which individuals belong. This dimension of gossip or oral communication around the activities of well-known names in mass media facilitates the tendency of people to be alert to status-dependent and context-dependent events or activities. This may take place indirectly as gossip and is an example that reflects the contrast between central and peripheral routes to persuasion in various strands of life. The central route to persuasion is carefully reasoned, uses algorithms and depends on the quality of the arguments involved. However, the peripheral route to persuasion is less carefully reasoned, uses heuristics and depends on superficial aspects (that is, attractiveness of source, source prestige and so on).[40]

UNCERTAINTY, FAMILIARITY, SPECIAL OCCASIONS AND HIGH STAKES

Another cause of context-dependent activities is that people prefer familiar activities or sources of information that mitigate the complexity and uncertainty of the contemporary environment. Complexity in current affairs and uncertainty about the outcome of certain decisions produce a greater need for familiar people, technique types and sources of performance. This need leads usually to the emergence of networks which are useful because they promote familiar names and top performers. In this environment, the success of a top performer is actually self-fulfilling. This phenomenon implies that there is an increasing rather than a declining preference to view, or to receive the services of top performers repeatedly. This tendency stands in contrast with traditional economics where the more we consume of something the less we want to pay the price of it.

Another cause of our preference for positional sources comes from studying the phenomenon of gift-giving and the celebration of special occasions. In a poor society, a man can express his love by giving a rose, but in a rich society more expensive gifts are usually considered suitable.[41] The celebration of a special occasion is important for the development and projection of our identity. People prefer to enjoy celebrations with friends at special restaurants, clubs and travel destinations. This induces them to be more attentive to the special information that comes from positional activities or sources.

The demand for a well-known or positional product or service may also stem from a desire to avoid regret over possible adverse outcomes attributable to having bought less than the best. The executive who hires the blue-chip consulting firm, which is based in the Wall Street area or in the City of London, does so because they protect themselves from the criticism they could possibly face if things do not go as wished. Thus the choice of the premium consultant appears natural, especially when the stakes are high. The pressure to hire a well-known name is often substantial. Fear therefore of adverse outcomes induces people to prefer positional sources and superstar professionals because with them there is a feeling that everything possible has been done to avoid an unfavourable outcome.[42] Therefore, social influence often determines the choice of products and professionals.

RISK SHIFTS

Overall, risk-taking and the behaviour that accompanies it play an important role in decision-making.[43] For example, in a large market people are unlikely to know the number of their competitors and to be able to assess information about their relative strengths and weaknesses. The lack of information leads individuals to overestimate both their own abilities and their luck. The same result occurs in superstar markets, because of the visibility of higher standards and the cultivation of ambitious aspirations. As a result, people are inclined to become more risk-takers with regard to their occupation paths. Yet the behavioural evidence about people's attitudes towards risk is contradictory. For example, people appear to enjoy gambling, even when the odds of winning are not great. Risk preference therefore is essential to explain such phenomena. The more risk-taker is one decision-maker, the more attractive they will find their participation in a superstar market. However, a risk-averse or a risk-neutral participant in a superstar market will find this sort of experience confusing and less attractive. Yet if the number of risk-takers in a given superstar market is high, it influences socially more people to enter these contests.[44] With the flow of information, the prevalence of aggressive role-models in the mass media and the high visibility of positional activities, the number of people who are willing to compete in superstar markets has grown dramatically during the last decades.

HAPPINESS, RELATIVE INCOME AND INTERPERSONAL COMPARISONS

Another pertinent consideration that requires examination is the role of non-monetary incentives in relative position competition. Thus there are factors other than money, which contribute to our well-being. The objective of people is to experience frequent and intense levels of positive affect, or low levels of negative affect when situations become painful. People who experience this pattern of emotions are considered happy from a stereotypical viewpoint.[45] Intense levels of positive and negative emotions characterize highly emotional people, while those with mild levels of positive and negative affect are considered to be more phlegmatic.[46]

From a philosophical point of view, the ultimate goal for individuals is not stereotypical happiness. Since antiquity most philosophers talked about *eudaimonia*, happiness that is associated with positive affect, with some stressing that the avoidance of negative affect, or *ataraxia*, that is, a persistent feeling of tranquility, is what must be sought by people. In any case and whatever happiness is, freedom of choice is an indispensable characteristic of the quest for happiness. In addition, according to recent evidence self-esteem and extraversion in personality, which are important factors in sustaining freedom of choice, can directly explain happiness. Yet among the lay theories, only factors such as optimism and contentment were proved to be associated directly with happiness, which, however, are fundamental forces in the burgeoning literature on positive psychology.[47]

Additional evidence shows that many decisions are influenced primarily by relative income considerations and, broadly speaking, by relative comparisons.[48] The well-known typical study of the 'ultimatum-bargaining game' in economics demonstrates an interesting result.[49] According to the game, $10 is distributed between two people, the owner of the money who is called the Proposer and the one who demands a fairer distribution who is called the Respondent. The Proposer in principle can offer the minimum pay, say $1. The evidence of this study suggests that the Respondents will accept on average $2.59 or, approximately, 25 per cent of the total amount to be distributed to them, while the Proposers offer on average as high as $4.71 to the Respondents, which is a surprising outcome.[50] Thus happiness and individual satisfaction are influenced not only by relative income considerations but also by fairness judgements about beliefs that are different across people and influence bargaining expectations.[51] This example shows that interpersonal comparisons are useful because they facilitate the exchange of views on fairness. This information is important for lower-income people with lower status while richer individuals of top positionality seek legitimacy.[52] In this example, a trade-off between fairness and legitimacy can take place between $4.71 and $2.59. Within this range, it is a win-win game, if an agreement is actually reached. The Proposers gain the legitimacy of their privileged status (after all, they were given the $10) and the Respondents earn a share that they believe is fair. Overall, this example shows that beliefs about fairness and legitimacy are important in the organizational context of societies because they induce individuals to conduct interpersonal comparisons.[53] For this reason, there is a stronger motivation to participate in relative position competition and context-dependent activities.

STRESS AVOIDANCE AND SELF-ACTUALIZATION

Since happiness is not possible in the presence of repeated negative affect, avoiding stress that causes negative emotions provides a great psychological award. People's perception of material wealth has an important temporal or spatial element. People compare what they have with either what they had in the past or what their neighbours have. In stagnant economic periods, people are more likely to focus on comparisons with the neighbours. This leads to frustration that may be exacerbated by the fact that the value people assign when they are in a losing situation is higher because people are in principle loss-averse. Loss aversion means that people will exercise more effort to avoid a deterioration of their relative position to their neighbours or to the new lifestyle standards, by engaging in a relative position competition rather than to win a clear absolute advantage. This behaviour deepens the pressure on lower-income individuals and creates greater frustration for them, since their odds are worse relative to high-income individuals.

Besides avoiding stress, there are other factors that enhance utility considerations and induce individuals to forego greater levels of consumer spending.[54] The list of those factors include vitality and exercise, socialization, free time and travel, and activities that contribute to a sense of autonomy and self-actualization. All these activities create greater and consistent levels of positive emotions, and provide an incentive to individuals to spend less on consumption goods. This incentive matters more to individuals of moderate levels of income. This raises a question with respect to the distribution of incentives attributed to the operation of status markets. In those markets, positional incentives are stronger for richer than for poorer individuals. It is more difficult for lower-income families to catch up with the Joneses because of income constraints, loss-aversion and lack of information. The frustration that usually accompanies these difficulties leads to discouraging interpersonal comparisons and can complicate the decision-making capacity of lower-income individuals.

THE LACK OF SELF-CONTROL AND SOCIETY VALUES

Another force that generates a bias in favour of positional goods and activities relates to our inability to impose self-control in many activities. Even if our mental capacities were perfect, we were able to predict our level of satisfaction over time and we were not influenced by the repeated sirens of commercial advertising, we would still have a strong preference for positional goods and services because of our inability to impose self-control. The more positional one activity is, the more tempting it will be relative to an ordinary one. Studies in social psychology provide evidence, according to which, although we may know what is best for us, we prefer nevertheless to engage in inferior activities. It is not easy to abstain from being involved in positional activities when there is a lack of self-control. These tendencies resemble the evolution of ordinary individual habits such as eating fast-food meals, excessively drinking alcohol and drug abuse. Early benefits increase the attractiveness of an inferior activity such as cigarette smoking in a manner that is inconsistent with the long-term benefits of abstaining from it. For an individual, it is more advantageous to adopt an attitude that secures the enjoyment of long-term health benefits. The introduction of external enforcement such as insurance penalties for those that prefer the short-term benefits of an inferior activity is not a justification for avoiding self-control. When self-control is absent we tend to engage more in habits of positional consumption and to participate more in activities, in which context is important.

STATUS ROLE IDENTIFICATION

People also make consumption choices that communicate 'symbols of class status'.[55] The classification of the social environment takes place around certain spheres of individual subjectivity such as the individual self, gender, age, family, class, religion, nationality and ethnicity. Other categories such as religion and sexual preferences are also relevant. There are also derivative classes since for many individuals the facets of their subjectivity are mixed in various ways, such as when nationality and religion merge.

The tendency of the post-modern individual to project intensely aspects of their subjectivity is supported by the television culture. For many years, television programmes such as soap-operas in the USA, have projected the stereotypical, positive image of white, family-oriented, rich, professional Americans or Northern Europeans. These stereotypes have the capacity to channel the understanding of people with regard to social classification. As noted earlier, social classification that is based on subjectivity can in fact be very wide, from a basic core of categories to a broader range including religion, sexual preferences, education, urban or rural identification, political preferences and so on. Yet even within a broad spectrum of subjectivity, we are able to discern social classification, for example, one class identified as mainstream and desirable and the other identified as disadvantageous or deviant. In our times, positional goods and context-dependent activities are projected as normal, familiar and desirable. The projection of social identity is obviously a psychological process. The child gets pleasure because the act of looking allows the real self to mix with aspects of the desirable symbolic self. Similarly, television viewers feel pleasure when they see celebrities that melt the imaginary with the real experience. Since the imaginary relates to the real, it becomes very accessible and, therefore, identification with it is possible. Actually, the identification with superstars from different walks of life from Nicole Kidman, Tom Hanks, Richard Branson to numerous other celebrities, is very widespread. In contemporary television culture, viewing has become so fundamental that the childish tendency to identify with the imaginary is eventually inflated heavily by the huge supply of signs and symbols. These signs express individual representation in a manner that is definitely pleasurable to the viewers. Thus our imaginary, subconscious desirable constructs are culturally injected from what we see from television and do not constitute some invariable aspects of our human nature. Therefore, this imaginary experience is social, cultural and to a great extent ideological.

To understand further the social nature of cultural classification we need to analyse television programmes in such a way that the social constructed subjectivities surface.[56] An example is gender differences in tastes. For example, in general men seem to denigrate women's tastes in television, their mode of watching or their talk about television programmes. Women's talk about television is 'gossip', as opposed to men's 'discussions'.[57] Women's attitudes towards television programmes are not homogeneous of course. Some women may adopt a masculine way of thought and denigrate other women's tastes as trash. However, other women remain attached to their own cultural tastes and to gossip. This attachment would be more rare if these women had a different, more assertive position in the family power structure.[58] The pleasures that women find in soap-operas and talk-shows have obviously a relation to their gender attitudes but often are injected and inflated by their situation in the family and by their intention to differentiate from masculine power and attitudes. This is often understood by men and that explains why gossip is characterized negatively by them. Gender differences show that stories in television programmes connect viewers to each other and establish a relationship between them and the imaginary world. But those relationships are rooted inevitably in the social background of the viewers and their social position. The psychological tendency of the viewers to identify in a pleasurable manner with the symbols of super-stars supports their drive to get involved actively in context-dependent activities and relative position competition.

STEREOTYPES AND PREJUDICE

As the example of gender differences in tastes has shown, many activities are influenced by stereotypes. These are often linked with the presence of prejudice among different groups of people.[59] There are different frame-works, which explain how stereotypes and prejudice develop. First, there is the cultural approach, according to which the individual emerges as the product of a culture that promotes stereotypes and prejudice.[60] Second, there is the motivational approach, the advocates of which consider prejudice as the product of hostile motives.[61] Finally, several social scientists support the cognitive framework, in which stereotypes and prejudice are simply the result of pernicious beliefs about people.

Another relevant framework is realistic conflict theory, according to which, when groups are in competition for material resources, in-groups will become more cohesive and hostile to the out-groups.[62] Alternatively, the frustration–aggression theory focuses on the fact that stereotyped prejudice against some groups is in essence the product of latent aggression towards someone, or something else that has caused frustra-tion earlier. Research on stereotypes has focused on issues of the development and persistence of stereotypes. There is substantial evidence that indicates that if people have a prior theory that two things are related, they will see a relation between them even when there is no actual real relation. In addition, if people encounter a member of a group who does not fit their stereotype of the group, they will decide for that very reason that the person is not typical of the group, and they will not revise their impression of the group as a whole.[63] In conclusion, with the exception of the frustration–aggression theory, all other approaches imply more or less that stereotypes and prejudice emerge from specific motives to protect a territory over material goods, and that these attitudes can be inflated if there is a culture that promotes such processes. Thus the research on stereotypes and prejudices provides a useful explanation why relative position competition emerges in status and superstar markets. Participation in such contests involves often stereotypical comparisons as well as manifestations of prejudice against other people or groups since relative position competition augments the polarization between in-groups and out-groups.[64]

BEHAVIOURAL POLARIZATION SHIFTS

Polarization causes shifts that can be explained by social comparison theory. Social comparison theory involves two basic ideas, the notion of shared reality and the process of self-evaluation. Regarding the first idea, when people are confused about certain aspects of their shared world, they tend to use other people's views in an attempt to understand that world. In addition, people see themselves as willing to take risks to attain certain high objectives. This self-evaluation may be explained by the fact that risk-taking is a desirable quality in the contemporary world and it seems to be more prevalent among young people.[65]

In social comparison dynamics, an explanation for risky shifts is that people compare themselves with other people and want to be thought as being greater risk-takers. This tendency involves the comparison of one's attributes and one's beliefs to those of other people. In contrast to this view however lies another framework, the persuasive argument theory. In this context, risky shifts are caused by the fact that people compare the arguments they hear with the arguments they know. In retrospect, relative position competition and polarization shifts associated with stereotypes and prejudices are explained better by social comparison theory. Yet persuasive argument theory stresses more the role of culture in terms of how we compare arguments. If culture dimensions promote a dynamic attitude then people will adopt arguments consistent with this attitude. Group communication produces either a risky or a conservative shift. Thus in an interactive environment, groups tend to become more polarized and adopt positions. The tendency towards polarization in a culture that promotes individual aggressiveness explains people's increasing involvement in a relative position competition regarding positional activities.

SOCIAL COMPARISON, RELATIVE POSITION AND DEPRIVATION

The theory of social comparison focuses also on another process, namely, the social comparison that takes place when we experience loss or deprivation. Psychological evidence shows that people feel deprived not when they focus on their own well-being but when they compare themselves with their reference group.[66] This process is a fundamental aspect of relative deprivation theory.[67] Social psychologists attempt to develop the relative deprivation theory better by studying the details that encompass people's feelings of resentment when they fail to possess something they desire and when they see that other individuals, similar to them, have it.[68] Certainly, there are complex repercussions such as cross-cultural differences in self-serving or self-enhancing motivations. Finally, besides causal attributions of success and failure and self-reference judgements, recent evidence highlights the relevance of factors such as judgement about in-group conditions and readiness to accept either positive or negative feedback about the self.[69]

The feeling of deprivation can be especially inflated when some people feel entitled to possess something, when they think that it is feasible to possess it and when they do not blame themselves for their failure to possess it. These explanations link relative deprivation theory with equity theory because the relative deprivation approach stresses the importance of moments when people perceive their situation as inequitable. An idea like entitlement can be incorporated in equity theory, since it is assumed that people expect or feel entitled to receive the just benefits of their contributions.[70]

Moreover, resentment seems to be greater in cases where one 'almost' achieves something.[71] The explanation of this phenomenon lies in the observation that people project a referential measure by means of which they compare reality with their imagination.[72] Here references play an important role. Thus there is a connection between the heuristics approach, especially the heuristic of availability and Boudon's 'reference group' approach. In both contexts, lower-class agents are less expected to be successful and they lose less in social recognition for not being so.[73]

In any case, equity theory is based on the assumption that people are motivated to seek equity. One implication is that people do indeed have a general idea of equity in the sense that they do believe that rewards must reflect inputs.[74] This is the same as saying that people believe that they are entitled to rewards that reflect inputs. Naturally, the way people feel entitled varies from culture to culture. People prepare themselves in most of the circumstances they face in everyday life with respect to their perception of entitlements because they are influenced by their culture's conceptions about what they should do in certain situations to protect their own interests. In cases of failure, overexposure to status markets strengthens the feelings of entitlement, creates relative deprivation and reinforces the motivation for individual involvement in relative position competition.

The nature of individual adjustment in status markets may be variable. People experiencing cognitive dissonance between status-seeking and social recognition can adapt their behaviour with regard to what is status-worthy. Thus individuals are able in fact to choose which status game to play. For example, status may be more important to individuals who spend more in leisure activities than in their consumption of material goods.[75] Thus the minimization of discomfort associated with cognitive dissonance in positional markets is associated with alternative paths of positional orientation or reorientation. This explains why some individuals may in fact choose to be involved in a 'leisure status game' rather than in a 'consumption status game' and to adopt a snob strategy rather than an emulation approach. In this case, there are more options available to rise in social rank and fewer reasons to experience relative deprivation.

DISSONANCE, DEPRIVATION OF THE DISADVANTAGED AND ECONOMIC PROCESSES

The observed real behaviour depends on the interplay of various forces. For example, stronger self-confidence fuels motivation.[76] A side-effect is that this motivation makes individuals more willing to change or manipulate their self-perceptions. For example, if current self-confidence is projected in the future, it results in perceptions of more confident future selves. This process is beneficial because it tends to weaken procrastination. Furthermore, the time-inconsistency problem that young people usually face, that is, to have to work now in order to reap rewards in the future is minimized. Yet this mental process inhibits the danger of overconfidence, which may lead to the choice of ineffective career projects. Thus the manipulation of self-perception and overconfidence may result in harmful excesses because people may seek alternative ways to justify self-handicapping. For example, people may choose over-ambitious career projects to avoid negative inferences about their ability. Alternatively, they may choose to worsen their performance to provide justifications of self-handicapping. Overconfidence enhances also selective memory and self-serving beliefs regarding one's own advantages and positive traits. This process of psychological immune system can result in sizeable individual costs because it motivates people to look at the bright side. In certain situations in which losses are realized, it is better to accept more realistic and honest accounts of self.

These considerations show again that dissonance reduction and cognitive adaptation become important. Individuals who are not successful in the relative position competition internalize dissonance or psychological discomfort. As it has been mentioned earlier, this feeling arises precisely because of the incompatibility between the objective lack of social esteem and the individual need for self-esteem. This psychological discomfort can be reduced by either committing greater resources to positional lifestyles, or by adjusting individual attitudes especially with respect to those factors from which an individual derives worthiness and self-esteem.[77] In fact, much of the behaviour of the underprivileged arises through a process of dissonance reduction through which attitudes towards status-seeking are modified, especially when the power of traditional incentives is small.[78] Even so, inefficient outcomes that relate to traditional lifestyles may still arise and represent the norm. Thus financial redistribution can reduce feelings of dissonance and discomfort experienced by those being in a disadvantageous position.[79]

MORAL COMMITMENTS AND VALUES

Feelings of resentment and relative deprivation that are experienced in positional competitions become smaller once we introduce a framework of societal culture, in which moral values play an important role in decision-making. A basic insight of social psychology is that the concept of an individual is not independent. The individual and the community interface with each other. In many cases, the society is not a 'constraint' to the activities of an individual but serves as the domain within which individual activities are shaped. This stands in contrast with the traditional economic wisdom, according to which, preferences of individual liberty are given, and they cannot be manipulated by social force. In the neoclassical framework of social economics, preferences are exogenous and the effects of education, persuasion (including persuasive advertising) and the influence of leadership are minimal. 'Economic man' is perceived as a 'biological-psychological miracle', born fully formed, say in his mid-twenties.[80] The individual preferences appear 'immaculately conceived', as it has been quite insightfully argued.[81]

When we extend the analysis beyond the neoclassical behavioural framework, we view the relative position competition for positional goods, services and activities from a different angle.[82] More specifically, individuals can be viewed as being able to make moral judgements about positional choices. Morality is a route through which externalities are introduced into decision-making. Sometimes, these externalities stand in contrast with the utility derived from pleasure. Yet in many cases moral actions are less costly and constitute a less coercive mechanism for conducting social relations than public incentives that are assumed to take place in the neoclassical framework. As a result, there are two sets of preferences that can be in conflict at a single point in time.[83] When people maximize their immediate preferences, the 'doers' act. Instead, when people choose to act from a moral viewpoint, this happens because the 'planners' act. Thus in every individual resides a mixed doer/planner self that attempts to achieve certain goods. Moreover, morality is closely related to the notion of moral commitment. Moral commitment is important because it stands as an independent value other than just striving to be better off. The question whether moral commitment is an important idea in decision-making reflects however the deep differences in behavioural methodology. This is so because morality implies a sense of internalization on the part of individuals. Moral internalization is an important difference between neoclassical and deontological behavioural frameworks. Neoclassical behavioural theories imply that there is no internalization of any kind, either moral or otherwise. Then again, moral internalization can eventually turn constraints into preferences.[84] When individuals cannot exploit opportunities because of the presence of certain constraints, then it is easier for them to experience feelings of deprivation and resentment. This implies that the degree of relative deprivation that people feel when they fall back in relative position competition for positional goods and services will be lower if the societal culture supports moral values. This type of culture can benefit people easily once one considers that moral and altruistic behaviour is an inherent part of the human personality.

ALTRUISM AND PUBLIC GOODS

The traditional economic mono-utility idea is problematic in the case of public goods and collective activities. The neoclassical notion of public goods refers to those items that can be 'used by many persons at the same time without reducing the amount available for any other person'.[85] In this framework, the basic proposition of the neoclassical school of public choice is that 'the only assumption essential to a descriptive and predictive science of human behaviour is egoism'.[86] As a result, individuals do not need to allocate resources to public goods unless side payments will reward them individually for this allocation. In fact, people are expected to free-ride whenever they feel that they can escape costs or later punishment. Finally, people are expected to free-ride in larger groups. These presumptions of the public choice theory stand in contrast with symbolic moral attitudes such as, for example, ideological preferences, party identification, or ethical stances on issues that are common attitudes in western democracies. Indeed, to the extent that civility or moral commitment to democratic society is solid, then it must be expected that individuals are willing to allocate resources to public goods. This happens because, as it has been mentioned above, individuals act simultaneously on the basis of two distinct sets of factors, their pleasure and their moral duty. These factors can operate with different degrees of strength in various historical and societal conditions. In any case, when one analyses injurious effects of positional competition such as relative deprivation, a framework in which both forces of self-interest and moral duty are functioning is more suitable.

EGOISM, MORAL COMMITMENT AND AMBIVALENCE

The interaction between self-interest and moral commitment is complex and full of conflicts, but it can often produce compelling outcomes.[87] The differences of these forces are easier to describe. For example, the more individuals act under the influence of moral commitments the more they are likely to resist uncomfortable circumstances in the future. That said, when market changes occur the more individuals act out of self-interest the more likely they are expected to take advantage of them. Clearly, there is a trade-off between moral commitment and self-interest in various situations although there are cases of co-existence. For example, moral commitments seem to reduce moral hazards, that is, the transaction costs associated with hedge protection when circumstances change unfavourably.

Yet one can discern that the approaches that are followed between mainstream economists and the majority of psychologists are essentially different.[88] The latter assume the combination of motives of self-interest and moral commitments as being highly possible. On the contrary, neoclassical economists argue that in the very end it is the action that matters. This action may in fact represent various motives endured into one preference. This approach however overlooks the benefits or costs that emotions carry as well as possible behavioural repercussions at a later date. Subsequent outcomes show that it is not easy to substitute moral and pleasure preferences because in the end they are qualitatively different. Furthermore, there are cognitive biases involved in the operation of these different types of preferences. For example, the broader demand for credit cards since the 1980s is due to the fact that they permit people to undertake debt obligations without having to experience the dissonance between their feelings that 'debt is wrong' and their desire to use credit cards.[89]

The conflict that takes place between pleasure and moral preferences, whether expressed in the form of guilt, denial or some other type of psychological symptom involves a cost. This happens because the conflict diminishes the performance and the productivity of the individual. The cost of this type of conflict differs from the standard information or transaction costs assumed in traditional economics. Overall, the feelings that are associated with moral commitments or preferences, which influence the productive capacity of an individual, cannot be precluded from studying individual behaviour. In addition, when moral preferences prevail we see a different process from the one assumed in utility preferences, dominated by self-interest. For example, in certain cultures choices are influenced so highly by moral commitment that it is difficult to reverse them, especially after a threshold.

Psychology is more useful in dealing with these kind of costs and the extent of relative deprivation that people feel when they are involved in relative position competition. As a result, psychological considerations hold even when classical economists and some psychologists argue that people seek equity even in cases where they are more eager to be involved in something associated with moral commitments or preferences.[90] For example, marriage or love involves equity because in many situations the absence of equity leads to the dissolution of marriage or love affairs. Still, this mechanism is not sufficient to overlook the effect of feelings and cognitive attributions on the behaviour and well-being of individuals.[91]

FURTHER CONSIDERATIONS ON THE ROLE OF EMOTIONS

What is viewed as equitable is to a great extent influenced by the values that people hold. People use references in order to judge whether certain prices are fair.[92] When those prices exceed the reference levels, people think that there is no legitimate reason to justify them. This holds even when prices are adjusted towards lower levels. In general, the environment in which individuals live plays an important role in shaping their values, their references and hence their opinion of what is legitimately fair or not.[93]

Moreover, the neoclassical analysis implies that pleasure and non-pleasure preferences are distinct entities. This comes in sharp contrast with the fact that most people prefer a mix of work and leisure rather than work or leisure alone. Both options offer intrinsic rewards and it is possible to model such mixed behaviour.[94] For example, the conflict between pleasure and non-pleasure activities can be resolved as a 'tie-in sale', an idea used in marketing when buyers who desire one good are offered to buy some proportion of another good they desire less. Thus it is possible that an allocation between self-interest and non-self-interest activities can produce better benefits than activities induced by self-interest alone.

There are problems attaining balanced combinations because cognitive biases may induce individuals to shift their allocation over time depending on what preference supersedes the other. This difficulty does not preclude the possibility of a balanced mix at different points in time so that in the very end normative-affective factors eventually shape the options that we choose. Yet moral or affective considerations become so strong sometimes that individuals prefer to stick to decisions based on these forces even when self-interest, or rationality is against them.[95] Moreover, individuals stick with their behaviour and their decisions on the basis of prior commitments expressed either publicly or to one's self.[96] In many cases, new information that is inconsistent to prior commitments is denied, or is undermined since people believe that it was difficult for them to foresee it. Once a person is involved emotionally in their decisions it is difficult to change them on the basis of sensible reasoning especially after a threshold.[97] These observations are not made in an attempt to deny the usefulness of rational decisions based on self-interest; rather, they are put forward to stress that in reality people's decisions are influenced by emotions and by internalized cognitions. In the case of unfortunate experiences, this mechanism results inevitably in the realization of personal costs. These losses cannot be easily overlooked in dealing with sentiments of relative deprivation in positional contests.

Psychological analysis helps us understand better in what ways emotions produce a heavy burden on individual performance. There are many strands in psychological analysis that can be utilized from Freudian analysis and cognitive approaches to systems analysis. Even humanistic psychology is useful because, in this framework, emotions are viewed as constructive in decision-making. In fact, emotions as the joy of self-actualization and the confidence that arises with it are viewed as fundamental needs of human beings. As emotions constitute an end by themselves therefore, they are sought by people as wholesome experiences and not as mere signals for rational decision-making. We need to value better the role of emotions, the behaviour they trigger, and their impact on the performance and the well-being of individuals. Recent neurological evidence demonstrates that viewing signs of high status in an individual differentially engages perceptual-attentional saliency and cognitive systems. Although neuroeconomic studies of this sort have not been developed extensively, it is noteworthy to mention the relevance of visibility in the neural human reactions to signs of social status.

CONCLUDING REMARKS

Subjective considerations in positional activities reveal that people do not hold preferences for certain goods, services and activities themselves, but instead for the specific material benefits that these items confer, and also for the purpose of internalizing positive affect or satisfaction. This psychological process is important because it is associated closely with individuals' perception of self-worth. The involvement in the consumption of positional goods or services surpasses the material benefits that are associated with these activities because of the working of a signalling effect that aims at demonstrating high competence and territorial control. In addition, certain psychological limitations exist in situations of great uncertainty in which there is lack of prediction and visibility. For example, cognitive limitations in processing too much information leads to the phenomenon of benchmarking or seeking for references for positional material possessions and activities. This mechanism holds also for individuals that are more visible and appear more familiar than others and trigger feelings of certainty with regard to possible outcomes. While this sort of analysis explains why people may shift their preferences towards positional concerns, the influence of cognitive dissonance and the impairment of self-worth are crucial in explaining why the existence of status markets can cause feelings of social deprivation. This process takes place in a context of social interpersonal comparisons between the privileged and the less privileged. It leads also to a reactionary behaviour with the objective of catching up with the dominant groups by using as references the behaviour of superstars when making consumption, lifestyle-activity or occupational decisions. In the context of relative position competition, the subjective incentives to signal self-worth, efficiency, territorial control and special identity are stronger in the case of successful and competent people. Thus there is an evident personal waste in the attempts of the less privileged to catch up with the superstars, the celebrities and the top-tier consumers with higher status. This waste is reinforced by the greater difficulty that less fortunate people experience when they try to succeed in superstar markets, leading to situations of relative deprivation. People who succeed to compete in status markets are classified socially as competent and normal while the less privileged people who do not fit the successful stereotype become the object of social prejudice destined to stay out of the competition for material resources. Here the role of overexposure to inflated successful stereotypes through the media is unquestionable, since individuals tend to internalize aspects of social roles that they visualize repeatedly in the media in order to establish their own social identity. When this takes place in reference to the dominant, more visible, mainstream, privileged and, eventually, positional social identity, there is no question why feelings of social deprivation and motives for an otherwise difficult adjustment to social competition materialize.

5. The anthropology of popular culture and identity formation

INTRODUCTION

Although the social psychology analysis of status markets provides several important insights, we can still enhance our understanding by examining their relation to aspects of our everyday life. This constitutes essentially an anthropological inquiry of positional concerns. More precisely, the objective of this study is to uncover the human aspects of everyday routines, which interface with status markets. The post-modern life today is in many ways radically different to what the industrial experience was in the past. People today experience their lives amidst greater expectations and enjoy more entertainment, free expression and aesthetic fascination through media and popular culture. A key anthropological question that must be addressed is how our individual feelings that appear in the context of post-modern life interface with the development of status markets. Another economic anthropology issue is how particular forms of social phenomena, which relate to consumer society, popular culture and media reality, facilitate the exposure to superstars and celebrities and trigger relative social competition. These manifestations may include brand projection, excessive sexual promiscuity, aesthetization and fashion novelty. In our post-modern world, symbols and myths play an active role in the process of shaping preferences and in individual decision-making. From an anthropological viewpoint, it is important to explore how myths and symbols, which surface in status markets, link with human aspects of everyday life, such as experiences, hopes and emotions. Here it is also useful to examine the channels, through which our emotions, whether positive or negative, or our experiences, whether pleasurable or painful, relate to signification and role identification.

EXCITEMENT AND NOSTALGIA

When one observes the western daily routine of middle-class life, one cannot easily escape the impression that with events such as pop festivals and market fairs popular tradition provides a symbolic escape from civilized mainstream life. In this routine break, individuals are again capable of feeling emotions and the intense bodily pleasures associated with food, drink, sexuality and artistic beauty.[1] These situations are in fact opportunities, in which the boring everyday life is reversed, the forbidden fantastic acts are possible and the ability to dream can be practised without guilt. These needs are normally suppressed because individuals that usually come from the upper and the middle classes predominantly have developed an ability to control their emotions as part of their civilized everyday life. They can only break with this norm in places of cultural escape.[2] In contemporary times, these places have become global as international fairs, the city of London, the traditional villages in Sicily, the seaside in the Aegean Islands, the exclusive resorts of Bali and St Lucia, or even the exotic bays of Vietnam, and produce the material for excitement, dreams, nostalgia and even identity development.[3] This sort of escapist excitement has become in turn a favourite topic in art, literature and popular entertainment.[4]

The escape from everyday routine has historical roots in the industrial era. The department stores, the grand national and the international exhibitions that emerged in the second half of the nineteenth century, as well as the theme parks and the shopping malls, which were developed since the 1960s, were some of the institutions of urban market and urban lifestyle that served as sites of ordered disorder or packaged dreams.[5] These institutions provided the characteristics of a fantastic world in the expression of imagery and simulation of exotic locations and experiences. Thus the department stores and arcades, which were developed in Paris and subsequently in other large cities since the turn of the twentieth century onward became 'dream-worlds' for millions of consumers.[6]

With the passage of time, 'dream-worlds' did not remain in the centre of metropolitan cities as spin-offs in the form of shopping malls and pop-culture development projects (that is, Disneyland and other entertainments parks) were developed in the suburbs.[7] Moreover, 'dream-worlds' expanded in meaning and scope. For example, the museum has evolved to be not only a magnet for tourists but also an icon for post-industrial urbanism.[8] The cultural experience became an indistinguishable part of the market worldwide. The globalization of 'edutainment' (a term coined by the Disney Corporation) through urban cultural development involves a considerable infrastructure that is developed with the aid of signature architects, leading-edge artists, marketeers of branded chain stores and footloose performers. These synergies are necessary because they manage to offer maximum economic and cultural capital returns.[9]

POPULAR CULTURE AND SYMBOLIC ANALYSTS

The trend for the aesthetization of everyday life has narrowed the chasm between grand and popular culture. During the last decades, people have observed the collapse of many barriers that existed between art and everyday life. Gradually, the sacred status of high art as a protected commodity has disappeared. High art is used in many popular applications, such as in industrial design and in advertising. The professionals who work in these crafts, deal with symbolic images and they are called the 'new cultural intermediaries'. These professionals constitute a share of a broader 'creative class' and are engaged in developing cultural symbolic goods and services.[10] The 'creative class' consists of a creative core group that is considered innovative and is made up of knowledge-based workers. The creative core group creates commercial products and consumer goods and encompasses a wide range of occupations from science to research with cultural intermediaries forming a small subset. Cultural intermediaries include the marketing, advertising, public relations, radio and television producers, presenters, magazine journalists, fashion writers and the helping professions (social workers, marriage advisers, psychologists, diet specialists and so on). Their common characteristic as a group is that they are in essence the 'new intellectuals', who adopt a learning attitude towards life.[11] They place a great importance on identity, presentation, appearance, lifestyle and morality. Their understanding of the broadness of experiences open to them, the lack of self-reference to a particular locality, the learning attitude, the ambition for a higher social identity explains their tendency to refuse to be classified. Life is perceived as essentially open-ended and changing. There is an obvious quest here for distinction through the cultivation of lifestyle, and often through positional lifestyle. Thus the adoption of an almost artistic life made possible through distinctive poses and projects has been an important aspect of relative position competition that is observed in the lifestyles of this new middle class of professionals.[12]

This expressive life is the result of an important transition in the twentieth century. Traditionally, only artists and intellectuals since the Romantics used to adopt an emotional openness and informality, which stands in contrast to the behaviour that is observed in economic life. This particular attitude towards emotional openness helps exploration and artistic ends. Obviously, the sexual revolution which took place during the 1960s and early 1970s played an important role in the rise against emotional restrictions. Since then, an enormous pop culture industry has developed with the objective of provoking good or intense feelings.

However, the emphasis on the aesthetic experience of life, which constitutes an important trend in advanced societies, has created already a reaction and a call for a traditional revival.[13] These traditional accounts emphasize radical social changes towards utopian paradigms. Yet it is difficult to understand clearly the dynamics of new popular culture movements as we are constantly immersed in their symbols. Often, new social and cultural experiences are analysed in a particular context. For example, they can be understood as part of an analysis of rapid culture change, which requires a theoretical framework of social processes.[14] As a result, they can be accommodated easily within a theory of social development that is based on conflict theory utilized in Marxist analysis. In this theory, post-modernism is viewed as the cultural dominant theory and is related with the social changes that took place in the post-Second World War era.[15]

Thus the new social phenomena such as the rise of symbolic analysts and superstar markets are explained in terms of an analysis of post-modernism that is viewed as the cultural mechanism of late market economy. In this context, the current culture changes 'express the deeper logic' of the 'late consumer, or multinational' capitalist social system. In this radical account of cultural study, there are certain parallels drawn between functionalism and market economy, modernism and monopolistic economy, and post-modernism and consumer economy.[16]

Although this analysis seems simplistic, it is quite useful because it raises culture as having an impact 'on the superstructural levels'.[17] With regard to post-modernism, there is an interface between relative position competition and popular culture. Culture becomes the 'very element of consumer society itself, no society has ever been saturated with signs and images like this one'.[18] This saturation leads to the destruction of high culture and its relative autonomy.[19] Instead, there is a prodigious expansion of popular culture in the social process.[20] Everything in our social life has in fact become 'cultural'.[21] This integration has become possible because of the boost in hyperreality signs and senses. The real and the imaginary have become mixed.[22] In modern times, aesthetic fascination has become a major force, which pervades various social experiences. Simulation, indefinable distinction and aesthetic pleasure merge and provide new experiences. What in fact individuals internalize is a sort of simulational post-modern culture.[23]

For example, one of the first and most celebrated forms of simulational culture was MTV.[24] This medium seems to exist in a timeless present.[25] There is a tendency for film genres and art movements from different historical periods to blur boundaries and the sense of history. Our structure or hierarchy of aesthetics in real life has certainly collapsed. In addition, one major quality of simulational culture is that it is figural. For this reason, it turns on primary processes (desire) rather than derivative ones (the ego).[26] The medium is images rather than words. Spectators get lost, or live in the object as distances collapse. These qualities support individual de-differentiation and the possibility of a new synthesis of individual interests, which relate to the projection of social identity.

In the sphere of continuous identity changes, status is achieved both by contributing to group output and by non-productive, social activities that involve signalling in social politics. Competition based on merit can push group members to work hard.[27] Status achieved through positional social tactics can result in lower overall performance. Factors such as the size and the productive performance of the group may influence the outcome of the competition for relative position.[28] Increasing the group size reduces every individual's marginal reward for effort, and thus encourages competition for status rewards.

CONSUMER SOCIETY, AESTHETIZATION AND FASHION NOVELTY

Signs, symbols and images have become so important that culture plays now a significant role in the reproduction of the basic process of market economy. Culture is 'the very element of consumer society itself'.[29] In many cases, individuals do not live in reality but live in a dream, or in a virtual reality. Advertising and the display of goods in the 'dream-worlds' of department stores such as Harrods or Macy's and in city centres such as Paris or London provide signs, mixed meanings and social identities that are traditionally treated as separate.[30] In this vein, they create an unusual and novel synthesis. When consumer goods are advertised in terms of qualities such as luxury, beauty and romance, it is difficult to memorize the real aspects of these products.[31]

Here television and, more broadly, electronic mass media through the Internet and mobile phones become important. This is because the images and sounds of electronic mass media alter our understanding of reality.[32] Individuals live in a world of signifying culture, a simulational world that upsets severely the distinction between the real and the imaginary.[33] People already live in an 'aesthetic hallucination of reality'.[34] The loss of the understanding of reality is replaced in many situations by nostalgia for the real. Thus the turn towards traditional values and the attraction of a simpler life on the farm or near the beach is often explained by the desperate quest for real people, real values or even real relationships. This explanation contradicts effectively consumer culture and the domination of electronic mass media, through which values are turned upside down since artistic forms cannot be distinguished easily.

In the development of these forms, fashion glitz serves as an important role. Fashion allows both the contradictory tendencies of imitation and differentiation to be at continuous work and fusion.[35] The dynamics of fashion are powerful because of its almost endless capacity to present imitation as novelty. This practice proves to be a major force in everyday life because it shows the power of fashion to create a mass of signs so that it shapes tastes with regard to consumption and leisure activities.[36]

Novelty adds a premium to fashion products and services. High-status individuals seek to buy these goods, which will later be the object of desire by latecomers, who are usually lower-income consumers. The high price of fashion goods is a distinguishable component in the creation of fashion cycles. Novelty arises because it efficiently demarcates the differences between high-income and low-income people through the expression of their different tastes. It is novelty that prohibits status conscious individuals from buying the same fashion product from the same fashion firm.[37]

As a result, fashion helps produce popular cultural goods in a distinctive way that implies once again that the production of goods and lifestyles cannot be reduced only to the economic process. Rather than relying on economic analysis solely, it would be more reasonable to acknowledge the autonomy of particular practices such as the shape of taste through fashion forms. Certain practices need to be explained in terms of principles and processes, which are different to the mechanisms examined in economic analysis. However, although fashion is an everyday consumer practice, there is still a need to explain analytically its aspects as a means of communicating one's commitment to certain contemporary values and identities.[38]

For example, individuals of the creative class, who act as cultural intermediaries and provide symbolic goods and services, typically invest in cultural and educational capital.[39] This group differs from both the traditional middle class and the working class because it adopts upper-class qualities and is attracted to the associated characteristics (such as style, distinction and refinement). This does not take place initially in terms of competition for relative position but in the pursuit of expressive and non-constrained life. Yet social validation and social addictions are useful ways of life, especially when it comes to explain the dispositions, which eventually shape tastes. These individual unconscious dispositions are in fact classificatory schemes, which are too powerful to dismiss simply as genuine preferences.[40] They also express themselves within an area of individual appropriateness in the choice for cultural goods and practices such as art, food, holidays, hobbies and so on. Social practices can transform into habits, which do not influence only social behaviour but are inscribed into the body. For example, many individuals seem to be uneasy with their bodies since they actively attempt to watch and correct the presentation and the gestures of their bodies through special diets and beauty programmes. Fashion determines tastes with regard to the image of the body because it intervenes in the cycle of desire itself. Through fashion, the body is decoded and recoded in order for individuals to reclaim social validity.

Yet the predominance of fashion leads often to reactive actions. A special feature of the industry for cultural goods is that in fashion and art the obvious way for the marginal groups of low-income individuals to resist the condemnation to invisibility and exploitation is to insist on being seen and heard. This reaction explains the rise of cults and subcultural styles as a new social experience of our times. These cults serve as a medium for group visibility, which is achieved often through a radical or unsettling behaviour in relation to the mainstream. However, one should not ignore the interplay that takes place between the visibility of diverse and stylistically distinct groups and patterns or trends in advertising and the media. During the last years, we have encountered a paradoxical situation, in which marginality has become a valuable enterprise for certain social groups. With the prevalence of cultural goods, individuals can speak from the margins and claim representation in ways in which perhaps they did not or could not twenty or thirty years ago. Although there are negative side-effects to this development, most notably a false sense of self-determination, this representation gives the opportunity to overcome cultural barriers across classes and to liberate people from their social identification.

It is for these reasons that the analysis of marginalism has attracted the interest of social scientists. There is an increasing awareness that the initial market economy model that emphasized administration and repressed freedom has shifted to a 'post-Fordist' phase, in which diversification rather than standardization is the name of the game despite various relapses.[41] Around this theme, there is a growing hope that the market economy itself can produce in the end a situation in which diversification and cultural freedom will enable a social change.[42] Thus developments in the area of culture make it possible to view some of the positive aspects of late market economy society.[43] Obviously, this view is rather optimistic and involves a certain risk of contentment. As a consequence, in this type of framework the critique of the failures of market economy on the basis of social principles loses much of its effectiveness. It is also uncertain that in the future the social process will necessarily take a determinate twist towards freedom through the representation of large groups of people. The mission to broaden representation may simply prove an illusion because the capacity of marginalism to alter real social relations is narrow.

TOURISM, IDENTITY AND REPRESENTATION

A characteristic example that describes how people realize an upgraded identity in our times is the experience of tourism. This activity evolves around tourist places that are capable in provoking individual desires and tastes. People of all ages and various incomes pay considerable chunks of their earnings to fly around the world to set feet on a long-desired ground.

Tourist places are seductive and images of perfect holiday paradises trigger tourist dreams.[44] Places like beaches are suggestive of identity and individual representation. People do not just go to the beach for the sheer pleasure of a swim. Instead, they live scripts or 'ethnographies' of beach life.[45] In this context, differentiation and marginalism are frequently observed because different individuals or groups opt for alternative and sometimes eccentric destinations as their holiday paradises.

In a sense, tourism serves as a strategy for the projection of an identity through an accumulation of photographs, videos or through colourful storytelling to friends, neighbours, associates and family in a cozy corner at home, at a nice café or at a restaurant.[46] By way of analogy the choice of specific positional goods and services which become visible helps to project a social identity. The experience of travelling is relived as tourists essentially perform scripts and roles tracing, interpreting and performing particular identities when they visit tourist sights and attractions.[47] The situation can become extravagant sometimes as the tourist identity is not limited in its materialization to beauty or idyllic sightseeing.[48] In the quest for a marginalist identity, the most unlikely places have started to become tourist sights (from the very poor Brazilian favelas to high-rise suburbs and industrial complexes).[49] Thus tourist places appear as sights that facilitate the projection of identity to travellers in a process that links cultural, economic, political and social networks.[50] However, tourist places are realized through the development of different factors such as policy-making, networking, service-development, shopping, sightseeing, strolling and socializing.[51] Overall, the example of tourism demonstrates vividly that social identities are often formed and treasured on the basis of remote rather than immediate everyday experiences. This provides certain implications about the power of media in providing information to project social identities.

TELEVISION, SYMBOLS AND REALITY DISTORTION

The most important medium of symbols and signs is television. The development of television technology was followed by the widespread growth in new communication technologies such as cheap, high-quality video conferencing and mobile technology. These new technologies are transforming, and will continue to transform the communication functions of the marketplace. In addition to new communication technologies, new information technologies, such as the Internet provide superior access to information for consumers, investors and managers.[52] This development produces in turn its own audience of advocates and critics with respect to market and societal developments.

The new technologies produce a world where values, culture and economics interface continuously, creating new symbols, concepts and products.[53] Human culture and human values are influenced largely by new technologies in electronic media. Through electronic media, social groups have access to the commercial marketplace to shape their values. While the Internet and its applications such as social media appear to individualize electronic media, they are powerful because they incorporate material from television and the press. 'YouTube' depends on the visual content provided by television while blogs use extensively material from journals such as the *New York Times* or *Le Monde*. Through Internet applications, traditional media such as the press still exert a powerful influence while television remains the ultimate platform of collective identity formation.

Television has substituted the family in reproducing values.[54] There are accounts of average teenagers watching twenty hours of television per week while spending five minutes per week alone with their father and twenty minutes alone with their mother. On the contrary, an activity like training to acquire a new skill requires work, time and money. Watching television does not require effort. Thus there is a tendency in the USA towards an overexposure to the messages, the signs and the symbols that television offers.[55] The same tendency has been predominant in other regions of the world like Europe and Japan.[56]

The transition to visual media changes the manner that individuals think, evaluate options and act. There are several examples that illustrate the inconsistency between rationality and emotions in television culture. For example, as recorded in various surveys, the public chooses to react in a certain way to negative political advertising campaigns. From a national point of view, negative political advertising sabotages the comprehension of the political process. This situation seems to have an emotional impact and is often efficient in winning elections. Thus perception becomes more important than reality in a television world. This type of process shows the immense power of the media on a global scale.[57] For example, if we believe that we live in a safer world, chances are that we behave likewise. In recent years, murder rates have been falling in cities across the USA (in some cities, such as New York, dramatically), and some attribute this development to the influence of the media. As a result, television culture becomes a medium that in practice replaces various aspects of the real world. When it comes to developing our mental pictures of reality, real culture and real people lose frequently their own importance. The transition to television culture makes important the value of speed and instant gratification. The time of television shows and movies is fixed and instant gratification must be ascertained so that viewers stay to watch advertisements. A great deal of this gratification goes to ego massaging because it is associated with materialism, consumerism and private ambition. Yet these expectations and pleasures do not come without cost. In television culture, we do not communicate with real people but with virtual or, in some sense, mythical people. For example, the television family is far wealthier than the real average family (about four times as wealthy) in the USA.[58] This leaves real people with a false and exaggerated understanding of how comfortable and wealthy the average people really are and alters their own frames of reference. Yet relative comparisons lead many individuals to experience feelings of relative deprivation. As a consequence, to compensate for this perceived difference, many individuals undertake a risky shift in their lives and careers to attain status and the privileges that accompany it.

TELEVISION AND EMOTIONAL SOCIAL IDENTITY INTERNALIZATION

Business culture and television culture fit together nicely since both are interested in making money. Yet their inherent values are not identical. Much of business culture is associated with productive activities. By contrast, television culture focuses on consumerism and instant gratification. One important aspect of status markets is that they are 'hot'. This feature is promoted by the media, which present exciting accounts of the lives of successful people. One representative account is given in soap-operas or television sitcoms.[59] Here the audience identifies with the virtual lives of superstars.[60] For example, the pleasure of watching popular series such as the *Bold and the Beautiful* or *Friends* is eventually the pleasure of 'implication', a controlled identification with characters that necessarily involves believability and truth.[61] Here the subjective criteria of internalized norms of feelings and overall behaviour become critical. The conventions of soap-opera or television sitcom realism require that a pair of characters act in such a way so that a believable natural conclusion will be reached and, therefore, be internalized.[62] The representation of superstars in television programmes has in essence a cultural meaning.[63] This representation is categorized according to the tastes of viewers and, as a consequence, various subcultures exist. Some of these subcultural perceptions may go against traditional values. For some analysts, a subcultural perception of Rihanna or Britney Spears among young girls involves, for example, the projection of 'tartiness' and seduction, traits that become acceptable with them although with other celebrities or superstars would have been out of context. The projection of 'tartiness' is not an isolated quality since in this case it represents social values.[64] Projections such as 'tartiness' or 'gentlemanship' are also critical in endorsements of products by superstars, who act as the virtual Joneses. This signifies the importance of the pleasure of remote implication provided by television, which has been overlooked in accounts of immediate positional comparisons with neighbours or peers, that is, the Joneses of real life.

In addition, the individual charateristics that show up in television programmes are best understood not in their uniqueness, but essentially in terms of a simple structure of social values that pervades the characters (such as the hero, the heroine, the villain and the villainess). In these programmes there is always a particular structure of social values, a 'myth' that points to a particular conclusion. Each television episode seems to be a transformation of a structure, which may be shared with other series of the same kind. For example, one fundamental structure of characters which operates in soap-operas is centered around the battle between good and evil, or between the hero and the villain.[65] The distinction between good and bad is also evident in reality shows and elsewhere in the form of more concrete connotations.[66] For example, these include the distinction between western and non-western individuals, white-collar and blue-collar workers, middle class and working class, attractive and unattractive people, traditional and non-traditional families, single or married individuals and so on. In many situations, the conflicting values describe implicitly the difference between successful and unsuccessful individuals. One could argue also that this distinction is expressed in many instances in the difference between masculine and feminine, active and passive, or leaders and followers. For some sociologists, the distinction between good and bad stories applies also to news reporting. An example is a study of labour strikes in hospitals where the presentation of the news story from the television newscasters involved in essence a political rather than an industrial dispute. The worker-strikers were presented as the villains against children, moderate unionists, government and, in general, the mainstream.[67]

It is obvious that television carries in its programmes the signs of structures of social values and promotes certain 'myths'. In market economy societies most myths represent the values of the dominant social groups and their interests that appear natural for all. Radical narratives are rare except in areas like politics where there is institutionalization of ideological movements.[68] A radical myth of the role of the labour unions is possible, whereas a radical myth of, for instance, the family, is not easily presented in contemporary society. Radical ways of understanding social structures and internalizing social values are conscious and presented against the mainstream ones. With the help of myths, the views of the contented need no explanation or defence since they have become the 'common sense' of the society. Quite often, television programmes promote myths of the white, male middle-class television characters who often function as a reference for the majority of viewers, even for radicals, for understanding and internalizing social values. As a result, there are feminists, who find pleasure in the conservative representations of women in *Housewives* although they know the contradiction of their own behaviour.[69] There are surveys which indicate that radical people watch mainstream programmes like *The Young and the Restless* or *Friends* because they help release primitive feelings such as love, hate, disgust, sadness and nostalgia.[70] Although for many radical people leisure activities might predominantly be alternative in context, when it comes to watching television programmes, their emotions are released through the sexiness or the attractiveness of conservative middle-class or upper-class superstars.[71] With emotions, the identification with the television personalities and the social attributes of their roles becomes possible.[72] People loved and hated characters like Sue Ellen and J.R in *Dallas* some years ago because these characters related, even as an overstatement, to emotions that people have in their everyday life.[73] In this sense, people from all strands of life are hooked on mainstream television programmes. The inner contradictions that these people experience because of their own different social values happen when these people relinquish for a moment their partisanship to experience emotions, through the help of expressive mainstream role models. Therefore, many people today need to reconcile within themselves the contradictions between their own values and the social values that are internalized in mainstream television programmes.

Yet the internalization process that takes place through television programmes has other dimensions too. For example, soap-operas and reality shows focus on casual problem-solving, intimate conversation and the feelings which are experienced in everyday life. This contrasts to action series, in which dialogue is minimal and sharp. In these series, the determination to succeed, the physical movements and the fast clear-cut decisions replace feelings, intimacy and dialogue. Also, for women today the alternative roles for heroines, either in a state of jeopardy and as a victim or as an avenger, are easily represented within the context of standard myths.[74] In this context, status-seeking appears normal. There is a relation of status and gender, which is fundamental and must be studied at a deeper level. For example, evidence from evolutionary anthropology explains the emergence of status over the five million year history of the human race as a process that facilitates the coordination of simultaneous competition (for mates and resources) and cooperation (against external threats).[75]

TELEVISION, INSTINCTS, INTERCHANGEABILITY AND SELF-PROJECTION IN POSITIONAL LIFESTYLES

Television programmes are powerful because they influence the experiential and emotional reactions of viewers through a process that stimulates basic instincts such as sexuality and fear. It is therefore no accident that for early social critics of television programmes, soap-operas were seen to focus on seduction as a process that involves sexuality.[76] In these television programmes, seduction functions in essence as a pleasure that emerges through the continuous postponement of an objective.[77] Here the experience of difficulty after difficulty is very important to the rise of desire. The perception of time plays also an essential role. For example, in soap-operas there is a similarity between time and real time. The same is also true with regard to the newer genre of reality shows. In contrast, action sitcoms seem to compress television time as there is an emphasis on achievement and on action that escalates so that a certain thrill is attained.[78] Here there is neither memory nor intimacy and no pretence of living life between episodes.[79] By contrast, the masculine characters live in the moments of performance. An important aspect of role projection television is the segmentation of scenes within the same series. Anthropologists, psychologists and sociologists became aware very early of the seductive, almost sexual, aspect of television programmes. Pleasure and joy express two different categories that are initiated by a process that involves perception of television messages.[80] The pleasure is associated with the meaning that is produced by the reader. Thus there is a psychoanalytic perspective to pleasure from this point of view. In essence, this framework expresses to a certain extent Freudian theory. Finally, the increasing capacity of people for fragmentation and interruption, the growing habit of channel-jumping, the intensifying absorption of television in its new forms (what Umberto Eco named 'neo-TV') where television takes itself and its participants as its own subjects through chat shows, award ceremonies or news programmes produce a post-modern psycho-cultural dimension of television.[81]

The television world and the simulations it produces have transformed the physical structuring of social life in a dramatic way. Earlier periods were characterized by clear-cut differences between private and public life, and between the subjective and its perceptions and the objective real world.[82] These differences seem to have lost much of their power today. In this fusion of perceptions, the projection of self into positional objects to sign wealth, advantageous context and skill (as in positional goods like luxury cars and premium holiday houses) is now clear because there is an interchangeable play between positional symbols and the perception of self.

Television expresses literally 'the real world of postmodern culture, society and economy ... of real popular culture driven onwards by the ecstasy and decay of the obscene spectacle'.[83] As such, it has an immense influence without precedence in other types of media such as social media. Thus active individuals can become passive and assume the identity of viewers. Social groups are also defined as packaged audiences, who are influenced by the trends promoted by media and other elites.

The world of flat images transforms or replaces the world of experience in what may be considered as the victory of the culture of signification. One important aspect of this culture is novelty, which influences fashion, and in certain cases complicates people's lives. Fashion expresses one of the purest and most developed forms of commodity market economy. The compulsive desire to produce novelty for the sake of novelty seems in a sense similar to the motive to accumulate for the sake of accumulating. Through fashion, desires are stimulated, multiplied and in the end never satisfied. This happens because the need for novelty that is created through fashion produces unsatisfied people.

STATUS IDENTIFICATION

Despite its importance, empirical studies of identification with superstars and celebrities and its impact on individual preference for status goods have not been conducted extensively. Still, there are some clues from research in similar areas. Here I present certain findings from different research approaches on the effect of images of success and stereotypes on positional consumption. This type of research examines the impact of media displays of success on the desire of consumers for luxury brands.[84] In a pilot study and three additional studies, it was demonstrated that reading a story about a similar and successful other, such as a business major from the same university, increases consumers' expectations about their own future wealth, which in turn increases their desire for luxury brands. However, reading about a dissimilar but successful other person, with a major quite different to their own but from the same university, lowers consumers' preferences for luxury brands. Therefore, familiarity and identification with other people such as superstars or celebrities may influence the decision about which category of status goods and services matters more.

Another example of promising research focuses on the process of wishful identification, especially with respect to occupational choices. Television often shows work-related activities of characters and is one of several important sources of occupational information for young people. In telephone interviews, a sample of economically disadvantaged young people named their favourite television character and the character's job and rated their perceptions of this career and their wishful identification with the character. The respondents also identified the job they would most likely have. Results show that income and education expectations of respondents are positively correlated with the attributes of the characters' jobs. Wishful identification is stronger for characters in jobs with higher income, which required more education, were seen as more realistic, and were perceived as providing greater extrinsic values such as respect and benefits.[85]

Another study of wishful identification included measures such as perceived attitude similarity, perceived character attributes (smart, successful, attractive, funny, violent or admired) and wishful identification with the characters. Wishful identification was identified with the desire to be like or act like the character. There was evidence of greater wishful identification with same-gender characters and with characters who seemed more similar in attitudes. Men appeared to identify with male characters who they perceived as successful, intelligent and aggressive, whereas women identified with female characters who they perceived as successful, intelligent, attractive and admired.[86]

In another study, the extensive reach of popular culture through media visibility is examined. This study provides insight into the powerful influence that celebrities can exert on those who identify closely with their mediated images. An ethnographic study was conducted of Elvis Presley fans. Results indicate that Elvis fans and impersonators develop strong identification by consciously role modelling their idol's values and by changing their own lifestyles to emulate him.[87] This form of identification is not confined only to superstars but extends to other classes of people such as celebrities.[88] Another line of research studies refers to the adoption of stereotypical sex relations. A recent study confirmed that TV's abundant yet stereotypical portrayals of sexual relationships do indeed mislead young viewers. Frequent and involved viewing was associated with students' support of the sexual stereotypes surveyed. Women exposed to clips representing a particular sexual stereotype were more likely to endorse that view than women exposed to non-sexual content.[89] Yet the impact of self-other similarity on the outcomes of social comparison effects is not well understood. It has been argued that the extent to which this similarity is distinctive is a key to understanding such an effect.[90] Two experiments demonstrated that when self-other similarity is distinctive (unique), assimilation is more likely, whereas when self-other similarity is non-distinctive (common), contrast is more likely. These results suggest that what matters is the type rather than the quantity. Similarity on one distinctive dimension leads more readily to assimilation than similarity on numerous non-distinctive dimensions. This suggests that individuals seek distinctive aspects of a profile in order to assimilate to successful prototypes.

In addition, results of research on identity suggest that the multifaceted nature of identity provides a strategic basis for reducing the threat involved in upward social comparisons. After performing worse than a comparison standard, people may strategically emphasize aspects of their identity that differentiate them from the standard, thereby making the standard less relevant for self-evaluation. On the basis of previous research showing that persons with low self-esteem are less likely to make effective use of self-protection strategies, it was hypothesized and confirmed that the strategy of deflecting the threat involved in upward comparison (that is, decreasing perceived comparability by emphasizing an unshared social identity) would be used primarily by persons who are characteristically high in self-esteem.[91] Moreover, the use of this strategy caused more positive affect in response to threatening upward comparisons.

Other studies point out to the possibility of self-deception.[92] Four experiments demonstrated that self-threatening social comparison information motivates consumers to lie. There were several factors related to self-threat. These included relevance of the social comparison target (that is, the importance of the comparison person), comparison discrepancy (that is, the magnitude of the performance difference), comparison direction (that is, whether one performs better or worse), nature of the information (that is, whether the comparison is social or objective) and perceived attainability (that is, the possibility of achieving the compared performance), as well as influenced consumers' willingness to engage in self-deception. These results extend social comparison theory because they demonstrate that comparisons that threaten public and private selves cause self-deceptive behaviour. To sum up, social comparison strategies are more complex than what is implied by immediate comparisons to neighbours or peers and involve practices, which include identification with superstars and celebrities, distorting preferences and self-deception.

TELEVISION WORLD AND THE SOCIETY OF SPECTACLE

Some useful ideas for assessing the impact of the television world on the formation of preferences originate from alternative perspectives such as the one put forth in the *The Society of the Spectacle*.[93] This radical analytical approach was developed on the basis of alienation and commodity-use theories. When these theories are applied in a contemporary framework, there is a greater attention on phenomena such as excess consumption, new types of communication and the massive growth in the electronic media. People now live in a world that emphasizes the social meaning of images provided by media.[94] The analysis of the society of the media involves the spectacle as 'the moment when the commodity has attained the total occupation of social life'.[95] Thus the show is not only a collection of images but it is transformed to a social relation among people with the help of images, symbols and signs. In modern societies, there is an immense accumulation of shows. Everything that is directly lived can be also relived through its representation.

Through media, the spectacular and almost mythological world presents itself as natural; time and historical accounts are often forgotten within culture. However, lived experience is packaged and is merchandized in a manner that is consistent more with mainstream social values. For example, in the spectacular world there is little room to represent social critique and change. Thus people need to develop a social understanding and critique beyond the influence of the virtual system.

CONCLUDING REMARKS

The study of anthropological aspects of status markets demonstrates the emergence of popular culture as a central locomotive for the post-modernist expressionist lifestyle of post-modern individuals. This life-style is certainly stimulated by the aesthetization of our everyday life, which is created by the rise of media but is also the product of nostalgic and imaginary reaction to massive consumption and work alienation. The rise of popular culture brings forth its critics and analysts in the form of symbolic analysts, who constitute the creative class. These individuals place a great importance on presentation, appearance, lifestyle and morality. Such qualities are internalized by post-modern individuals as aspects of social identity, social validation and addictions. Despite reactionary movements that call for a revival of traditional values and lifestyles, individuals today internalize expressions of simulational culture filled with aesthetic pleasure, mixed meanings and identities, and artistic novelty. These phenomena do not operate in a vacuum. In contrast, they are indispensable pieces of a process, in which social validation, identity and a sense of self-worth are determined. This sense seems to be a valued commodity because even marginalized individuals attempt to preserve it, or inflate it by appropriating a marginal part, sometimes a small one, of this mixed simulational culture. Thus we must acknowledge the fundamental collapse of traditional social distances, which constrained large groups of people in the past. Yet the virtual hyperreality provided by the media and more notably by television promotes symbols and myths of a social world that is mostly mainstream, upscale and comfortable in its representation. Through the pleasure of 'implication' with real-life emotions, this social world is internalized in individual feelings, perceptions, tastes and, eventually, social identities. Thus emotionally internalized social validations and addictions through positional lifestyles explain individual unconscious dispositions and the formation of tastes. Accordingly, the assumption that preferences or perceptions of social identities are exogenous or genuine runs into great difficulties. To a great extent, they are not only endogenously determined but also emotionally internalized through the pleasurable process of identification with symbols and myths of virtual hyperreality. Since most of these symbols and myths are mainstream ones, it is easy to understand how established and discriminating social boundaries or structures are reproduced with the internalization of social identities and social values. Moreover, the relation of the ecstasy of media spectacle and the formation of an individual 'virtual' identity implies that in the fusion of perceptions the projection of self to positional objects to sign wealth, advantageous context, skill and to reaffirm individual self-worth really occurs through the interchangeable play between positional symbols and the perception of self. Thus status-related choices do not always represent free choice and independent individual tastes as the proponents of orthodox economics seem to argue. Yet any counterbalance to the society of the spectacle, that is, to the society that emphasizes the social meaning of images provided by virtual reality, which is consistent with the social values of the contented upper and middle classes seems difficult. The only exception to this impasse comes from the possibility that excessiveness and own contradictions may initiate processes that will eventually produce policies aiming at social correction.

6. The sociology of distinction, superiority and deprivation

INTRODUCTION

So far, the inquiry has concentrated on the analysis of economic and behavioural forces. It is now time to turn to the study of the sociological processes that are relevant because the rise of status markets that we witness today applies in the social context of late market economy. Factors such as the media, information technology and the mobile phone exercise an immense influence and tend to amplify the subjective psychological forces that result in the rise of status markets. These markets are relevant to different social groups, who assume differing social roles. The social dimension implies that the study of status markets must be conducted from a sociological perspective. There are certain significant issues that need to be analysed through the application of the sociological methodology. Such questions refer to the environment of contemporary social groups, which influences tastes or preferences; or, how factors such as the media or advertisement shape the social identities of individuals, who act within or across social groups. Another sociological issue refers to phenomena such as sensationalism, virtual communication and an endless appetite for novelty. An important question to ask is how the social identity of different individuals is cultivated and in what manner this identity influences positional concerns for distinction and, in certain cases, for social discrimination. Another sociological issue is the relation of social identities with symbols or myths provided by contemporary media and advertisement. This opens the path for an interesting discussion that explains how symbols and myths, which are used by individuals for the purpose of the formation of social identity, interface with the impact of diverse structures in the society. The interaction of different social groups creates modes of social discrimination, which are utilized for social territorial competition. Finally, one last question that must be addressed is how the process of relative position competition alters social dynamics and the way social change is envisaged by people today.

THE POST-MODERN SOCIETY OF TELEVISION, SENSATIONALISM AND EXCESS CONSUMPTION

The new technologies create an environment in which values and economics become interdependent and create a fertile ground for the development of new activities and products. Human culture and values are influenced by the virtual reality that is created by television and other media. As a result, many social activities are shaped today by the values and the role models which are promoted by the forces of media.

Screen productions in the form of movies or television shows are an important medium to reach mass audiences. Many professionals shift their activities to interface with the mass audiences of television because the commercial influence of television is enormous. Young people (and professional adults in many instances) communicate with vocabularies taken from television shows. Some people choose to express their feelings by imitating film or music superstars in their gestures and vocal tones, and to project a different image than their own. Thus the transition from the written word to a virtual and verbal mimetic narrative that is taken from the media changes individual behaviour.

An example of such a change is the case of the negative political advertisements in the USA. Although the public says that they dislike political advertising because it is cynical, market surveys show that negative political advertisements are quite effective. Therefore, in a television culture perceptions of reality are in fact more important than actual reality. One could argue that the media becomes essentially a secular religion replacing shared history, national cultures, real religion, families and friends, as it is the dominant force that creates our mental pictures of reality. In the world of instant gratification, television shows promote consumption as the core of life and the only means for individual ambition and fulfilment. Television series such as, for example, *Housewives* or *Dynasty* in the past, portray typical American individuals or a typical American family far wealthier than the real average. This type of representation leaves Americans (and, equivalently, European viewers of similar programmes) with a false and superficial perception of how wealthy the average American or European is. In fact, the virtual family is a wealthy mythical family that pushes many people to internalize feelings of relative deprivation. In trying to catch up with more affluent lifestyles people tend to become overworked or make false occupational decisions, because they strive to overcome the cognitive dissonance between reality and virtual perception and the deprivation that comes along with what the television shows bring. To this extent, the quest for private material accumulation is consistent not only with market economy values but also with the television culture.

THE 'FEEL-GOOD' SOCIETY, THE RISE OF POPULAR CULTURE AND THE FORMATION OF INDIVIDUAL PREFERENCES

As it has been noted, the appearances of the most popular and successful professionals today are reproduced at low cost. Film, video, television, radio, recorded music, books and newspapers are the means of access for the public to the world's most talented actors, comedians, singers, authors, columnists, athletes, politicians, self-help coaches, financiers and other successful professional people. A greater demand for cultural products and services is evident since cultural events, books, performances, sports and television programmes provide the means of social reference and social identification.

As leisure and entertainment have become an important part of western life the demand for cultural goods and services in its broad sense has increased.[1] This excess demand creates excellent profit opportunities for the producers of these services. *Ceteris paribus*, the producers prefer the services such as books or the attendance of well-known or celebrity professionals at events rather than unknown ones. Given the uncertain character of cultural goods and services, it is reasonable for the producers to seek for some sort of certainty in their expected profit margins with the choice of well-known professionals. Yet the choice of popular performers cannot always guarantee results.

Moreover, there is an emphasis on sensationalism, whether from television shows or from movies, books or concerts. This comes as no surprise when one considers people's fascination with sensational issues such as sex scandals or nudity portrayed in media and culture. It is true that historically, to some extent, this fascination with sensationalism has always been present, but with the media technology that is available today, the supply of sensationalism has exploded. With the remote control, television viewers are free to choose whatever kind of programme they prefer. Yet the same appliance obliges television executives to seek for the most sensational issues to keep the attention of television viewers a little bit longer to their shows. Furthermore, television executives are challenged today to create a sort of television culture that can influence the preferences or the tastes of the public. While some tastes are rooted to primal drives, such as those for food and sex, there are other tastes such as those for style, music form or art that are shaped by cultural considerations. As style now becomes more and more important in the routines of people, the influence of the cultural environment on style becomes more discernible.

Thus tastes today are not formed only by exogenous biological factors but are shaped in many instances and through various different channels by modern culture. To the extent that there is a market for culture, it influences culture and preferences. Generally, the cultural market is characterized by the same forces of supply and demand that apply to basic commodities. For example, since instant thrill is for many a source of entertainment, there is a demand for thriller movies to which the market responds with the production of a rich menu of this type of movie. However, the rise of such a market influences social responses and the perception of the public towards violence. The pulsar culture is so influential that it pervades its impact on the determination of preferences. There is ample clinical evidence which shows that the exposure to a certain social or cultural environment influences the human neural system. Moreover, the environmental dominance of simple sensational images over complex social reasoning influences people today to such an extent that individual attitudes such as patience, a good work ethic or principled reaction are becoming less frequent in contemporary life.

In such a sensational and formulaic routine, superstars and celebrities emerge as mediators of gossip and self-reference.[2] The role of media in any form, from television to magazines, cannot be underestimated easily because they are full of reports from the lives of the 'rich and famous'. In this social background, in which the majority of people are preoccupied with the lives of the celebrities and with their values, it becomes increasingly difficult for individuals to identify and pursue their own interests against the flow of the information they receive. People also make decisions and take promotions in many situations not because of what they know but of whom they know and of what this person prefers. Social networks of community or at work are very strong and information from the media serves as a traditional benchmark for reference and communication in networking.

ADVERTISEMENT, ENDOGENOUS PREFERENCES AND RELATIVE POSITION COMPETITION

An important dimension of the contemporary corporate world and popular culture is advertisement. The influence of advertisement has escalated because advertisement messages use social psychology know-how in order to convince consumers to buy certain products. Thus the consumer today is exposed to biased information that comes from advertisement and forms meta-preferences or second-order preferences that differ from their initial desires and, in this sense, the consumer does not act rationally.[3] There are various accounts that describe how consumption is influenced by advertisement.[4] This is a point that was emphasized by Galbraith and is shared to a lesser extent by Frank. Nevertheless, consumption patterns become biased towards activities or products that involve context and status although on principle people may in fact want more time for themselves and their friends.[5] The role of advertisement is highly influential because it does not highlight quality activities or spontaneous free time but instead products such as cars, appliances and clothes that can be easily related with context and status. Since positional goods and services are usually more visible than private quality activities, the impact of advertisement in increasing the visibility of positional goods is indisputable. It is no surprise therefore that there is far-reaching evidence in social psychology tests which support the view that consumer decisions are heavily influenced by information that is provided by television advertisement. One main aspect of this evidence is the representation of a repeated massage in novel ways to provoke a sense of immediacy and emergency among viewers.[6]

In essence, the influence of advertisement is in itself a characteristic pattern that manifests that preferences are endogenously determined in a context of positional lifestyles. This situation happens because preferences with positional concerns are a form of reference-dependent preferences. As such, preferences are not autonomous but they depend on perceptions of activities and behaviours.[7] Cognitive responses require the use of a reference point and, therefore, they are relative.[8] Thus preferences can be perceived relatively on the basis of a reference point. Relative perceptions affect the process of dissonance reduction. For example, on the one hand the selection of a reference point, which is not too higher from the level that is consistent with one's financial situation, makes dissonance from the experience of positional lifestyles easier to reduce.[9] In the case of the poor, less 'anomie' is internalized. On the other hand, the selection of a reference far beyond one's means results in the realization of an individual psychological cost. The more worthy the rewards from positional activities, the more difficult it is for an individual to change their attitude towards participating in relative position consumption. In the absence of appropriate policies, financially disadvantaged individuals are essentially encouraged to 'keep up with the

Joneses'. This will eventually motivate them to work harder to improve their social position.[10]

It must be noted that preferences are endogenous not only in a behavioural type of analysis through the choice of a reference point but also in a rational-choice context. When individuals place a great importance on safeguarding self-esteem, there are patterns of habituation, withdrawal and the compulsive re-emergence of an abandoned habit.[11] This shows that even in a rational-choice framework the formation of seemingly undesired preferences is an important process which relates to positional consumption. Not only this, but the dominance of undesired tastes results in pollution when it comes to marketing.[12] This deprives people of their own desires since markets do not provide intrinsic rewards to their initial inclinations as much as to their status-oriented preferences. The result of these proclivities is the appearance of suboptimal outcomes with respect to first-order individual preferences, a phenomenon that manifests clearly in the occurrence of market failure.[13]

THE HYPERREALITY OF POPULAR CULTURE AND SOCIAL DISCRIMINATION

As the world has entered an era in which information technology, the media, popular culture and the 'aestheticization' of reality prevail, communication is inflated to reach new levels. In some situations, there is a complete ecstasy and imagination since what we observe is in fact simulated.[14] This is also evident in the virtual manifestation of social media from Facebook, Twitter and Instagram to other less well-known but upcoming outlets. People today live in a world of imagination or hyperreality. In this world, it is difficult to identify the difference between the imaginary and the reality especially since the modern landscape of our experiences is full of diverse cultural manifestations from new religious movements and special communities to modern shopping malls and new business practices. This fragmentation can suppress or modify individual behaviour. It is in this context that the individual can be viewed as a temporary idea, a concept which emerged in a particular period after the Renaissance and was developed during the industrial society. The notion of 'man' is eventually a narrative of industrial modern society that becomes problematic in today's hyperreal world because positional consumption and fragmented lifestyle preferences are used to make discriminatory judgements. These evaluations identify the taste of the consumer with themselves and render it visible to other consumers. The range of discriminatory judgement is vast and may vary across different occupations and class groups.[15] The world of tastes and lifestyles, with their distinctions or grades, constitute in essence a large space, in which discriminatory judgement takes place everywhere.

Understanding changes in tastes and preferences may require skills and knowledge of new goods. This knowledge includes also methods, through which new goods are used as representations of taste and exclusivity. This process pervades all grades of class spectrum from the new rich and the new middle class to skilled or unskilled working class. Various commodities and services can be used for symbolic consumption, from television and concerts to self-improvement, motivational counselling and personal relationship counselling. The objective of symbolic consumption is to create a symbolic pose or lifestyle, which in conferring status, can provide satisfaction and a sense of fulfilment.[16]

Globalization and the rise of exotic local cultures to prominence make it increasingly difficult to determine the type of commodities or services that can be utilized as benchmarks in the formation of individual discriminatory judgements. Yet despite localism in a global environment, there is sufficient homogeneity, which allows the existence of a polarized structure of cultural goods and lifestyle activities. One such representation of partitioned structure has already been proposed within the French sociologist tradition. This approach broadens the scope of analysis because it describes characteristics such as body shape, manner of walk, tone of voice, style of speaking as being in essence classificatory schemes, which involve discriminatory judgements.[17]

THE POLITICAL ECONOMY OF THE POST-MODERN CULTURE OF SYMBOLS AND SIGNS

Since the 1980s, there has been a great interest among French sociologists in consumption, commodification and the conflict that the signalling process creates in a framework of political economy. These thinkers apply a Marxist mode of thought when they examine the semiology of consumerism and the social behaviour that is associated with symbolic consumption. Of course, in Marxist analysis there was traditionally a tendency for an economization of life in terms of the tradition of political economy.[18] Thus these sociologists attempted to develop a 'political economy of the sign'.[19] Furthermore, some of these thinkers tend to examine the field of cybernetics as an important process and conclude that this process creates a new social order. Their view goes beyond the analytical domain of classical Marxist theory with its emphasis on class conflict. This extension happens because of the rise of virtual reality and symbolism, in which goods, services or activities are emptied from their original meanings in order to be rearranged in a different context or order. In this perspective, the notion of 'man' is not an independent entity anymore, but an actor or a facilitator of various popular cultural experiences. An example is the manner in which a post-modern person is consummated through various television images and their dependency on them.

However, the analysis of status markets solely in terms of the importance of the representation of hyperreality and virtual man is not easy. There is still space for the autonomous individual although the distance between self and their new environment is gradually losing its meaning. Yet there are numerous cases in which it is difficult to distinguish between external and internal factors in individual experiences, since information and the prevalence of communication have made this distinction useless.

The rise of the imaginary, the sensational and communication for the purpose of instant gratification and the suppression of the individual who is transformed into a facilitator of the hyperreal, have led thinkers such as Jameson to describe the post-modern culture as a 'depthless' culture. In this framework, post-modern culture is viewed in essence as an excessive consumption society in which there is a saturation of images and signs to such an extent that many aspects of social life are influenced by them.[20] In addition, popular culture rises to such levels that it competes with high culture. Hollywood and entertainment theme parks compare with the Teatro alla Scala in Milan and the British Museum today because the ecstasy of communication has diminished their differences. The radical line of thought with its emphasis on the role of popular culture eventually interfaces with mainstream concerns about the impact of consumerism. Still, one problem with this particular radical understanding of popular culture is its tendency to view with no exception cultural products as homogeneous and dangerous to individuality and creativity. Yet there are examples in which popular culture is fun and reinforces creativity and innovation. There is a need therefore for a deeper and eclectic analysis, which will reconcile the homogeneous and heterogeneous aspects of post-modern society.

INDIVIDUAL LIFESTYLES, SYMBOLISM AND SOCIAL DISCRIMINATION

The surge of consumerism with its excesses and oversupply of goods that carry a symbolic classification is widely observed today. People become easily confused as they observe the diverse symbolism of consumer goods that they are exposed to through the media and the social networks in which they participate. This symbolism and the gratification that many consumer goods provide are often instant. As a term, consumption is an activity that implies destruction, exhaustion or waste. The symbolism therefore that is carried with the activity of consumption in our times is easily exhausted as there is a need to project novel signs of status after a period of time.[21] Hence, an explanation of the oversupply of symbolic popular cultural goods and services lies in the fact that their symbolism is instant and novel.[22]

The question that arises however is how symbolism operates to provide a system of classification. For example, Barthes shows that images or ideas constitute a first perception of meaning. This implies the existence of a signified and a signifier united by a symbol. The symbol exists within the function of a myth. The original meaning is emptied out, and it becomes a classifier for a second, mythical meaning. The symbolic consumption can hide discriminatory dispositions such as racism or sexism. For example, the contingent representations of consumer goods that are bought by the new rich appear to be natural and eternal. There is a process of transformation from the original meaning that applies to a wide range of products and services from cars to perfumes. There is a semiological similarity with the manner in which the fashion system operates. Thus the world of fashion as depicted in the magazines *Elle* or *Vogue* can easily become a theoretical and empirical field of study for analysing context-dependent activities.

From the catwalks of Milan or Paris and the purchase of an evening dress for a summer night out in the Hamptons or Capri to buying sprees at mass tourism destinations in Florida and Spain or at the nearest mall in Athens, there is a symbolism or semiology that changes over time. This semiology dictates to people how they can combine fashion items so that they become fashionable. Often, the process of eventually becoming fashionable involves the contempt for the common and the unfashionable. Thus discrimination is inherent in judgement involving fashion, which can be examined in semiological terms as texts, scenarios or narratives that require to be decoded into second meanings.[23] Certain activities in the entertainment industry, from music hall concerts to hip hop dancing venues, are viewed by some sociologists as providing texts that can be decoded and rearranged to bring forth hidden secondary discriminatory meanings.

DISTINCTION, SOCIAL RELATIONS AND DISCRIMINATION

A certain aspect of consumerism is the positional identification or the status that certain products assign to the consumer. It is not just high-end luxury goods such as expensive cars or waterfront summer houses that assign positional privilege or status, even basic commodities like a bottle of wine or a branded t-shirt can confer a sense of status to their owner. The tendency for social distinction takes place not only in the case of expensive items, in which prestige is gained through the implication of high exchange value of products. Even less expensive products, for which the price does not have to be mentioned frequently, can carry symbolism, demarcate social relationships and confer exclusivity and distinction. With a moderately priced bottle of French vintage wine many enjoy exclusivity not because it will be consumed in reality but because it will be consumed symbolically. With symbolic consumption, products are actually viewed, are part of gossip and transform to expressions of desire as well as to representations of values.

Symbolic consumption provides also a great deal of satisfaction to the owner. Since the symbolic connotations of the product become important, symbolism plays a fundamental role in the design of the production and marketing. The symbolic associations of commodities are stressed by the designers because they help shape values, lifestyles and social relationships. There is now considerable research on the various ways through which the purchase of commodities is used to demarcate the lines of social relationships.

SYMBOLISM, HABITUS AND SOCIAL INEQUALITY

Individuals are able to develop strategies to acquire the required cultural capital to secure particular positions in the social hierarchy. This may include the possibility of feedback of tastes from the bottom to the top of the social ladder. The feedback takes place when individuals of the upper classes adopt certain trends that are common among bottom-tier income groups, which then distort and eventually frustrate the aspirations of the middle classes. The middle classes experience confusion and frustration due to insufficient stocks of cultural capital to understand this deceptive tactic.[24]

Social distinction and the tactics for obtaining it has been analysed in economic sociology in terms of Bourdieu's notion of *habitus*. This process takes place in a context in which there is a differentiation between the cultural and economic capital held by individuals.[25] In this context, lifestyles and motives vary horizontally, cutting across the social hierarchy. *Habitus* is still the capacity to develop classifiable practices and the skill to differentiate and appreciate those practices and products (taste), which are utilized as a system of discernment influenced by social position power.[26]

In this context, the notion of gentrification is an additional area, in which various combinations of economic and cultural capital are used by individuals of different groups in their attempts to achieve distinction from each other. Gentrification also involves a process of reclassification. An example of this rearrangement is contemporary middle-class preferences, which are influenced by status, style and cosmopolitanism. Gentrification covers all aspects of life such as housing, leisure, consumption choices and portfolio decisions. In this process, new elements of distinction are introduced continuously so that in practice there is always a variable 'gentrification premium'.[27]

SOCIAL STRATIFICATION AND INEQUALITY

Bourdieu's theory implies that persistent inequality is due to the ideological domination of the upper classes, which discourages the aspirations of lower-class individuals. Such an effect takes place by creating an environment to form self-fulfilling beliefs that drive them towards more reasonable educational and occupational tracks. This approach provides an explanation why upwardly mobile agents are more often treated as the new rich in Europe rather than in the USA, which offers greater incentives for upward mobility. In Europe, when this is possibly perceived to take place through effort and ability alone, it is often considered to be unlikely. For this reason, individuals just focus on maintaining their initial social position.[28]

It is interesting to note again that the major intellectual and political conflict among French sociologists dates back to the early 1970s when Bourdieu's theory of persistent inequality stood in contrast to another prominent sociological approach advanced by Boudon, who developed the reference group theory.[29] The advocates of the persistent inequality theory were critical of the reference group theory because the latter attributes the inadequate performance of lower-class individuals to their weak motivation.

This idea of the reference group theory was considered as being very conservative and the debate between these two theories raised important policy implications. If, as maintained by Boudon, individuals are mostly motivated by social status and lower-class agents do not have much to lose from adopting an attitude which results in poor economic performance, then there is no strong rationale for policy intervention that increases efficiency. However, if persistent inequality is due to statistical discrimination and/or imperfect rational learning as implied by the analysis of Bourdieu, then political action should be taken to minimize inequality. The policy implementation may take the form of the imposition of quotas, affirmative action or simply measures for the reversal of the dominant discourse.[30] Still, there exists a possibility that both theories may contain elements of relevance or truth for different social groups. For example, the reference group theory may be applicable to lower middle-class individuals but does not explain adequately the behaviour of members of the lowest classes. By contrast, the hypothesis of persistent inequality can explain this situation better.

POST-MODERN CULTURE AND THE DOMINATION OF SIGNS

As it has been mentioned, popular culture and the rise of the media have been the subject of study by various sociologists who conduct their work in terms of the notion of a post-modern society.[31] This type of society recognizes knowledge and information technology as important and productive forces. The post-modern society is in fact a knowledge society. Moreover, the introduction of culture in radical accounts of thought interfaces greatly with the analysis of the post-modern society. The term of post-modernism was first used by Federico De Onis in the 1930s to indicate a minor reaction to modernism.[32] The interest in post-modernism has increased over the years. Thus there have been various important contributions by well-known social theorists such as Bell, Kristeva, Lyotard, Vattimo, Derrida, Foucault, Habermas, Baudrillard and Jameson.[33] Of course, the post-industrial stage can be described in other terms such as, for example, on the basis of certain ideas utilized in Marxist analysis. One such term is the idea of late capitalism that was adopted by Jameson. Whether a post-industrial or late-capitalism analysis, there is a clear tendency to view the knowledge society or post-modern society not as an independent entity but as one mode of free-market economy.

In the new Marxist account of post-modern culture, the characteristics of late capitalism or the last stage of free-market economy include the international new division of labour, the prevalence of information technology and the media, as well as the emergence of the new rich.[34]

These factors do not deviate much from the ideas of various mainstream thinkers, who point to the very same themes as being important in the evolution of the post-modern world. However, the mainstream approach differs from modern Marxist culture theory because the latter departs radically from prior analysis that was based on the economization of life and because it considers various aspects of the contemporary social realm as being cultural. Not only this, but for some Marxist sociologists like Jameson, popular culture stands at the core of post-modernist society and its dynamics. The implications of such an approach are insightful although they support the notion of complete popular power or imperialism of the leading classes.

DIFFERENT ACCOUNTS OF POST-MODERN SOCIETY

These radical sociological approaches do not constitute a homogeneous line of thought because there are different views on post-modern society. For example, for Baudrillard technology and information are basic aspects of the shift from a production reality to a social context order, in which simulations and signs become more important and the distinction between the real and the imaginary disappears. However, when Lyotard examines the impact of what he calls the computerization of society on knowledge his analysis seems to be rather optimistic. The emergence of diverse signs and symbols of universalism, which replace the fixed traditional local meanings, is considered as a positive development that is associated with greater freedom and individuality.[35] This conclusion is part of a more general sociological approach, according to which, the temporary and the periodical can be incorporated in the traditional understanding of experience.[36]

Jameson has however a different periodical idea of the post-modern and of the essence of a post-modern society.[37] In his context, post-modernism is not confined to epochal terms only because it is considered as the cultural equivalent or structure of the last stage of market economy, that is, late capitalism that has taken place since the 1970s.[38] Here the notion of 'post-modern man' contradicts the idea of 'modern man' who, as a hero, constantly attempts to invent himself.

In Jameson's framework, the depiction of reality as images and the fragmentation of time into a series of diverse moments are critical in the life of 'post-modern man'. Due to the importance of images, the media exercise a substantive influence on the behaviour of individuals in the post-modern society. However, despite the emphasis on the role of the media there is little discussion of the actual experience of watching television by different people and in different social settings. Thus the heterogeneity of reactions to media messages is actually undermined.

This homogeneous framework contrasts with Baudrillard's analysis, in which today's simulational world is described as the result of the rise of information technology and its use in production. Information technology allows the 'triumph of signifying culture' that reverses the causality, in which social relations are determined. As social relations become saturated with shifting cultural signs it becomes increasingly difficult to describe social changes in terms of a polarized relation such as class conflict, and this development diminishes the importance of social policy interventions. In its extreme form, this may lead to 'the end of social' experience. Overall, post-modern conditions include the appearance of aesthetic self-consciousness and reflexiveness, as opposed to rational reflexiveness, the rise of simultaneous experience as opposed to a linear narrative form, the prevalence of exploration over traditional certainties and, more generally, the emphasis on dissolution of structure. The post-modern conditions in art include the reduction in the differences that separate life and art, mass culture and high culture, the mixing of signs and traditional social communication, eclecticism and everyday life. The dissolution of structure that is prevalent is an everyday reality that cannot be easily overcome.[39] This situation poses a difficulty to the development of a sociological discussion of status markets.

CULTURAL DOMINATION, STRUCTURE AND COMMODIFICATION

In early accounts of the distinction between modernism and post-modernism, the fundamental cultural assumption of modernity is the principle of the autonomous self-determination in the behaviour of the individual.[40] The post-modern archetypes of individualism are the entrepreneur in the economic field and the artist in the cultural field. In addition, there is definitely an interface of the three domains: polity, culture and economy.[41] In these approaches, there is no use of the relation between base and superstructure. Thus economy is not analysed as the base, changes of which lead to new cultures. Post-modernism is envisaged as a mix of different tendencies of the modern era.[42] However, Jameson's analysis goes beyond this understanding and refers to cultural logic in a broader sense. Additional emphasis is attributed therefore to alternative connections of culture with the other areas of contemporary society.

In contrast, Lyotard's approach implies that the study of the influence of culture cannot be discussed within structural analysis alone. Thus a sociological explanation of cultural trends and forces is destined to fail as it cannot avoid holistic perceptions or systematizations within the modern grand narratives such as science, humanism, Marxism, feminism and so on. There is a need therefore for a sociology that allows for deconstruction and the creativity of the aesthetic world. This type of post-modern sociology would reject its generalizing social science objectives and instead attempt a synthesis of the ironies, the inconsistencies and the creative forces underlying post-modern culture. Yet an alternative tendency of post-modernism is to examine the relation of culture with other forces in economic terms. One such term is the idea of commodification, which is used to explain how in a situation of excess consumerism the dominance of the symbolism of the exchange value of goods constitutes use-value.[43] Commodification is a basic idea of the Frankfurt School that is present also in the work of Baudrillard, who emphasizes the role of semiology in the active manipulation of signs during the consumption process. Thus in his analysis sign and commodity interface and produce what is known as 'commodity-sign'. The analysis of commodification is used to argue that in market economy goods become signs because of the meaning that is attached to them by the consumers. Thus the relation between the analysis of the production of goods and the consumption of signs requires special examination. Mass consumption is influenced by the internalization of media images. The consumer culture and the media have developed a mass of images and symbols that leads to a simulational world.[44] As it was mentioned above, in this sphere the distinction between the real and the imaginary tends to disappear. Moreover, there seems to be a broader agreement in sociological inquiry that is summarized by the claim that the culture of post-modernism or post-industrial society is less unified now than in earlier stages of market economy. In this context, the exposure of contemporary citizens to the mass of signs and images is regarded as a case of schizophrenia that brings in mind the example of continuous television channel hopping.[45]

This schizophrenic representation of post-modern life marks the elimination of any structure in the relationship between signifiers and signified and the breakdown of a sound perception of serial historical time. Yet it would be a mistake to conclude that individuals today are removed of any power in conceptualizing the schizophrenia of the contemporary experience. There are effective individual resistances to the saturation of signs of post-modern life. The contemporary consumer conducts their aesthetic, emotional and hedonistic exploration on the basis of personal calculations, which induce a special attention to beneficial social relations.

LATE MARKET ECONOMY AND CULTURE CHANGE

Jameson describes the contemporary global world as an intensification of the forces that govern market economies. There are three eras of market economy development. First, there is 'market capitalism' with the rise of industrial capital in national markets. Second, there is the rise of 'monopoly capitalism', which coincides with a period during which national markets expanded into world markets organized around nation-states. This expansion was based on the exploitation characteristics of colonialism that secured cheap raw materials and labour. The third stage is 'multinational capitalism' with the emergence of globalization, international corporations and the explosion of international trade. Thus multinational and consumption-led market economy is the 'purest form of capital yet to have emerged, a prodigious expansion of capital into hitherto uncommodified areas'.

This line of thought implies that the new area of commodification for global market economy is pre-eminently representation itself. In traditional Marxist social theory, culture is part of the ideological struggle to hide or to enforce the real economic and social relations.[46] The studies of the production, exchange, marketing and consumption of cultural forms takes place in a broader framework. Such forms are examined in an extended sense including advertising, television and the mass media generally. These services play an important role in the progress of economic activity. The images and the styles of individuals appear to be accessories to economic activity but, to the extent that they are tied to self-esteem, they are the goods themselves. This process is facilitated also by the explosion of information technology that makes information not only a mediator of economic activity, but a very precious good itself.[47]

THE DYNAMICS OF POST-MODERN CULTURE CHANGE

The analysis of the post-modernist condition often appears to be inconsistent with traditional analysis and accounts of long-term social change. For this reason, there is a transcendence of any sense of discomfort with the difficulties that long-term narratives and perspectives face today.

Post-modernist culture is grasped in a dialectical manner in both its positive and negative aspects, just as Marx could possibly perceive the dialectics of progressive forces, which were inherent during the rise of capitalism. Today there is a sociological concern with the impact of international corporations in an environment of globalization marked by an increasing pluralism of cultural trends. These trends produce endless creative and diverse possibilities, which arise from the saturation of signs and symbols. A very important exercise in this connection is to imagine the limits of post-modern plurality in order to produce exogenous, if possible, references. As the future lies 'entangled in that unrepresentable outside like so many linked genetic messages', these exogenous benchmarks can be useful in the formation of alternatives to what seems an inescapable present from sign and symbol saturation.[48]

Another issue is the examination of the antinomies that underlie the relationship between post-modern change and permanence. Individuals witness both an unparalleled rate of change on all levels of social life and unparalleled standardization of everything. As a consequence, there is a need to reconcile homogeneity and heterogeneity. In a post-modern world, every principle of heterogeneous excess seems to have been programmed to meet the needs of the very system it seems to exceed. In post-modern theory and post-industrial economic practices alike, there is a contrast between any kind of philosophical foundation and the ecological revival of thinking in terms of the idea of nature and between the universal obstacle of utopian thought and that irrepressible impulse of the utopian. The quest for the utopian hides in almost every form of post-modern collective life despite appearances of compromises with a conventional life.[49] Thus it seems that the quest for external measures, which limit post-modern signs and trends and the study of the antinomies between change and permanence in contemporary life, provide an ambitious challenge to research in order to overcome the rigidity and the ineffectiveness of traditional social theory.

Even if the advocates of an utopian approach appear to try too hard to reconstitute the basis for some form of a grand narrative of social and culture change as we know it from the past, nevertheless their quest sets explorative questions, which can help advance our understanding of contemporary changes. This interesting inquiry mixes with an intention to use a structural approach that distinguishes the operation of forces into stages from industrial production and commodification to the marketing of goods. The change of tastes, values or information is a third stage, in which the market is 'corrupted' completely by relative position competition and a social signification that is reminiscent of demarcations that take place in the consumption side of market economy.[50] This structural approach is however a development in Marxist social theory because it emphasizes the interdependencies between economic activities and psychological forces, which are active in relative position competition. In the interdependence between culture and economy, the importance of the former rises and everything becomes culture. Production, consumption, culture, communication, signification and symbolism relate to each other to develop what we know as contemporary post-modern experience. When this is understood, Jameson's analysis of aesthetization of the contemporary that refers to the flow of signs and images, which saturate almost everything in contemporary society, is reminiscent of Marx's idea of fetishism of commodities. However, the functional analysis that is based on the interdependence of post-modern society and on the notion of fetishism seems to be less of a critical force in radical analysis relative to the analytical quest for external and more permanent references. Permanent references can be utilized as the basis to design effective policies to curb the post-modern domination of signs and trends.

CONCLUDING REMARKS

Understanding the phenomenon of status markets from a sociological perspective is a valuable and insightful task. This phenomenon takes place within the broader world of post-modern society, which is influenced by forces such as the culture of the media, popular culture and advertisement that are capable of changing initial individual preferences. The influence of these forces has increased immensely and has altered the social stereotypes so that the standards of wealthy, very successful or very visible individuals are considered to be an important reference by many. The lifestyles of these individuals have become the context of everyday talk and social reference. With the explosion of media, people perceive, act and internalize information provided by the virtual hyper-reality to which they are exposed. In this imaginary environment, perceptions of real social boundaries disappear and the crossing of social boundaries is thought to be possible even when in reality it proves to be highly problematic. In essence, individuals form meta-preferences or endogenous preferences influenced by forces such as popular culture, advertisement and media.

Thus relative position competition to assume status becomes more intense. The quest for relative social advantage is not limited to income rises or wealth accumulation but also to social distinction and superiority achieved by lifestyle poses with the aid of signification processes. These signification processes evolve around signs or symbols provided by media, advertisement and popular culture. Symbolic consumption, activity or occupational engagement is part of a post-modern culture, which implies classificatory dispositions that show social advantage and distinction, and aim at redesigning the social relations between individuals and social groups. The symbols or signs that are used in classificatory processes are usually provided by the popular culture of virtual hyper-reality and are often characterized by fashion novelty.[51] In many cases, positional activities redesign the map of social relations because they take the form of social discrimination and exclusion. The disadvantaged internalize feelings of unpleasant relative deprivation that needs to be alleviated. Thus the rise of status and superstar markets express to a certain degree the social and cultural domination by the financially comfortable and contented individuals, who enjoy considerable positional advantages. This cultural form of domination determines the perception that people have about the norm in society and about who is legitimate to intervene in the society. Correcting this distortion through long-term policies to overcome social discrimination and domination can run into great difficulties because in our post-modern world of saturated signs it is difficult for individuals to separate real from imaginary preferences. This in turn poses obstacles to the design and implementation of measures to promote culture change in order to overcome the social losses associated with status markets. Thus culture change also must take the form of developing effective policies with the objective to rearrange social references in the society. Overall, the sociological inquiry on status markets refers to the impact of general but powerful forces. Although they differ from economic micro-foundations and their analysis, sociological accounts provide the canvas for the discussion of important social realities, which pertain to status markets and the influence of superstars, and to their symbols in ways that economic analysis has been constrained to produce so far. Thus economic sociology paves the path to enhance economic foundations in a manner similar to the impact of psychology to behavioural economics.

7. Contentment, politics and the philosophy of superiority

INTRODUCTION

The operation of status markets involves directly or indirectly an individual attitude towards certain forms of social discrimination. This raises the issue of possible political implications that are relevant for the formulation of appropriate public policies. For example, if status markets generate social costs and the contented resist to acknowledge them and do nothing about these problems, then appropriate policy remedies should be imposed in a decisive manner. One way to discuss political repercussions is to apply principles that are drawn from the literature of political economy with respect to the behaviour of the upper and middle classes. A question to address is whether in the presence of a widening gap in income distribution, there are visible political interventions by the privileged to contain the complaints of the less comfortable. More specifically, it is useful to examine whether status markets enhance the perceived differences between the comfortable and the less privileged and whether they interfere in any form with the political debate between advocates of those groups.

In terms of a philosophical discussion, a point of departure is the inquiry about philosophical principles that may facilitate our understanding of the rise of status markets and of possible solutions. In particular, it is important to reflect on what kind of solutions will be more appropriate and how they relate to philosophical dialectics. Although this discussion seems to furnish a lateral rather than an immediate analysis of status markets, it is constructive because it contributes to a better understanding of the nature of institutions and policy commitments that are required. A special question is whether there are any alternative frameworks besides those described by the traditional dichotomy between pragmatism and idealism that are useful, even to some degree, to the adjustment process of correcting the problems arising from positional markets. Overall, the political and philosophical inquiry is useful because it enhances our understanding about the political and ideological impact on status markets and the manner in which policies are shaped in relation to this process.

I THE POLITICAL PROCESS

Status Markets, Political Economy and Income Distribution

The rise of status markets has definitely caught the attention of several social scientists. Despite some promising steps no decisive progress has been made so far to explain the political aspects of the interplay that exists between status markets, excessive consumerism, the new rich, relative position competition, social discrimination and economic inefficiency. Thus it is useful to expand the analysis from standard economic theorizing to political dimensions of status markets.

For some of the founders of political economy, capitalism is characterized by forces that lead eventually to inner fragility. Forecasting the outcome of this instability could be a reason for disagreement. For example, for Ricardo the market economy survives in any case because there is no visible alternative. On the contrary for Marx, there was a better alternative, socialism, which in reality did not work out. Their works in political economy deal more with issues such as inequality and poverty and less with status. The first type of analysis in the political economy literature that examined status and social contest was provided by Veblen's *Theory of the Leisure Class*. In this book, Veblen attempts to explain certain social aspects of inequality. Some of his observations are striking, especially with regard to the detachment of the new rich from serious social problems and to the relative position rivalries that take place between members of the new affluent class.[1]

Income Distribution and Politics

The issue of inequality seemed to attract less and less interest until the Great Recession in the USA. The decline of interest in inequality and in policies that express the political intervention to mitigate the wide distribution of income since the 1980s is an issue that certainly needs further explanation. One explanation for this decline is the reduction of poverty and the emergence of a large middle class. However, a simple observation would suggest that great inequality is still present. Yet some decline in inequality during the Great Moderation, either objective or perceived, must have been under way otherwise social upheavals would be present and intense in a way that could endanger the legitimacy of market economy.

An alternative explanation of the decline of interest in income distribution issues can be based on some of the consequences of western democracies, which provided a new social context in which to perceive the rich. With their wealth, the rich enjoy a greater freedom with respect to power, physical possessions and self-esteem. However, the subjective freedom for the less wealthy, such as for individuals from the middle class and even from the lower middle class, has improved drastically. In contemporary times, there is less resentment for the rich because the differences in subjective freedom relative to the degrees of wealth have declined. Here the role of subjectivism and inner self seems to be important. One factor that certainly contributes to the increase of subjective freedom is that today individuals communicate, shape their values and go ahead with their actions in a dream world of hyperreality or virtual reality. They can dream for the materialization of their financial success and they can hope that nothing is impossible.[2]

The decline of interest in issues of income distribution coincides also with the appearance of other problems, more notably, global uncertainty. The accumulation of wealth and the attempt of entrepreneurs to safeguard their affluence is a natural and quite obvious process. Yet despite serious improvements in the economic and the business environment, the security that businesspeople sense is fundamentally fragile and does not necessarily bring peace of mind. The existence of an economic, financial and business environment that is inherently and continuously uncertain is a conclusion that finds supporters even among economists or social scientists from conventional backgrounds. Although the uncertainties regarding the prospects of depression and inflation have been reduced during the years of the Great Moderation, other uncertainties such as those related to international financial instability, frequent deflations and recessions, political tension, immigration and environmental problems are still present.

Politics and the Paradox of Power

An alternative explanation is that the comfortable have successfully contained the resentment and the complaints of the less privileged due to the emergence of market phenomena such as globalization, financialization and the decline of unions. During the 1980s and in the midst of the Reagan and Thatcher administrations, in the USA and UK respectively, policy-makers adopted a neoliberal economic growth model, which utilized asset price inflation and credit expansion to substitute productivity-related wages, and a commitment to sustain aggregate demand towards full employment. The result of this process was the widening income distribution. Thus there is a relation between politics and market activities which involve transactions of commodities that resemble 'more like a heat exchange than an exchange of social greetings'.[3] Politics extend beyond individual tactics associated with the quest for status and the rise of non-productive and positional activities.[4] There is a broad process, which relates to markets and refers to the 'paradox of power', according to which the rich become richer and the poor become poorer. However, this phenomenon does not hold in cases in which there is a strong determination by the poor to resist.[5] Thus there is a political dimension in income distribution that is influenced by the political determination of the poor. This in turn is a process that relates to the support of social policies. Therefore, the synthesis of economics and politics and the incorporation of the notion of power offer a useful interdisciplinary understanding. Critics of neoclassicism in social economics have long argued that traditional wisdom ignores any power relationships. However, their impact is substantive and relevant to various market processes including positional activities.[6]

The Opposition to Government Programmes

The power relations between social groups from different classes are often represented through contrasting perceptions of the usefulness of government programmes. For example, extensive evidence from surveys indicates that large groups of individuals from the upper and the middle class hold a negative view of the role of the government. Furthermore, many individuals who benefited from the development of new services and the operation of positional markets do not view great differences in income as a serious problem, which must be mitigated by public programmes. Those policies are usually mocked by conservative commentators in the USA for their inadequate services and their complex regulations. Overall, they are pictured as an obstacle that needs to be reduced drastically, if not to be eliminated altogether.[7]

Yet there are areas in which there is conventional support for government intervention. These areas include certain forms of social security, medical care at higher income levels and financial guarantees to depositors in small regional savings and loan institutions. Thus the critical stance towards government programmes is not universal. However, those programmes seem to be consistent with the interests of middle and upper classes. Thus the exceptions that the 'contented majority' makes to its criticism of government and its interference to economic progress are eventually associated with activities that are better undertaken by major market interests and intermediaries. For example, military expenditures associated with third-party suppliers constitute in aggregate the largest part of the federal budget in the USA. These businesses use their strong political influence through public sector lobbying. In contrast, the government expenses for low-income individuals, such as expenditures for welfare, low-cost housing and health care for the very poor, are considered often quite excessive by individuals who belong to the comfortable and affluent social groups.

Besides, there are supplementary cases of selective opposition and bias to government plans. An example is the attitude of the comfortably situated towards the cost of financial crises, whether international or domestic. As in the 1980s with the savings and loan bailout experience, the bailout of banks during the international financial crisis 2007–2008 demonstrated the need for public intervention with the money of taxpayers contrary to stated principles of the fortunate. The cost of financial rescue was not resisted by the comfortably situated. In this particular case, the role of the government was accepted. It is no accident therefore that Galbraith took the opportunity to describe similar cases as clearly displaying 'the controlling principles of contentment'.[8]

The critical attitude against government plans for the underprivileged is also related with the view that any form of public intervention is possible only through the imposition of higher taxes. Higher taxes are resisted not only by the very rich but also by the great majority of upper and average middle-class professionals. Taxes are viewed by those individuals as preventing them from attaining their own financial goals. This belief however does not take into consideration the cost of social problems that exist in the society. Thus the fact that public services and taxation are viewed selectively by the contented electoral majority in the USA explains what characterizes from year to year tax and fiscal policies. The benefits from public services remain always an area of acrimonious political disputes. Yet it is evident that there is an inclination towards other issues, which favour the contented individuals.

In addition, the indifferent stance of the comfortable towards social problems has not been resisted boldly by the very poor. In the past, the reaction of the poor in many situations took the form of strikes and riots. Until the outbreak of the Great Recession, there had been a long period of relative social tranquillity compared to previous periods. One reason for this outcome is that with the decline of social democracy institutions the resistance of the underprivileged was softened ideologically and institutionally. Another reason is that this tranquility was attained because of a process of transition from a poor life to a more comfortable life, with the possibility of generational escape. Both those factors contributed to social tranquility since generational escape would not have been possible if the depressing needs of a poor life were still very presistent.[9]

Thus one can suggest that forces such as the escape from a poorer life, the prospects of generational jump, the growth of corporate culture, the rise of financialization and the decline of social partisanship have contributed to greater or lesser extent to contemporary social tranquility. However, we do not know whether the social tranquility of the past decades will continue in the years to come. Since the 2000s, there have been violent demonstrations against globalization that received wide media coverage in Seattle, Gothenburg and Genova at meetings of world leaders. After the international financial crisis 2007–2008, the Great Recession and the outburst of the Eurozone crisis, there has been a shift towards a greater awareness and social mobilization on the issue of inequality.

The Culture of Contentment

Financial interest, business objectives and social climbing are strong motives to pay less attention to the hardships of the less fortunate. Another force is the growth of corporations and the corporate culture. Despite the support of modern corporations to good causes as manifestations of corporate social responsibility, individual interest surpasses common sense or reasonable understanding of social problems. The spread of corporate culture links with the presence of professionals, who exhibit limited interest or capacity to address social issues. In the corporate culture, there is more emphasis on short-run comfort and on obtaining individual benefits. Of course, the homogeneity of corporate culture breaks down with the diverse approaches that entrepreneurs follow in today's global environment but here there are other mechanisms that serve a self-gratified society.

Nevertheless, individuals from the upper and middle classes, whose activities relate to the development of new services and status markets, live definitely what Galbraith described as 'contentment'.[10] There are many channels through which the culture of contentment is expressed. On pure theoretical economic grounds, contentment is broadly based on the principles of laissez-faire, which is the driving force of free-market operations. These axioms are posed against the idea of government intervention and more precisely against the imposition of government regulation. The government regulation is viewed by the mainstream as necessary only in particular or abnormal instances. Yet the reliance on the principle of laissez-faire does not always prove fortunate. In fact, there are serious obstacles to the working of free-market mechanisms: environmental constraints, international financial instability, political instability associated with Third World poverty, international immigration and so on. For example, in many situations financial recessions or depressions have induced different groups of people, including proponents of the laissez-faire principles, to share the view that the government must intervene in order to contain the disastrous economic spillovers of financial instability.

Still, there are supplementary principles upon which contentment can be easily situated. One such axiom that applies to wealth is that more is always better than less. This argument supports the pursuit and endless aggregation of riches. Since this accumulation is justified axiomatically, it appears that it cannot be easily overturned by requests for government intervention. Thus financial accumulation seems to be justified as a social objective for many privileged individuals. In such circumstances, there is definitely evidence of little sensitivity or responsibility for the unfortunate ones. Those who agonize financially are usually described by the comfortable as detached from reality and as being solely responsible for their own misery. While the poor, unemployed or struggling individuals are described simply as thoughtless, the comfortable are content to legitimize themselves as the only socially responsible group.

Global Market Fragility, Cyclicality and Public Intervention

These manifestations of justification or contentment are not able by themselves to undermine the inner instabilities of the market system such as a severe international financial crisis or increasing ecological strains and their effects on employment.[11] Actually, judging from the experience of the Great Depression in the 1930s, such developments are able to change the way people justify social problems for many decades ahead. During the Great Depression and the years that followed, there were radical electoral majorities that supported the policy measures of the Roosevelt Democratic government. Thus although radical ideology is inconsistent with the views of the privileged of the upper classes, it still survives because it highlights the great risks associated with the continuous cyclical manifestation of instability of the market system. When the inner fragility of free-market economy becomes apparent, the political scene changes, becomes self-corrective and leans towards progressive and radical views. In this vein, it turns into being inconsistent with the axioms that underlie contentment and reduced responsibility for the poor. The cyclical nature of the political and ideological process that is attributed to the intrinsic instability of the market system is what causes in the very end scepticism about the laissez-faire axioms and the justification of social apathy.

As it has been noted, there are several threats to the market economy system, from environmental catastrophes due to rapid industrialization, global or regional financial crises and political unrest due to corruption to population movements, global economic imbalances, race tensions and religious wars. However, until the recent experiences of the Great Recession and the Eurozone crisis, the possibility of social upheaval on the part of the less privileged in developed economies was appearing remote. Yet we cannot undermine further social tension if social troubles persist and intensify. Since social anxiety depends on discomfort relative to the past, we should not be misled by an extrapolation of past social calmness to the future, as it was in the case during the Great Moderation. Social problems are still present and are exacerbated by unemployment and poor access to necessary services. For example, there are social groups who are in a devastating position, mostly in the inner cities. This is a social problem that cannot be ignored easily. Thus substantive policy efforts must to be exercised so that life in inner cities will improve with better schools, better-paid teachers, more available counselling on drug addiction, improved opportunities for employment and training, enhanced public investment to support housing for the poor, an effective and accessible health care system, and more facilities for cultural activities, individual development and security.

II THE PHILOSOPHICAL INQUIRY

The Philosophical Roots of Superiority Complex and Thymotic Morality

In addition to the political justification of the culture of contentment, which accompanies the phenomenon of status markets, there are certain philosophical reflections that explain their expansion. In this inquiry, ideas such as subjectivity, intersubjectivity and thymotic morality can be used as instruments, which support a philosophical understanding of positional markets. The participation in status markets has primarily to do with the issue of freedom of choice. One can start at this point with Hegel's emphasis on 'subjectivity' as experienced in the freedom of people to act and think.[12] In this connection, the term 'subjectivity' carries primarily four connotations: (i) individualism: in the modern world, individuality without limit can be viewed as fundamentally good; (ii) the right to criticism: today, subjectivity is expressed by the ability of one to recognize themselves as something distinct from external influences; (iii) autonomy of action: with this we are able to carry in practice our own sense of responsibility; and (iv) self-consciousness: in modern times the emergence of subjectivity facilitates self-consciousness or self-knowledge.

There were many historical events through which the principle of subjectivity was diffused: the Reformation, the Enlightenment and the French Revolution. With Protestantism even religious faith became reflective and the religious world became a subjective matter in western societies. This was extended in many aspects of individual life. Thus the moral concepts of modern times follow from the recognition of the subjective freedom of individuals.[13] This notion is definitely grounded on the right of individuals to think and act on what they suppose themselves to be valid.

In contrast to the validity of free choice and its excesses, the concept of subjectivity serves as a departure for a different model of individual communication provided by a higher-level intersubjectivity, which leads to a communication community and a harmonic society. This process allows modes of cooperation, understanding and agreement among free and equal persons and leads to a greater sense of autonomy even against the institutionalization of common will.

Thus from Hegel and onwards, the possibility of expressing the ethical totality as a communicative reason inherent in intersubjective life was crucial. In this vein, an idealistic form of democracy and a framework of rights for all citizens, poor and rich, could be sketched. Not only this, but Schiller went further to contrast the ideal form of intersubjectivity with isolation and mass existence, the two opposite deformations of intersubjectivity.[14] Therefore, from a philosophical viewpoint, it is important to ask how status markets are capable of drawing us more towards or further away from the possibility of living in an intersubjective harmonic community. This inquiry is not an easy task especially when appropriate consideration is given to the discriminatory attitudes, which arise as an indispensable aspect of status markets.[15]

There are strands in philosophical thought that justify discrimination within the domain of the expression of subjectivity. Here the need for signification plays an important role. For example, sexual conquest is usually not just a matter of body pleasure as one does not always need a lover for that. However, on many occasions sexual conquest proves one's desire to signify a characteristic in order to be 'recognized' by the other.[16] The willingness to be recognized was expressed initially in the history of philosophy by a term, *thymos*. This can be expressed in two alternative forms, *isothymia* or the quest for equality and *megalothymia*, which is the desire to signify as having exceptional power or superiority. In a context that utilizes thymos, reason and desire are viewed as parts of the soul distinct from thymos. In many ways, reason and desire constitute important forces of subjectivity for the individual of our days. Yet certain phenomena cannot be grouped in their totality unless we utilize the idea of thymos. For example, we can comprehend better aspects of social upheavals when we turn our attention to the impact of thymotic anger and the quest for recognition, which exist among political and social leaders during social crises. In this connection, our sense of self-worth and recognition from others is usually described not as an autonomous force but is inherent in virtues like courage and generosity. Furthermore, this example makes obvious that the quest for recognition may not be confined within private interests, as is the case with status markets, but relates also to social activities and goals.

The desire for recognition has a negative connotation because thymos is a source of various miseries for the individual.[17] In any case, good or bad, there are benefits in so far as thymos is an expression of one's own worth.[18] This happens because thymos is related directly to the capacity of individuals to signify freedom of choice. In this sense, thymos is an important motive because it serves as an expression of 'self-respect' and 'self-esteem'. The desire to signify ability or superiority to other people has its roots in ancient Greece and in Plato's idea of megalothymia.[19] However, in a world of thymotic morality, people will be constantly in conflict. Their arguments will encompass almost everything, however small. This notion seems to be an expression of the ancient and (one may observe) contemporary Greek world and culture and can be expressed in many forms. For example it can express itself both in individual and in social life. What is at stake here is the recognition of one's authority on any matter from material possessions to artistic issues or to mere interpretations of everyday life. It is obvious at this point that the notion of megalothymia is useful in the analysis of status markets because the desire to establish authority in order to discriminate for social or market purposes or to dominate through taste or choice is an intrinsic aspect of status markets.

For ancient Greeks, megalothymia was important mainly for political reasons.[20] In *The Republic*, Socrates argued that megalothymia motivates the citizens to protect their city against its foreign enemies, who are ready to attack at any time.[21] The city can be saved by a class of guardians who will show courage and an interest in public affairs beyond their self-interest in material possessions and in the good life.[22] It is difficult to see courage and public-spiritedness arising from self-interest although the latter creates public benefits. Here metalothymia is a better explanation of the willingness of the guardians to protect their city and to be involved in emotions of anger and sadness for the sake of the city that otherwise would seem irrational.[23] This motive underlies often the actions of kings, politicians and warriors, all aspiring to establish their authority and to mobilize other people for the sake of the general good.[24] Thus thymos can serve both social purposes and private objectives.

Megalothymia and the Will for Power

In modern philosophy, the concept of megalothymia was predominantly used by Nietzsche.[25] This notion was used in a framework of nihilism and relativism.[26] In his account, man is able to elevate himself when he is able to evaluate, to distinguish good from bad and to act towards what is good for him. But in this context, the autonomy of evaluation can be safeguarded and protected by something external such as individuals' sense of self-worth and their authority to command recognition for their actions.[27]

Megalothymia is expressed in Nietzsche's idea of the 'will for power' which is used in a context appropriate to criticize the lack of pride and confidence that exists among economic men in western democracies. Again, the notion of megalothymia is used as opposed or as supplementary to those of reason and desire. Thus one can envisage the co-existence of thymos and desire or reason. The first two principles lead to betterment of material life. But man is not content with the economization of life alone.[28] Thus he pursues megalothymia, his own sense of superiority, or at least isothymia, a state in which he can be recognized as equal to other people.[29] The concept of megalothymia is useful because it is equivalent to expressions such as 'self-esteem' and 'self-worth' that are relevant in describing behavioural aspects of status and superstar markets.[30] The 'modern man' who lives in today's western democracies is a 'miserable man' for Nietzsche. Although modern man's calculations of self-interest secure him material possessions and comforts, he lacks thymos.[31] It is because of this deficiency that he is not able to stand above material needs.

The privatization of life on the basis of the pursuit of material self-interest would undermine the social communication that is necessary to proactive citizens in democracies. Early observations on the American way of life pointed to the claim that the master of an economic entity, the consumer, was experiencing their smallness both as a citizen and as an individual in the passage of events that take place in a large and growing country.[32] This weakness raises serious concerns about their ability to fulfil their subjectivity constructively in contemporary market economies.

Superiority and Resistance

Megalothymia, or the willingness to signify superiority is not expressed only through proactive behaviour as it can often be reactionary. Thus we are able to look differently on a series of other issues. For example, why the poor and the weak should accept the authority of the powerful and the rich? Nietzsche again here had the answer. The less fortunate have no other option but to resist but this is not because of higher morals or mere sentimentality. The resistance of the poor arises simply because of resentment. Here megalothymia enters implicitly again in the picture because it is the own sense of self-worth that makes the less fortunate resent the idea that the powerful will look after them on their own.[33]

In the past, it was megalothymia that pushed people to look for a more powerful reason or force that would oblige the rich and the powerful to submit. This reason can be an all-encompassing essence, God or a revolting proletariat or enlightened sovereign to come. In those reasons, people find traditionally non-contingent and therefore influential allies against the rich, the powerful and the greedy. Thus major social initiatives can be used as potent forces against social deprivation. Here lies the essence of radical thought against piecemeal policies, namely that there are indeed deep inherent powerful forces that underlie market economy and cause its instability.

Utopian Politics and Liberalism

In this connection, one might prefer to follow radical initiatives rather than just reformist policies. However, in contrast to fatalistic approaches, there is moderate liberal theorizing, according to which radical traditional rhetoric should be abandoned. Underprivileged people should settle for something less than grand solutions. A possible path therefore is the correction of market failures within social democracy.[34] But even if there is a place in radical thought for a market economy with a role for the state, there is still a need to explain several characteristics of this economy such as status markets in terms of factors like greed, selfishness and the strategic behavioural pursuit of positional discrimination. This raises the issue of the identification of suitable policies, which reduce differential treatment with respect to goods and services, social discrimination and the waste of human, financial and natural resources in the pursuit of relative competition contests.

Such a synthesis does not deny the existence of deep forces underlying market economy but it distances itself from utopian politics. It is true that resentment and resistance are often associated with ideology and utopian politics. Radical political philosophy is a tradition that has produced so far what has been labelled as utopian politics, the kind of politics that found its first expression in works such as Plato's *Republic*. Utopian politics is not expressed only through Marxist ideas. The philosophy of Nietzsche and Heidegger produced another political utopia, the culture of 'last men'. However, this utopian prototype is inconsistent with the notion of self-consciousness and with the importance of the idealist paradigm of the 'wise man', which underlies modern reformist politics in contemporary social democracies.

Within the liberal approach, seemingly trivial terms such as 'greed' or 'discrimination', which are operative in positional markets, are theoretically founded as forces in social relations. In this approach, we can confidently expect that a policy or political intervention can be 'narrated' within the domain of contemporary market economy. This political analysis does not require the redemptive power of processes such as working-class dynamics. Hence from a philosophical perspective the analysis can be conducted in terms of its capacity to yield concrete solutions, however small, rather than utopian ones.[35] This is a difficult task since working on small concrete solutions requires often more effort than developing a grand narrative that manifests dramatic power and immediacy. Developing concrete solutions can be carried within various alternative approaches, such as pragmatism or positivism.

Politics, Pragmatism and Idealism

If people abandon utopian politics, one question which arises is to what possible extent can liberal reformism interface with pragmatism, if not with pure economic positivism. With respect to the pragmatist approach, the only act that seems to be required is to get rid of idealistic fallacies. This happens because notions from idealism and morality are still linked with pragmatism. In reality, caution must be exercised when touching the fine line between pragmatism and idealism. There is an important reference in modern sociology and philosophy, what is considered to be an important contribution of German idealism to American pragmatism. For example, within pragmatism there is still a need to apply principles of convention and organization because it is difficult to describe what constitutes a distinction between experience and the external world.[36] Like positivism, pragmatism explains only that truth works but it does not explain what it works for. In this sense, in a pragmatist context ethics is situational. Thus for pragmatists a major question is to help resolve people's moral and social conflicts in their everyday lives. Yet to achieve moral capacity in a social context embodies a sense of idealism. It is not easy to escape entirely the paradigm of the 'wise man', and thus the liberal framework. For this reason, an ethical justification of the truth of functionality requires an overlap between idealism and pragmatism. Thus although individuals today can focus their attention on pragmatist questions on social issues they must still have sufficient personal and social leverage to be able to answer more idealist questions with regard to obligations and hopes.[37]

The Conflict between Pragmatist and Idealist Approaches

Posing pragmatist questions can take place in advanced western democracies, in which everybody seeks to enjoy the benefits that other people enjoy such as wealth, material goods, freedom and time to pursue personal fulfilment through private and sometimes idiosyncratic ways. This is a world that is consistent with the liberal agenda. As it was mentioned earlier, this contrasts with radical approaches in which there is a universal and higher force that is communal in character. This force requires a considerable redistribution of private possessions beyond productivity concerns of factors of production and a rearrangement of the freedom to act. As the pursuit of universal external truths is central, judgements regarding mainstream everyday experiences appear trivial.

Yet one sees elements of the quest for universal truths in the liberal agenda such as the principle of enhanced happiness and/or reduced pain. Although this is consistent with the pragmatist approach for liberals, pragmatism is deficient in helping us understand various issues of modern societies, especially those which relate to distressing experiences of the less privileged. Thus the liberal pursuit of concreteness differs from pragmatism because of its interest in useful liberal truths, which are also different from traditional German idealistic approaches.[38] It is in this context that it is possible to analyse effectively the phenomenon of positional markets from a non-pragmatist view but with a special emphasis attributed to the repercussions on the less privileged.

In the liberal context, supplementary tools and practices are required, which are available to social democracies and their institutions subject to possible improvements. What seems as an obstacle to reform is that terms such as 'resentment' and 'greed' are psychological forces associated with market economy (and its phenomena such as status markets and relative social competition) that cannot be easily communicated within a universal framework and point of view. Thus it is useful to provide an analytical framework for what can be regarded as an esoteric obstacle to social reform as it is the case with greed and the longing to sign superiority through market activities.

Pragmatism, Political Commitment for Change and Social Engineering

Another important debate that takes place today is between post-modernists and modernists with respect to the need for political commitment that is associated especially with the validity of universal truth. Here pragmatists stand in the middle and favour a synthesis between the modernist and post-modernist approaches. For example, in the pragmatist framework, there is an acceptance of the post-modernist idea of the 'death' of meta-narratives or of universal truths.[39] However, the pragmatist analysis incorporates the modernist view that nevertheless people today have in fact the option not to give up on political commitment.[40]

The modern narrative relates closely to the pace of technological progress and the development of economic and social entities associated with this progress. The benefits of technological progress enable people today to be optimists and to have the confidence to be self-assertive. For modernists, as our ancestors achieved great goals, so we now and the future generations will succeed in attaining worthy objectives. This sort of confidence has produced the reformist politics and the social engineering associated with a free press, education, social care, the parliament and the rest of the institutions of modern democracy. It is this sort of confidence that is required to develop policies and institutions to accommodate new social situations such as the impact of status markets.

On the contrary, the post-modernist agenda implies that the rejection of universal truths must make individuals treat all political programmes as potentially totalitarian. What is left is just the development of local cultures that may be mutually incomprehensible and incompatible. Contrary to this pessimistic approach, the pragmatist synthesis implies something different. It is argued that even within local cultures, people can develop narratives of progress. For example, they do not need to define themselves according to a permanent universal truth. But there is no reason why they should not continue to press for the pragmatist vision, in which all opinions and options are set in free and open exchange. This objective goes beyond the rhetoric about increased tolerance and decreased suffering. What is required only is the relativist idea of tolerance. On the basis of this principle, liberals can continue to attempt to develop a world society based on liberal institutions.

Yet once again there are reasons to be sceptical with respect to this rationale. For example, one may ask why people should accept the all-importance of the idea of tolerance relatively to other principles. Here we go full circle to questions of principles that traditional philosophy poses. However, it is important to note here that pragmatism has gained momentum during the post-Second World War period compared with nihilistic or even apocalyptic approaches. It is in this connection that radical philosophical thought faces difficulties in coping with the contemporary social and cultural situation. This happens because the pursuit of analysis along pragmatist and predominantly reformist lines leads to positions beneath the dignity of radical advocates. It is no accident therefore that pragmatists criticize the emphasis on the roots of modernity and post-modernity as being in essence exaggerated because it points out to hopeless revolutionary or nihilistic solutions. By adopting this approach, radical intellectuals limit their influence to an audience that seems to be just the avant-garde of cultural analysts.[41]

Psychology from a Philosophical Viewpoint

On the contrary, philosophy has room for the psychological inquiry. For Nietzsche, the distinction between pragmatism and idealism does not exist. Therefore, the distinction between reality and appearance implies a relativist approach, in which the idea of using a universal context for all social issues should be abandoned. This relativist framework seeks to undermine the idealistic roots of philosophy and approaches truth through living, internalizing and thinking of people's contingencies. In this respect, it is implicitly more tolerant to the symptoms of status markets.

Here lies the philosophical acknowledgement of the usefulness of the psychological approach. To avoid the anxiety surrounding the inconsistencies of their lives people attempt to find universal truths and to escape from contingency rather than to acknowledge the eventualities of life, as poets do. Often, aspects of status markets are viewed as greater than what they really are and seem incomprehensible. In this connection, the role of psychology as a relativist approach seems to be useful because it helps individuals to understand the inherent forces of such phenomena. The fact that there are no philosophical principles in the psychological approach delineates the constraints of the potential concourse between psychology and relativist philosophy. What is dull, calculative, immoral or unprincipled for relativist philosophy can be an exciting account of unconscious contingency in psychology. This brings us back however to the issue of defining moral principles and the analytical territory in which these priorities emerge.

Relativism, Ironism and Social Issues

The attention on principles does not preclude philosophical approaches from dealing with contingency and relativism. Such approaches exist and they can be useful in the development of new social policies. For example, the ironist philosophical tradition is in essence a relativist approach that is based on certain elements. The first is a sort of scepticism for own expression in the sense that there is recognition of the expressions, narratives and vocabularies used by other people in the same or different areas of analysis. The second characteristic of ironism is the presumption that understanding own expressions cannot provide an all-substitution of other vocabularies or expressions. Finally, according to the ironist approach, people should not believe that their expression or way of thought is in the end a better representation of reality than other ones. In this sense, the ironist approach to philosophy shares many elements with art or style such as the incorporation of novelty, which is an important force in the cultural context of status markets.

Since novelty and antithesis are so important in the approach of ironist philosophers such as Nietzsche and Heidegger, ironism aims at developing a dialectical project reminiscent of idealist objectives. Thus an ironist's way of thought constitutes in essence some sort of synthesis between antithetical and critical viewpoints. The generic task of the ironist agenda is similar to that of the great and original poet: to create the final taste by which they will be judged. But the judge the ironist has in mind is one's self. The ironist approach is essentially narrative in form because its nominalism and historicism will not permit thinking of the analysis as establishing a relation to real essence but only as establishing a relation to the past. This has implications for policy-making with regard to positional markets that although certain phenomena may seem incomprehensible it may just suffice to establish cultural objectives that are different from the past.

Furthermore, within our increasingly ironist culture, philosophy has become more important for the pursuit of private perfection rather than for any social task. Today ironist philosophy acts as a facilitator for individuals to become private philosophers who can intensify the irony between nominalism and the historicism. In this connection, artists or symbolic analysts of all kinds can do something which is socially useful. For example, they can help people attend to the problems that arise from their participation in positional markets. Furthermore, the ironist approach can be useful in developing and understanding aesthetic alternatives to the sensation of status markets by doing what is common place in this paradigm, mixing and creating different traditions and cultures.

There are claims that ironism lacks moral responsibility and political commitment and this shows in the involvement of ironists to the deconstruction of the liberal vocabulary. But this is not so, if ironism calls for political action to unlock deficiencies present in liberal reformism. The only criticism that remains against ironism is that it does not produce political philosophy on the basis of which people could move out of political commitment such as liberal reformism to a new type of society. Still, the ironist approach may be useful in the context of the 'pragmatist utopia' of being open to all possibilities, discussing and, eventually, attempting to pursue some of them.

CONCLUDING REMARKS

The political and philosophical analysis, which is relevant to status markets, provides us with many useful insights. First, the privileged of status markets are detached from social problems and tend to undermine them. The urgency of the privileged to internalize the fact that they live in a growingly secure economic, business and financial environment leads them to publicly attempt to undermine the social problems of status markets. This political attempt takes mostly the form of a call against state intervention and public programmes to assist the less privileged. However, those who are at a disadvantage do not resist vigorously this adverse situation as was the case in the past. This phenomenon is partly due to the stable economic and financial environment of the last two decades before the international financial crisis 2007–2008, which is known as the Great Moderation that led many people to climb socially. A similar cause is the shift of the developed countries from industry to services. This shift became possible with the migration of industry to emerging economies, which led to the decline of the power of the unions. Another explanation is provided by the rising subjective freedom to physical possessions and by the self-esteem that the middle and the lower middle class enjoy. This freedom leads to less resentment for the very rich. Yet another explanation for the small resistance of the less privileged is simply that the rich have successfully contained their complaints since the call for less government intervention was implemented with the help of neoliberal policies since the 1980s. In this political environment, it comes as no surprise that a culture of contentment spread, with its emphasis on short-term comfort, private benefits and an aversion to address serious social problems. Yet contentment is in danger because of symptoms of fragility in global capitalism, which take the form of environmental problems, international financial crises, deep recessions and persistent unemployment, political instability that is associated with Third World poverty and international immigration. Thus the social justification of non-responsibility of the comfortable is inconsistent with the current intrinsic fragility of the global market economy. Overall, this discussion implies that complacency with regard to the effects of positional markets and opposition to public intervention, which takes the form of taxing the contented and introducing social programmes, are based on weak foundations.

In terms of philosophical discourse with respect to relative position competition, a useful notion to consider is thymos, which is associated with the desire to signify distinction, power and superiority. This idea relates to motives of internalizing self-respect and self-worth. Historically, this concept has its roots in Plato's notion of megalothymia, which was later embraced by Nietzsche. Megalothymia refers to the individual desire to establish authority in order to discriminate. In the case of status markets, this discrimination takes place for purposes of market or social differentiation and takes the form of distinction through taste and choice. The notion of thymos shows that it is possible to experience the pursuit for distinction in social endeavours that can benefit the society as a whole rather than just in positional contests of consumption and occupation choices. Resistance against social discrimination comes usually from resentment that the powerful will look after the less fortunate. This resistance can take either a universal utopian form (that is, as is the case with the pursuit of other forms of economic and social organization such as socialism) or a liberal and pragmatist solution-oriented scheme. The policies that are required to eliminate the social costs of status markets need to be defined with respect to the question of whether they will be universal in nature or part of a pragmatist agenda. In addition, defining the interlinkages between pragmatism and liberalism as well as between post-modernism and modernism, shows that it is possible to establish culture change policies in contemporary market economies. This inquiry determines in turn the type of political commitment that people must hold today in order to support concrete policies for culture change. Moreover, the philosophical acknowledgement of the impact of psychology and relativist philosophical approaches such as ironism, which emphasizes creativity, novelty and antithesis, are also useful regarding efforts to attain a balance between the pursuit of private perfection, freedom and social goals. Overall, the formulation of culture change policies can benefit from political and philosophical analysis so that it provides an enhanced and practical context for undermining extreme forms of positional markets. This context can be utilized also to reveal and correct deficiencies of reformist policies and to incorporate the impact of forces such as freedom of expression, novelty and creativity.

8. Alternative policies for positional activities

INTRODUCTION

It is now time to consolidate the analysis conducted in the previous chapters through the application of the interdisciplinary socio-economic approach on status and superstar markets. In what follows, I will discuss in what manner policy formulation can identify alternative types of intervention. A specific issue that will be addressed in this chapter is the political debate which concerns the effectiveness of each category of social policy measures. This review will highlight the benefits and the difficulties of each set of policy measures. It will also aid in examining the possibility of applying a mixed set of policies. A basic theme in the present study refers to whether redistributive rather than general horizontal policies are more effective in mitigating most of the social costs of positional activities. To the extent that redistributive policies are necessary, a fundamental task is to identify the social fields, in which this type of policy will eventually prove successful.

BENEFITS FROM POSITIONAL MARKETS

Despite the fact that positional markets involve high social costs we should not ignore that there are benefits as well. For example, status-seeking has important implications in financial decisions because individuals with a stronger incentive for social status to improve their capacity for wealth creation are more willing to accept increased levels of capital investment.[1] Thus the desire to participate in relative position competition can increase endogenous long-run growth although its impact may prove to be small. On the contrary, when the motive to seek status is rather weak, the impact on long-run growth materializes only if the initial stock of capital is high, a condition that is specific to developed countries.[2] Moreover, when heterogeneity in skills is balanced by some heterogeneity in preferences in the form of either a reflection of a moral norm or of sentiments of social-esteem, there is a stronger incentive for self-efficiency, which enhances self-governance and cooperation. Preferences for higher status enhance efficiency *ceteris paribus* as they result in stronger incentives and greater tolerance to heterogeneity due to improved self-esteem.[3] Such benefit can be undermined by the intervention of egalitarian institutions, which exist in modern democracies and normally would seek to impose corrective policies. Thus when policies to contain the exuberance of positional markets are examined the social costs must be carefully calculated against possible benefits.

STATUS MARKETS AND SOCIAL COSTS

The competition for superior relative position is manifested through excess consumption for context-dependent goods and services and through the pursuit of highly rewarding occupations. Besides rich individuals, the spread of media culture and the rise of information technology coupled with higher current and expected monetary rewards relative to the past, enable the middle class and parts of the working class to be involved in consumption excesses. But this could not be possible without the existence of a liberal credit system and financialization. Individuals belonging to these social groups buy bigger and more expensive houses and cars, jewellery, luxury fashion items and indulge in expensive recreational activities. Envy, superstar idolization and fashion emulation is widespread.[4] The frenzy for context-dependent activities can become insatiable. A bigger house in an upscale suburb, a fancy car, a holiday house or a small boat, are scenes of modern reality that can be recalled easily. However, many people cannot afford these expenses on the basis of their income. What begins as a lifestyle activity from frequent visits to beauty salons and spas, experimentation with brand name clothing and quality food, ends up involving high and often unbearable monetary expenses. In addition, an occupational choice to enter a highly competitive environment that is driven by high upward-mobility rewards, access to famous or influential people and the privileges which relate to such activities, may prove too risky. The evidence shows that people who do not belong to the social groups of the upper or upper middle classes cannot afford for long these types of positional involvement and end up deprived financially. In addition, they tend to commit severe mistakes with respect to their options in the labour market, which cause a negative impact on their savings and, consequently, on their financial situation. The feelings of financial deprivation become a reality especially for many young people because they end up in debt more easily. This happens because they try to sustain greater levels of consumption and ambitious career trajectories, in an attempt to keep up with the activities of the more privileged.[5] It is no accident therefore that the burden of debt has become too high for almost one-third of the incomes of lower-income individuals in the USA. Thus the credit boom during the last decades before the Great Recession created a burden of debt that superseded the financial means of consumers in lower-income families.[6] Still, financial pressure is not the only disadvantage of being involved in relative position competition for lower-income individuals. Struck by the huge rewards of superstar markets, many individuals decide to compete in them despite unfavourable odds.[7] Wrong occupational choices may be harmful if they are pursued for a long period of time. When it becomes difficult to postpone the financial pressure of excess consumption, lower-income individuals are forced to work more hours and to experience time pressure.[8] With family obligations, this difficulty becomes too stressful if, besides overworking and financial pressure, we consider professional training and other similar obligations.[9] Thus it is obvious that the correction of these social costs is helpful and can be coupled with the financing of general community goals, such as better education, better quality standards or better maintenance of infrastructure.[10] However, some of the corrective policy measures must be redistributive in essence to compensate for the extra costs and pain of the lower incomes, which arise from their involvement with relative position competition. For example, financing education programmes and community activities for lower-income families could have had a redistributive impact on members of this group and could help them resist the lures of excess consumption and positional occupational choices. Therefore, from a policy-making perspective we need to design policies that are feasible, beneficial for the community and redistributive for those who stand to lose more from the adoption of positional choices.

CONGESTION AND INEQUALITY

The question of whether correction policies on relative position contests must be horizontal or distributive requires an analysis that has to take into account the nature of their negative effects. If these repercussions are simply the result of congestion, then the most appropriate policy is an 'across-the-board' type of intervention. Relative position competition and status markets produce circumstances, which although seem harmless from an individual viewpoint, are damaging collectively in the end. An example is environmental pollution. A single motorist in Rome knows that their own car contributes to environmental pollution that affects all inhabitants of this city. But, because their own individual actions do not appear effective, they will not take action. Likewise, under the influence of positional concerns, relative position competition bears resemblance to situations such as traffic and environmental pollution, advertisement campaign rivalries and military arms competition. In the absence of a rule in terms of which rights can be defined, no individual party is in a position to take collective action. What is good for individuals separately harms the society as a whole. These problems are not only social as they often involve environmental costs. In principle, social status is defined in terms of the amount of time people dedicate to status activities, the value of time involved for status-signalling and the monetary cost of positional consumption as a percentage of total expenditure. Relative position competition to attain a higher social status through higher levels of consumption can result in principle in inefficient high levels of production. Thus there are important implications for ecological economics because environmental degradation is an obstacle to sustainable consumption. Sustainable consumption relates to the impact of policies to increase the consumption of products and services, which meet best basic needs and essentially improve the quality of life.[11]

INCOME INEQUALITY

Although relative position competition leads to congestion, it does not affect private stakes equally. Individuals do have a different bargaining position when the competition process takes place. In addition, the bargaining position changes with the pace of relative position competition. Individual parties are not necessarily ill-informed or undisciplined. Spending in various categories such as in positional housing or clothing provides pleasure and can be useful per se.[12] But when an individual's decisions start to depend on the decisions or the possessions of others, whether neighbours and peers or media superstars and celebrities, a social cost arises, which is distributed unequally against the underprivileged and latecomers. In this case, what is good for individuals separately harms in a disadvantageous manner certain social groups. This situation turns out to be a by-product of the fundamental harms of income inequality.

Another effect of status markets relates to the growth of income inequality.[13] From a policy perspective, the most important consideration becomes to ascertain that 'certain crucial commodities are distributed less unequally than is general income or, more precisely, less unequally than the market would distribute them given an unequal income distribution'.[14] There are obviously negative consequences because inequality produces greater psychological concerns in some spheres of life rather than in others. It is easier to tolerate the fact that income controls access to expensive cars than to tolerate its controlling access to good education, basic medical care and quality of life. The argument that the contented cannot be taxed because they will have fewer motives to work and invest productively is false.[15] In the past, status markets were less pervasive and, therefore, their impact was easily overlooked. However, with their tremendous rise today we need to intervene. For example, policy-makers can tax positional consumption to curtail its social costs and can use that income for those who are in greater disadvantage with regard to the operation of status markets.

HUMAN CAPITAL DISTRIBUTION AND DETERIORATION FOR THE LESS PRIVILEGED

Distributive policies to reduce the impact of relative position competition in status markets must be undertaken with respect to a number of indicators, which relate to the individual conditions of financial pressure, psychological well-being, recreational time and effective occupational choices. One of the outcomes of research of the Organization for Economic Cooperation and Development (OECD) is the recognition that the significance of social indicators lies in their normative function and that the first step is to set goals towards the areas that statistics have highlighted. This programme has identified several fields of concern with indicators on health, education and learning, employment and the quality of working life, time and leisure, command over goods and services, the physical environment, the social environment, and personal safety. More specifically, the research agenda includes indicators such as: the length of life and healthfulness of life, average working hours, travel time to work, paid annual leave, a typical work schedule, distribution of earnings, occupational injuries, work environment nuisances, occupational opportunities, free time activities, income distribution, social environment conditions such as social attachment and suicide rate, exposure to risk, fatal injuries, serious injuries, and perceived threat or fear for personal safety. All these conditions are related to human betterment and constitute what economists call human capital. This form of capital includes skills, education, talent, enthusiasm, drive and anything that may influence the performance and the productivity of an individual.

Similarly, status markets, the competition for relative position and the stereotypical discrimination they involve, compel many individuals to experience conditions of deterioration with respect to indicators related to work conditions, income distribution, social cohesion, perceived safety and access to occupational opportunities. This contrasts with the axioms of traditional economic thought, in which economic welfare improves only when there is an increase in real income, appropriately adjusted for changes in income distribution. Even so, an important issue to note is that increases in real income improve economic (social) welfare only if they are not accompanied by worsening life conditions arising from widening income inequality.

DISTRIBUTION AND PSYCHOLOGICAL DEPRIVATION

Some of these worse conditions relate to psychological difficulties. Individuals who are not successful in relative position contests internalize dissonance or psychological discomfort. This feeling arises because of the observed inconsistency between the objective lack of social esteem and the individual quest for self-esteem. A psychological discomfort of this form can be reduced either by committing greater resources to positional lifestyles or by modifying own attitudes regarding the criteria upon which an individual derives worthiness and self-esteem.[16] As a consequence, the relation between dissonance reduction and the modification of preferences or attitudes is important. The attempt to avoid or reduce psychological discomfort or dissonance does not necessarily involve irrationality. It is broadly acknowledged that the best policy in order to overcome poverty is redistribution of income from the wealthier to the poorer members of society.[17] This has also been the case with positional markets. Thus even in standard utility analysis, the correction of the observed market failure takes place by taxing positional activities, or through income redistribution from the rich to the poor that is made possible by taxation policies.[18] This type of intervention increases the direct or indirect monetary receipts of the poor and manages to minimize the cognitive dissonance and the relative deprivation of the less comfortable so that they are less likely to adopt low-class behaviour.

Everyone wishes to be status worthy and recognized.[19] However, although this observation is common it is also true that status matters more to the rich. In any case, policies that take into consideration the psychological adaptation of individuals and its relevance to economic developments are better equipped for dealing with redistributive issues. Such measures may eventually lead to the modification of individual disposition towards positional lifestyles because the incentives to emulate affluent attitudes may weaken and may produce substantive rewards. If redistribution helps avoid or weakens feelings of dissonance or *anomie* experienced by the disadvantaged, there is no pressure to be involved in costly attitude change.[20] The final outcome is to observe an increase in welfare.

Yet if the maintenance of the initial social position is the only relevant variable in the explanation of persistent inequality across generations, then there is a weak motivation for middle-tier individuals to work harder and to get involved in a process of upward mobility. In this vein, people from low classes are justified to exert little effort.[21] They do not care much about social position since they cannot change their situation much. Although it may sound paradoxical, welfare-improving policies should eventually have as their objective to assist people from lower classes to reduce their effort.

Thus although people from the bottom-tier social groups, such as those belonging to the poor segments of the working class or even the underclass, do not have any incentive for upward mobility through a behaviour change with respect to positional norms, this is not the case for individuals who come from medium-tier social groups, which may include individuals from the low middle class. People from these groups are responsive to positional lifestyles because they expect that they can achieve upward mobility. Thus it is better to have economies with a more egalitarian income and wealth distribution. This helps the accession through wealth hierarchy and improves social position.[22] Moreover, if there is manifestation of social waste such as the costs generated by positional markets with the support of a liberal credit system amidst growing financialization and excessive borrowing then redistribution should help improve social welfare. In the case of positional expenditure, even a small income tax for redistribution can prove to be what economists name Pareto-improving with respect to social welfare through a cross subsidy from the rich to the poor.[23] This happens because redistribution reduces feelings of dissonance or anomie experienced by the underprivileged.

ALTERNATIVE PATHS FOR THE REDUCTION OF COMPETITION FOR POSITIONAL GOODS: SIMPLICITY PROGRAMMES AND PRODUCTIVITY ENHANCEMENT

In our mass media and information technology-driven world, there are instances in which individuals attempt to react to the ills of industrialization, excess consumption and intense competition. One visible reaction to those problems is through the adoption of simpler lives. In some places like the USA and affluent regions of the European Union, we observe the emergence of reactionary autonomous social movements such as the voluntary simplicity movement. This platform calls for a simpler life, less consumption of positional goods and an enhanced sense of life satisfaction. In essence, this movement expresses the idea that achieving ever-higher levels of consumption of products and services is a 'vacuous' objective.[24] To a greater or lesser extent, the magnitude of the support for this position embraces all income groups. In fact, simplicity movements and their tribes such as down-shifters, simplifiers or voluntary simplicity advocates have been consensually embraced by the comfortable.[25] For example, music celebrities like Bruce Springsteen prefer to dress in worn boots, faded jeans and a battered leather jacket, while executives such as the CEOs of major information technology companies, including Bill Gates, Eric Schmidt and Scott Cook, appear easygoing even in quite formal situations. Likewise, what makes successful people embrace the simplicity principles to rarely attend charity parties, preferring to stay at home, is that they 'take pride in their relatively modest tastes and inconspicuous consumption'.[26] However to date, although it has received abundant media attention, the simplicity movement has not been strong among the middle class. Actually, there is criticism that the simplicity movement is just another fad or another pose of distinction among the comfortable. In some circumstances, this attitude is mixed with conspicuous consumption such as owning grand mansions or expensive boats. Yet for some experts the potential of simplicity movements among the comfortable might embody some hope for progress with regard to positional economies because it can assist in building foundations for a society that accommodates basic socioeconomic equality.[27]

Even so, there are other complications with respect to the effectiveness of the simplicity movement. Much of the growing interest in the simplicity movement comes from the belief that the new technological environment and the widespread adoption of information technology will provide many good part-time jobs, which will permit a great number of people to leave their demanding corporate careers. However, when part-time jobs are not plenty, voluntary simplicity practitioners are at disadvantage since there is a loss of productivity and individual income with foregone job specialization.[28] In some situations, being engaged in many unrelated and often temporary activities becomes a sort of solution. Perhaps, there is a potential in voluntary simplicity movements that could be supported productively with policy measures, which couple simple lives with job specialization in new technology-related activities and enhanced productivity.

CULTURE CHANGE INTERVENTION

This path is already visible in some countries, most notably in the Scandinavian countries. Yet in these countries social norms are characterized historically by a strong community, solidarity and social activities. In contrast, competition for positional goods is often viewed as a cultural ill. The reduction of competition for positional goods is achieved by adopting alternative social and cultural norms, which emphasize creativity, productivity, less competition and less excess consumption.[29] This is a situation that is relevant to culture change engineering and will be analysed in greater detail in the next chapter.

To sum up, the cultural dimension of such policies cannot be easily overlooked. A visible pattern by means of which excessive activities are discouraged has to do with social norms. This has been witnessed in various forms across different societies and social groups. In the past, religious activities were set to promote more low-profile activities such as self-discipline and relaxation of mind. In addition, excessive consumption by a newcomer in old-money neighbourhoods would often raise expressions of contempt as there were social norms against conspicuous consumption.

REGULATION

Besides culture change policies which will be discussed in greater detail in the next chapter, there are three alternative traditional forms of policy to curtail context-dependent activities: regulation, taxes and income transfers. Human capital improvement and culture change policy implementation aim at promoting an alternative human betterment way of life. In this last approach, human capital is not the only end itself. Another goal is life satisfaction, which differs from attempts to improve human capital.

Proponents of the orthodox laissez-faire tradition of thought argue that those policies interfere with the right of the freedom of choice that a potential consumer of positional goods must have. Furthermore, several other complications exist such as enforcement problems and issues arising from the difficulty of attaining agreement among different social groups. However, as we have seen, antagonisms in positional markets cause tangible losses both for the society as a whole and for the less privileged. Therefore, there is strong justification to support the legitimacy of undertaking intervention measures to discourage the conspicuous consumption of positional goods and the involvement in wasteful competition for relative position advantage.

Judging from the past, there are several types of measures that are capable of discouraging positional consumption. Such measures include regulation, taxes on positional goods and mandatory restriction either for the whole population or for parts of the population. History provides us with many examples of sumptuary laws, which were used as means of mandatory restriction to restrain the consumption of certain goods by the lower-income people. In contrast, the elites were not subject to these restraints. Even today such laws are active in several countries. Up until recently, this was also the case in the UK where all pubs were obliged to close by 11 p.m. while some licensed private clubs could open after that time. This shows that a similarity exists between earlier societies, in which the aristocracy was influential and our contemporary superstar society, in which the elite prevails.

An alternative approach, which is suitable for status markets as it has been proposed by Frank, is the imposition of a progressive tax on positional consumption.[30] With this measure, policy-makers will tax consumers on the basis of how much they spend. Thus substantive incentives are provided to cutback excessive positional consumption.[31] In addition, consumers who reduce their conspicuous consumption will find other ways to derive personal satisfaction. Since there are consumption items that fall under the category of luxury goods, it is simpler to tax different levels of consumption than different consumption items. There is ground to believe that the tax will distribute the cost of adjustment out of positional goods in a fair way.[32] For example, there are individuals who will adjust quickly to reducing their consumption on luxury goods while others may scale down their expenditures on positional goods. Then again, there are people who may still be willing to pay a tax premium to derive personal satisfaction for the improvement of their relative position.

However, regulation can be used as an alternative way to curtail context-dependent activities. Examples of regulation can be found in mandatory laws on political campaign spending, on litigation spending in Europe, on advertisement time on television or on bans of drug consumption in sports. Regulation is especially beneficial when safety is a crucial issue. For example, safety regulations discourage workers to undertake riskier working activities because of better pay. Laws that limit the risk we can take can also be found in cases when law-makers intend to discourage people in a given occupation from being able to take on additional projects. In this respect, people become less stressed because the competitive tension is reduced while sufficient room is made for newcomers.

Finally, regulation has been practised elsewhere to contain problems such as excessive pollution. However, the main obstacle regarding the effectiveness of regulation requirements is that they usually come close to general prohibition. In the case of the consumption of status goods and services, penalties could be the same for both types of consumers, those who actively pursue their passion for themselves and those who may occasionally purchase them. Therefore, it is very difficult in the case of regulation to establish a fair process of corrective adjustment.

Although regulation requirements may seem disadvantageous relative to the tax approach, there are cases in which they can be useful. An example is the case when taxes on excessive positional consumption fail to reduce it substantially because the drive of the society for that type of consumption is very strong. Another case in which regulation is preferred is when there are political disputes around the legitimacy of a particular tax or when there are practical or irresolvable problems regarding the enforcement of a tax. In this last situation, there is an option for progressive higher penalties for those who violate the rules. Finally, in the case of practical or chronic problems or of persistent disapproval by special interest groups, regulation may serve an often overlooked objective, that is, to provide obvious signals about the determination of the electoral majority to reduce positional excesses for educational, self-disciplinarian or culture change reasons. This type of regulation constitutes in essence an approach that is different from taxes or prohibitive regulation because it can be used as a policy signal to adopt cultural or societal norms, which are desirable to the majority of citizens in the society.

Another case is when the protection of status symbols is lax and there is signal deception among consumers with regard to positional goods.[33] For example, the consumption of counterfeit versions of prestigious brand-name goods is the most frequently used strategy of poorer individuals. In the case of successful deception, in which observers are mistakenly impressed, status-signalling costs are lower. The deception strategy is often so successful that there are even media reports of very rich people involved in the purchase of counterfeit brand names. In this case however, individuals from lower-income groups do not suffer from status loss because they may consume replicas rather than expensive original brand-name goods. Thus financial resources are saved relative to the situation in which there is conspicuous positional consumption.

However, a paradox arises because if there is a crackdown on counterfeit goods this will be disadvantageous to the welfare of poor consumers. These individuals may eventually experience frustration because their endogenously determined status needs remain unsatisfied.[34]

PROGRESSIVE POSITIONAL CONSUMPTION TAX

Alternatively, discouragement of excessive consumption activities is promoted by inducing the payment of increasing monetary penalties. For example, in luxury consumption legislation income transfers to a human capital improvement plan may be more desirable in order to encourage performance but this provides discouraging incentives to some people when it comes to competitiveness.

Consumption taxes come nowadays in the form of sales taxes. There are different types of consumption taxes, like one given by a single levy on the amount that individuals or families spend each year. Another example of sales taxes is VAT, or value added tax, which is broadly practised in the European Union. A deficiency of VAT is that it tends to be more beneficial for higher-income than lower-income individuals since it is calculated on a fixed rate. Therefore, VAT does not influence the consumption patterns of those who seek to increase their relative position and does not discourage low-income individuals from experiencing the strains of relative position competition. As I mentioned earlier, another type of tax is the progressive consumption tax that was proposed by the well-known economist Irving Fisher fifty years ago and was championed during the last two decades by Robert Frank. The progressive consumption tax is in essence a luxury good tax. However, it differs from the standard luxury good tax that is applied on a case by case basis because it is a single levy on different levels of taxable consumption. In contrast, a luxury tax can be charged as a percentage on all items of particular classes of products or services as with VAT estimation.

In the case of a progressive consumption tax, taxable consumption can be viewed as income minus savings allowing for income tax deductions. Therefore, if taxation authorities know the level of savings, they can determine in which bracket of taxable consumption a particular family stands, thus eliminating complex computations on different consumption items. Since savings are invested in some form of investment fund, the consumer will also expect a yield. Therefore, the benefit can be multiple for the consumer. The tax is progressive because at low levels of taxable consumption such as US$20 000 it can be 10 per cent while at higher levels such as US$100 000 it can be 40 per cent or even more. With this type of tax, all consumers of a particular positional good have an incentive to reduce their consumption and buy a less expensive positional good.[35] In this case their relative position remains unaltered, which is a desired policy objective in principle. At the same time they benefit from higher savings and profits from their additional financial investments. The state is also in an advantageous position because it has more income from taxes to pay for social horizontal policy objectives that benefit all. In addition, as we will see later on, the state has more money to pay for activities that have a redistributive effect between higher-income individuals who care about their relative position more and the lower-income individuals, who have less interest and information in pursuing a relative position advantage.[36]

The progressive consumption tax is currently supported by many economists and politicians, mostly liberals but also by some conservatives. The attractiveness of such a tax is based initially on the fact that it promotes savings, investment, and in the end, economic growth. A progressive tax can also save substantial amounts of money that is wasted on positional consumption patterns and can enhance the ability of the society to contain problems of this sort.[37] In addition, proceeds from a progressive tax can be used for redistributive purposes by educating those who are at the lower levels of taxable consumption how to make wiser decisions in status markets, in which superstars play a crucial role, and by helping them to derive greater personal satisfaction with less strain from their choices.

THE POLITICAL DEBATE ON A PROGRESSIVE CONSUMPTION TAX

Yet the feasibility of imposing a progressive consumption tax is questionable in some countries like the USA because it is an issue that raises bitter political conflicts. The issue of positional markets causes political debates that are influenced by social relations and conflicts. As a result, an analysis of the effect of power is important, an element that is absent in neoclassical economics.[38] Conservative policy-makers often express their reservations against the imposition of a progressive consumption tax because, according to them, there is no reason to discourage the consumption of certain individuals due to its negative effect on the behaviour of others. Thus they argue that a progressive consumption tax is not well-founded. Yet there are two problems with this reasoning. The first is that the interdependence of behaviour across producers or consumers is in fact an objective phenomenon that is usually explained in terms of what economists call external economies, a well-used idea in the sphere of public economics. As is well-known in economic analysis, the discouragement of negative external economies is a standard policy objective. In addition, the opposition of conservative policy-makers may express their concern for the redistribution effects of a progressive consumption tax. Since there is a strong indication that such a tax provides a more equal distribution of costs and rewards across different members of the society, the interests of the contented which are consistent with the proposals of laissez-faire economics lose ground. Furthermore, another reason that justifies these reservations is that a progressive consumption tax provides welfare benefits against wasteful consumption costs.

These considerations shift the domain of debate to matters such as which are the incentives for entrepreneurial and innovative productive activity, or which are the possible unfavourable effects on economic activity. Yet the uncompromising insistence on a position against a progressive consumption tax may indicate the existence of ideological and political considerations. We live in a period where taxes are used as a political tool to discourage voters. The advocates of higher taxes must respond to criticism from political opponents, who know or want to make certain by their political campaigns that taxes are not popular with voters. The advocates of a progressive consumption tax need to stress the welfare gains of such a tax for both the society and lower-income families. For example, the opponents of a progressive consumption tax argue that a progressive tax structure imposes penalties to many people with strong incentives to be productive. As a result, such a tax discourages them so that they will eventually take less risks and pay less attention to their work. This will cause a fall in their efficiency and in overall economic activity. It is true that incentives are important to individuals to restructure their consumption, production or investment patterns. Yet top earners may prefer to work a lot for much less of what they make without the imposition of a progressive consumption tax for the simple reason that they continue to earn large amounts of money. Therefore, the tenets of traditional laissez-faire economic theory do not apply in high levels of income.

There is evidence that shows that people eventually respond to tax incentives. For example, different tax incentives across regions or countries lead individuals or corporations to relocate. This was indeed the case with Sweden and England in the early 1960s when many high net worth natives relocated to other countries to avoid heavy taxes that were too high by recent tax standards. Yet there is an argument of conservative policy-makers that is founded on the principle of preference to substitute leisure for effort. This phenomenon is in essence a special case because it deals with the substitution effect that takes place for a very special group of people, the top earners. This group can recoup much of their income losses due to their privileged position in rebargaining their bonuses and fees. Finally, the payers of the services provided by top earners may opt for in-kind compensation and other transfers in order to circumvent a progressive consumption tax. Thus it is not necessary for top earners to substitute leisure for effort and reduce their efficiency.

Moreover, top earners can save a portion of the additional income that they will receive after rebargaining their fees by investing in mutual funds. This supports economic growth given the growing shift of households to capital markets investments and the size of portfolios of high net worth individuals. It also provides a strong incentive because the top earner's net worth is not diminished. Actually, although the consumption of positional goods might visibly diminish, we should nevertheless expect the net worth of top earners to increase through the receipt of dividends and interest payments. The better financial position of top earners will allow them to signal their superior relative position in context dependent activities, if needed. Thus the imposition of a progressive consumption tax can only delay for a while the excessive positional consumption of top earners without creating preference shifts in favour of leisure activities and without reducing economic performance. If however the proceeds from the progressive consumption tax are used in a distributive manner the situation becomes different. For example, if the choice is between leisure and effort, the market economy is inefficient in two ways because of the impact of attitudes.[39] First, average consumption may be so high so that if it is reduced through a distribution tax, many individuals will still prefer to continue with their positional consumption at the new level of average consumption. However, possibly too many individuals may prefer to be involved in recreational and leisure activities. In this case, policies face the task of reducing the size of the people who are leisure oriented.[40] To sum up, the imposition of a progressive tax on positional consumption can increase economic activity since it would stimulate savings, investment and productivity. Therefore, we may end up with a different result than the one prescribed by the standard incentive claim of the traditional laissez-faire economic theory.

Progressive consumption taxes can also stimulate savings through another route because they redistribute income to those who have the highest savings rates. There is strong empirical evidence that the impact of this type of redistribution is significant. Finally, since important differences in the propensity to consume exist, significant differences in tax payments and the relative capacity to save arise.

Possibly the most important argument in favour of progressive taxes on positional goods is that in essence behaviour is determined in a conventional manner, as was the case with Keynes' infamous beauty contest.[41] In this framework, the incentive to save and invest in response to a progressive tax on positional goods is influenced by the observed behaviour of other members in the same group. As soon as there is some shift for more savings and investment other top earners will follow and adjust their behaviour.

In addition, economic activity can be promoted because a progressive tax on conspicuous consumption can lead to a better allocation of talent across different occupations. There is ample evidence that top opportunities in media, sports, law, finance and other occupations attract more and more talent coupled with higher levels of drive. In order to pursue those opportunities, young individuals bypass careers in education, health, civil service or scientific fields. Yet there is overcrowding in the competition for top positions to the point that economic activity can grow more not by a further rise in top service positions but by growth in positions that exist elsewhere in sectors such as engineering, biology and health.

There are certain causes which are responsible for the misallocation of talent across occupations. The first is that with the rapid change in know-how, many contestants are ignorant about their ability to obtain a top position. According to social psychology tests, the great majority of workers think that they perform better than the rest. In addition, the contest for top positions leads often to overcrowding. This situation results evidently in reducing sharply the odds of obtaining a top position for all the contestants. Furthermore, the experience of overcrowding presses many contestants to take costly bets. For example, some may extend their job searches for long periods or may choose to attend expensive school programmes, which do not rank highest in their specialization. Overall, the appearance of superstar markets attracts many contestants whose relative ability to compete is fragile. For this reason, the imposition of a progressive tax is beneficial because it can support the finance of programmes that will improve occupational choices and economic activity.

PROGRESSIVE CONSUMPTION TAX AND ECONOMIC GROWTH AS A PUBLIC GOOD

Economic activity is not the only relevant variable with regard to the impact of incentives to save more as a response to a progressive consumption tax. For example, a shift from the consumption of positional goods to items that are related to the quality of life such as recreational, athletic, cultural or social activities increases the perception of subjective well-being for many individuals. The hike in individual benefit relative to what we spend will not be reflected in changes of national per capita incomes. Thus shorter working hours across all occupations associated with an improvement in well-being can be viewed mistakenly as a sign of economic decline. For this reason, there are already proposals to use smart accounting procedures on the basis of broader measures such as whole income. This measure is not confined only to earned income from economic activity but includes additional income that is foregone from voluntary action to pursue various activities, which enhance individual quality of life.

The claim of the advocates of traditional laissez-faire economic theory that a progressive consumption tax rate will result in a decrease in the economic activity is contrasted by ample empirical evidence. According to such evidence, up to the early 1990s, there was a clear inverse relation between income inequality as measured by the ratio of the income of the top 20 per cent of earners to the income of the bottom 20 per cent and national income growth rates for the vast majority of countries.[42] This result holds also along different periods during the last fifty years. Therefore, the support of a sizeable and dynamic middle class must be an important objective in the formulation of growth policies.

Finally, the legitimacy of a progressive consumption tax is grounded on the assumption that economic growth is in essence a public good. Frank supports the view that a high-growth environment may constitute a public good because it promotes goods such as democratic values, social harmony, scientific freedom and national competitiveness. In this respect, state policies that support growth objectives cannot be narrowly viewed as interventions that seek to restrict the freedom of various social groups. In addition, incentives still matter in a public policy framework. But as we have discussed, a progressive tax on positional consumption creates different types of incentives that make a society more competitive and productive. As a result, such a public policy supports a more equitable distribution of opportunities, greater income equality and economic growth. Yet there is a concern among economists and policy-makers with the fact that the idea of a progressive tax on positional consumption cannot be easily accepted. Since the 1980s, there has been a distinctive pattern of lower taxes in the highly industrialized countries, especially for tax payers in higher-income tax brackets. The support of the financially comfortable for this policy took place alongside a deteriorating perform- ance in relation to several public goods and services that range from municipal services, infrastructure maintenance, health insurance and services to support for education to promotion of cultural activities. Yet the public programmes that were cut in countries such as the USA were those that concerned the very poor citizens, especially social welfare services. Instead, programmes supported by special interest groups had a better chance. This points out to a link between the elimination of public programmes for lower-income families and the political influence of the financially comfortable.

THE ISSUE OF PUBLIC PROGRAMMES AND EMPLOYMENT

An important question for policy-makers is what share from the proceeds of a progressive tax on positional consumption can be allocated to support public service and community jobs, and therefore, employment. The level of this portion depends on the objectives we set. For example, besides financing programmes to correct the social costs of status markets and superstar emulation in consumption and occupational choices, the revenues from a progressive tax may be high enough to enhance training and employment opportunities. The support can be directed to that portion of workers who are typically represented in the actual average rate of unemployment, which in many industrialized countries is less than 10 per cent. However, the plan to provide employment and training opportunities for the very poor also involves a radical change in the political perception of the welfare system. This mechanism should be viewed not as a transfer mechanism that provides low financial support stipends but as a payment mechanism for those willing to accept a public service job. With the introduction of this new policy, the incentive structure will change. As a result, we may end up with the creation of new incentives, which may encourage workers in the private sector to shift to the public sector. This could raise a problem in the case in which relative wages across the private and public sector are not substantially different.

Although it may appear that public service employment imposes a great burden on poor people because it obliges them to work for sub-minimum payment, it is apparent that if poor people had the chance to choose between a public service job and a cash stipend, there could be significant improvement. Some may opt for the stipend on the ground of focusing more on their job search. Other unemployed individuals may choose to interact with other people during their search for opportunities and to maintain a positive attitude working in a public service job.

In contrast, the European experience suggests that there are other, possibly simpler, ways of improving the operation of the social welfare system. In many European countries, there is another system that relies simply on better organization. For example, in the UK and other countries of Europe social welfare payments are issued online with regular monitoring of the job search efforts of the unemployed. In concluding, whatever the problems are for paying for public programmes or for the support of employment, the benefits for the society as a whole are straightforward. It is feasible to have health insurance for all, better security in the communities and better education. Special programmes can provide a better allocation and use of funds that are designed to assist the less privileged.

RESOLVING THE POLITICAL DEBATE AND THE RELEVANCE OF CULTURE CHANGE POLICY

Besides differences in actual benefits, the extent of consensus across social and political groups is critical for the adoption of corrective policies by public authorities. An important consideration here is how these policies can be coupled with policies, which encourage and motivate agents.[43] For example, in the analysis of public policies (an extreme example is drug abuse), more effectiveness could be accomplished by encouraging acceptable behaviour rather than deterring the addictive activity.[44]

The objections to a progressive positional consumption tax come from the adoption of the laissez-faire approach to economic theory and policy. An implication of such policies is that we cannot do anything about the consumption of positional goods and services if that is what consumers want because it is in this manner that their needs are fully satisfied. In this perspective, state intervention is considered distortive, hence the fierce opposition to taxes. In addition, according to conservative policy-makers, freedom of choice enhances the well-being of a person because they will be able to be as productive as they know best. In this respect, an individual can experience higher levels of security and individual growth and can have better access for themselves and their family to education and health.

Yet the most renowned advocates of taxes on the rich are traditionally progressives and radicals. Some of the theoretical origins of those approaches are theories of class conflict and exploitation. Those theories stress the victimization of workers and consumers and their manipulation by the influence of the powerful and the pervasive impact of commercialism and mass media. The radical approach presents the consumers as helpless since they lack information and self-discipline. These social critics seek to impose obstacles to the influence of the powerful with the imposition of regulation. This form of policy is more evident in the European Union than in the USA because of the stronger position of social democratic parties and the left tradition of political movements and unions.

However, a standard objection to the adoption of regulation practices is the orthodox economic claim that state officials are inefficient because they are uninformed about consumption patterns as consumers. But taking into consideration that policy-makers can base their decisions on research evidence, consumers are also not informed. There is no freedom of choice for better access to scarce goods or to goods that are desired due to the patterns of positional consumption that often lead to congestion in the markets. In positional contests, the choice of one person is rarely independent of the choices of other people.

Overall, the debate about the imposition of a progressive consumption tax is fierce. One explanation is that both the arguments of the laissez-faire conservative school and the progressive school are substantive. Yet the arguments in favour of containing status markets for general social programmes and redistribution policies are superior. If this type of policy is adopted carefully through a well-studied and designed culture change plan to overcome bureaucratic ignorance and maintain freedom of choice, there will be obvious social benefits that will materialize. Acrimonious debates therefore show that there is a bitter political and ideological opposition underneath regarding nothing less than privileges for the comfortable.[45] This is an aspect of the policy process that cannot be easily overlooked. Given the high political tone of the issue and the opposition it faces, the actual imposition of a progressive consumption tax is in essence a sort of regulation and a process of social change. The imposition of such a tax mainly shows the determination of the electoral majority to send a political message to the comfortable who may remain in opposition even when all their arguments are defeated.[46]

Debates cannot last forever and in the end the majority has to decide what kind of society it wants. If this society is not based on a manipulated sense of freedom of choice but on authentic individual freedom, justice and social efficiency then these forces must be translated to a social policy proposal. To the extent that such a proposal is accepted by the majority of citizens this ends the acrimonious political debate. Moreover, it establishes a different social and cultural norm than what we know so far in western market economies. In short, despite efforts of the advocates of progressive consumption tax to render it an active policy instrument, it is very unlikely to be accepted in countries like the USA in the near future. Given the level of shock that it would exert to the neoliberal establishment, the imposition of a progressive consumption tax resembles a regulation ban. However, there is no reason to wait a long time for such a form of enforcement. Public policy measures with distribution effects can be implemented now in the area of culture change with regard to status and superstar markets. Until a progressive consumption tax is realized, these policies can prove effective as they have similarly been in other sectors such as in health and education in the UK.

POLICY SIGNALLING AND NUDGING

Finally, one relatively recent approach that contributes towards this direction focuses on social marketing and good choice architecture.[47] Through this intervention, consumers are 'nudged' or encouraged to correct their flawed choices. According to the nudge framework, individuals can improve their behaviour in various ways regarding their health, wealth and happiness. Policy-makers act as good choice architects and intervene in several areas including incentives, assisting agents to understand mappings, providing feedback, producing defaults, facilitating expectations of errors and structuring complex choices. Transferring the objective of these interventions to status and superstar markets implies that policy targets such as the realization of similar social benefits takes the form of social choice architecture. In this case, policy actions are different from progressive consumption tax or regulation. This happens because the correction of the excesses of positional concerns in consumption and labour markets does not take place at a general macro-level. Instead, it occurs at the micro-level since social choice architecture interventions are carried out to create individual improvements at the individual level. Areas that are commonly discussed in the nudge literature, such as health or happiness, do provide valuable hints as to how this approach can be applied in positional markets. For example, useful information can be given to participants of positional markets through mappings and feedback. One likely example refers to real-time electronic information that might be given through credit cards to assist consumers correct their purchasing choices. This form of intervention is considered a very mild form of regulation by the proponents of good choice architecture in the sense that it nudges consumers to review their budget constraints.

Emulation is described in the social architecture literature as the power of social nudges, which encourages teenage girls, overweight people, TV personalities, college students and judges to imitate the behaviour of their peers in activities such as pregnancy, obesity, mannerisms, academic efforts and decision-making respectively. As we discussed earlier, this tendency has severe psychological ramifications, which include conformity effects and collective conservatism. Collective conservatism is an attitude that explains why in an era of commercialization individuals stick to established trends such as positional concerns even when new demands emerge. Besides, peer pressure and cognitive biases regarding information processing, another social influence is the power of priming. People are primed into certain forms of behaviour, when they are exposed to salient and visible features such as simple and apparently irrelevant cues by direct marketeers or, even indirectly, by peers through gossip of television material.

The nudge theory provides effective but rather insufficient instruments to combat losses from positional involvement. For example, its advocates propose that public and private institutions assign advisers who act as choice architects to assist individuals. With regard to savings, this form of counselling involves the utilization of calculators to decide about the age of retirement and savings plans: on financial investments, practices such as avoiding frequent judgements, diversifying and going beyond simple rules of thumbs; on debt, taking default options, structuring debt decisions, mapping and visualizing consequences and looking for more incentives to process information; and on credit cards, taking advantage of innovations in automatic transactions to collect valuable information. Interestingly, another option for the libertarian paternalism approach, which pervades nudge theory is to avoid debt in order to support savings. Extending this proposal in the context of positional interests, recommendations could potentially include counselling to reduce positional consumption and abstention from occupation decisions in risky markets that produce superstars.

However, although a promising policy path, intervention through nudges in positional markets appears to be currently minimal or at the initial stages of development. Future research must be directed towards understanding the various implications of this approach. There may be situations where there are difficulties in applying nudging. For example, this form of intervention is essentially a soft form of policy since it encourages individuals to adopt a better attitude rather than punishes them for choosing the wrong strategy. Nevertheless, it may help resist widespread entrepreneurial practices related to advertisement, promotion of sales and facilitation of consumerism, and it may support social marketing, which is a component of culture change policy as we will see in the next chapter. However, for good choice architecture to be effectively transformed to social choice planning, policy interventions must be based on strong political support.

CONCLUDING REMARKS

There are three main alternative traditional forms of policy to curtail context-dependent activities: regulation, taxes and income transfers. Although regulation requirements may seem disadvantageous relative to the tax approach, there are cases in which they can be useful. The attractiveness of a progressive consumption tax is based initially on the fact that it promotes savings, investment and, in the end, economic growth. A progressive tax can save substantial amounts of money that is wasted in positional activities and can finance both horizontal and redistributive policies. However, as there is strong opposition to this form of tax in the USA given the level of threat that it exerts to the neoliberal establishment, its potential imposition is akin to the regulation of social norms. Proceeds from the progressive consumption tax can finance income tranfers to programmes for the benefit of the less privileged with respect to the impact of positional activities. This is a feature of culture change policy, which can combine regulation, taxation, income transfers and nudging as a form of social marketing in a behavioural model of policy intervention.

The examination of the various facets of the alternative policies leads to a few important conclusions. First, economic policies that are imposed in the form of a progressive consumption tax on positional goods and services are the subject of fierce political debates. The advocates of a progressive consumption tax win the argument against their conservative opponents because there are indeed welfare benefits of this tax that support economic growth. Furthermore, the application of such a tax can alter the behaviour of economic agents towards savings and investment in a manner that will offset the negative effects of internalizing smaller individual incentives to compete. However, the use of regulation with its emphasis on the imposition of penalties is preferable when the drive of the society towards positional activities is very strong and the resistance of special interest groups to accept economic measures is highly fierce. Thus the imposition of a progressive consumption tax on positional activities in an environment, in which there is a strong positional appetite and political resistance reminds us very much of regulation tactics. Of course, to the extent that the application of regulation influences the behaviour of individuals with respect to their disposition towards positional activities, there is certainly a cultural effect of regulation. Thus in some situations there is interdependency between the application of economic policies such as distribution, regulation and culture change policy. The culture change policy aims at shaping individual behaviour by promoting public programmes that emphasize creativity, productivity and real-life enjoyment at the expense of positional activities.

9. The political economy of status and culture change policy

CULTURE CHANGE LEADERSHIP

Policies about positional markets can involve to a great extent a form of cultural engineering. In this connection, moral leadership is an important issue in social policy formulation and implementation.[1] When moral leadership is weak, few social projects that require substantive changes will be undertaken because the voluntary support of people for them will also be weak. In our post-modern environment, individualism causes poor social participation and becomes the main source of individual emotional rewards. For example, people may prefer to derive satisfaction and positive emotions by identifying with branded products rather than by participating in voluntary work. However, the social costs of positional feel-good lifestyles have been underestimated because we live in a world of intense commercialization. Thus a different form of leadership than the one that we observe nowadays is required to overcome pessimistic considerations with regard to political costs and campaign financing.[2]

Today there is growing recognition of the problems that result from both unmitigated self-interest and impulsive choice. In this framework, the support of norms is an important movement to strengthen trust in order to eliminate attitudes associated with positional markets.[3] These attitudes involve often opportunism or prejudice. Yet culture change leadership policies can be adopted that discourage the gratification of emotional branding. Naturally, public intervention may not prove an easy task. Difficulties may arise during the implementation of policies imposing social norms.[4] In addition, culture change leadership requires a creative framework as innovation does not work in a top-down fashion, and requires fresh debate and high levels of individuality.[5] Furthermore, top-down approaches may alienate people who seek to act in a spontaneous way. Finally, another difficulty is that political leaders face strong incentives to implement their political agenda in the mainstream conservative sphere rather than getting involved with innovative projects that may create controversy.

All these considerations lead to the conclusion that cultural engineering involves some degree of uncertainty. The process in setting new
social norms may in fact involve strong uncertainty in some cases.[6] This
happens because the feasibility of options is tested on the basis of action
after choice, not before. Thus the notion of trust and moral leadership can
involve radical uncertainty.[7] In this vein, social or cultural engineering of
norms imply that trust is not easily manageable as a subjective probability.[8]

Thus one issue is to what extent social and cultural engineering
deviates from the economic doctrine of self-interested rational choice. To
put it conventionally, one problem is how do leaders know what norms
are functional. The answer is that they may not initially know but they
must act as there are observable market failures attributed to the
workings of positional markets. Furthermore, as models of culture policy
may be adopted from the experience of different countries and tested in
practice, there is less uncertainty. In this context, rational decision-
making can eventually take place on the basis of international experience.

This brings forth the issue of cultural differences across different
countries that must be taken into account in adopting culture change
policies towards positional markets. For example, in the North American
cultural environment, happiness tends to be defined in terms of personal
achievement. Individuals engaging in these cultures are motivated to
maximize the experience of positive affect. Moreover, happiness is best
predicted by self-esteem. In contrast, in East Asian cultures happiness
tends to be defined in terms of interpersonal connectedness.[9] There is
sufficient evidence from cross-cultural differences in self-serving or
self-enhancing motivations, which focuses on causal attributions of
success and failure, and self-reference judgements. Recent research
points out to additional factors such as judgement about in-group
characteristics and readiness to accept either positive or negative feedback about the self.[10] The introduction of cross-cultural differences is
important in studies in which both self-esteem and social harmony are
decisive in predicting happiness. For Europeans and Americans, happiness increases as more independent goals are achieved, while for Asians,
happiness increases with more interdependent objectives (such as bringing happiness to parents).[11]

Thus in European and American culture the failure to achieve
independent goals and in reaping the rewards associated with them leads
to severe deprivation. Developments in American culture that emphasize
the benefits of positional advantage leave those living in poverty in a
situation of *anomie*. The underprivileged feel deprived because of the

observable inconsistency between cultural goals (enjoyed by the privileged) and the means available to them to fulfil these goals. This may lead to the adoption of alternative and often radical behaviours. In extreme cases, a breakdown in traditional norms may take place and deviant behaviour may emerge.

The above considerations have started to catch the attention of policy-makers. In some parts of the world, attempts to form policies of cultural change are under way. For example, the notion of sustainable consumption is subject to many interpretations. These approaches range from the United Nations Agenda 21's hopeful assertion that governments should encourage less materialistic lifestyles based on new definitions of wealth and prosperity, to the view that green and ethical consumerism will be sufficient to transform markets to produce continuous and clean economic growth. This green and ethical interpretation is prevalent in international policy agenda. These different perspectives are examined using a conceptual framework derived from cultural theory, to illustrate the fundamentally competing beliefs about the nature of the environment and society, and the meanings attached to consumption.[12] Cultural theory argues that societies should develop pluralistic policies to include all perspectives. Using this framework, the UK strategy for sustainable consumption must be related to cultural theory doctrines and identify policy failures. In the past, the UK strategy favoured individualistic, market-based and neoliberal policies, and responded ineffectively to the problem of unsustainable consumption. In this context, the policy recommendation is to include measures that utilize inputs from competing cultures to realize the potential for more collective, egalitarian and significantly less materialistic consumption patterns.

FRAMING, INEQUALITY AND POLICY SUPPORT TO LOWER-INCOME INDIVIDUALS AND FAMILIES

Rising inequality during the last three decades has produced considerable losses for middle-class individuals from relative position competition. Status and superstar markets grew with the income gains of the people at the top of the income distribution. For individuals at lower levels of the income distribution, positional consumption and achievements alter the frame of reference and habits as to what form of commodities and services are appropriate. While it may be argued that it is changes in the frame of reference rather than pure envy of the fortunes of the wealthy that cause social emulation, the evidence shows that media visibility of positional activities and superstars affects heavily the frames of reference and individual strategies of emulation and snobbery. Expensive houses, cars, trips, decorations, clothing, leisure activities, schools and universities of higher-income individuals and families have led those in the middle to allocate much higher shares of their income for status goods and services, and to reduce their expenses in other areas of consumption. When middle-income families make allocation decisions between different types of goods and services they tend to choose lifestyle combinations such as between housing or annual spending on consumer goods and schooling that they cannot afford. Despite budget constraints, these families cannot give up easily on their wishes. These decisions are not obtained rationally but depend on behavioural processes and psychological considerations, including repercussions of envy.

These lifestyle changes create sizeable losses as we move along at lower levels of the income distribution. While status is justifiable for those who manage to realize their work and lifestyle goals and, therefore, appear to produce a return on personal investment in items such as clothing, cars, housing, university attendance and so on, there are collective losses for those who share these concerns and are not successful in consumption and occupation tournaments. Inequality has been associated with deteriorating conditions in health, commutes to work, morbidity and mortality, sleep deprivation, psychological stability and stress, family stability and divorces. However, relative deprivation manifests itself from psychological pressures that arise from financial losses due to overconsumption and overambitious occupation choices and their impact on debt, savings and pension levels.

Thus quite apart from the relation between productivity and the impact of a progressive tax rate on consumption, we must reconsider how superstar markets enhance income inequality. For example, although superstar markets to some extent manifest productive synergies, their unequal income structure is a burden to many who seek the opportunity to develop further their skills. Income inequality increases the burden of stress to several low-income individuals and leads to inadequate accommodation, improper nutrition, illness and poor educational opportunities. In such a stress-related environment, many young people coming from poorer families miss the opportunity to be productive, enhance their skills and work like productive individuals from higher-income families. As labour markets can be viewed as a succession of elimination tournaments, a prerequisite for one individual to be competitive at the current stage is that they have performed successfully at the prior level. Different incomes and, therefore, different opportunity trajectories, lead two individuals of the same talent to substantially different career paths. In many instances, this situation is unfair because the occupation ranks that are not reached by many individuals coming from lower-income families are in essence career opportunities that could be captured otherwise by their own talent alone.

These prospects are exacerbated by the multiplier effect provided by the elimination tournament character of labour markets for superstars. Through this tournament process, a small difference in income will lead to great spreads in individual stress and disappointment with respect to education opportunities and other potential benefits. This impacts negatively the productive capacity of a nation, especially if we take into consideration the missing potential synergies.

Another issue that requires a substantive redistributive strategy is the pressure that is put on many lower-income or middle-income individuals to follow fashion trends and to consume more than what they can afford. In this vein, their capacity to save adequately is in jeopardy. If these savings are put in the foreseeable future into an investment plan, they will certainly expand the opportunities of those who save. Yet the temptation of a better relative social position, the tracking of trends and conspicuous consumption of positional goods make the expansion of the map of opportunities for the unprivileged impossible. A progressive positional consumption tax would help many to save at rates that they feel are justifiable. This effect would be more powerful for people with lower incomes since their need to save for retirement or to invest for personal growth is greater than those in much higher brackets of disposable income.

ALTERNATIVE APPROACHES TO EQUITY AND DISTRIBUTION

The orthodox economic theory is represented by subjective expected utility models, which underlie rational choice models and are often grouped in the subjective expected utility theory. Utility maximization is attained by relying on assumptions that are highly restrictive. According to rational choice theory, preferences are stable and exogenous to the model and individuals have complete information. In contrast, behavioural economics has produced several processes, in terms of which rationality does not hold. In this connection, processes such as hyberbolic discounting, framing and inertia are relevant. For example, inertia manifests when individuals face a difficult decision or one involving too many choices, and so they may prefer not to alter their behaviour at all.[13]

The orthodox economic theory supports policies of libertarian paternalism, which assures that government does not constrain individual behaviour however this arises. More recently, nudge theory has been advanced as a behavioural approach that is consistent with the framework of libertarian paternalism. The government utilizes social nudges within an unaltered map of financial incentives and benefits. While libertarian paternalism interventions are more influential in the USA, there are remarkably different approaches in Europe. Besides policies associated with the European social model that is practised in Scandinavian countries, behaviour change interventions are visible as well in other European Union countries. For example, in the UK the HM Treasury Green Book envisages the implementation of government intervention to support both economic efficiency and the achievement of a social good 'such as promoting equity'.[14] While most behavioural models do not address directly equity concerns, policies utilize explicitly economic tools to mitigate the negative effects produced from inequality. The principle of social justice promotes equality of outcomes and distributional equity, which are broader entities than equal choice or opportunity. A supplementary reason for incorporating equity is that unfair interventions are often ineffective because they may provide an incentive to the public to oppose them.

By contrast, some radical approaches have traditionally emphasized technological determinism, which views environmental forces as ultimately determining attitudes and rendering them predictable. Subsequent approaches, however, such as structuration theory with extensions on social adaptation and systems theory, point to a different direction. In this theory, social structure and agency or social changes co-exist and provide feedback to each other.[15] The social and cultural capital framework stands within this structuration tradition as economic, social, technological and environmental forces clearly influence attitudes and values, although they do not constitute the exclusive determinants.

CULTURE CHANGE POLICY AND DISTRIBUTION

While status markets influence the supply of public goods, their effect is felt differently by individuals from various economic and social strata. This issue must be taken into consideration in the formation of relevant policies. Policy-makers must examine specific dimensions of status markets that influence the personal routes of various individual profiles. As it has been noted, the negative outcomes of positional emulation in consumption and occupational choices include: higher levels of debt, longer working hours, higher levels of anxiety and frustration, greater loss aversion that results in inactive behaviour, greater pressure to adopt a behaviour that signals compatibility in social status, a greater lack of information in a changing and uncertain environment, wrong choices in occupational choices and career inertia, a greater lack of opportunity for steady jobs and, in the end, greater income inequality.

People respond differently to the impact of these outcomes. For example, in assessing the personal paradigms of reactions to status and superstar markets an important distinction is initially made between those, who aggressively adopt behaviour to participate in them and those who do not actively participate but nevertheless are passively exposed to their effects. Thus the latter group of individuals will not be exposed to higher levels of debt and longer working hours but will still experience greater frustration and a greater need to convey some sense of social status at a low cost. Furthermore, in a changing working environment, these individuals will be exposed to the elastic conditions of the labour markets and to information noise with respect to occupation choice. This takes place even if they do not actively adopt an aggressive behaviour of exploiting the opportunities offered in superstar markets and even if they do not undertake the relevant costs.

However, when the behaviour of individuals who actively participate in superstar markets is analysed, the negative effects are more evident in the case of the most disadvantaged to succeed or to the latecomers. By contrast, the more an individual succeeds in establishing a superior relative position, the more able they will be to allocate financial resources to ameliorate some of the negative effects of superstar markets. In higher-income echelons, it is more likely for an individual to possess better information and to make wiser occupation decisions. Even so, they may not be able to overcome their personal commitment in working longer hours and in facing greater pressure at work.

In this context, certain conclusions can be drawn. First, superstar markets broaden the income gap between higher-income groups and lower-income groups. Second, the members of lower-income groups who actively participate in superstar markets may succeed but at a disproportionate high risk of failure. In addition, individuals of lower-income classes who choose not to participate in superstar markets succeed to escape the higher risk of failure but at the cost of experiencing personal frustration and information noise from the influence of superstar markets.

When we take into consideration superstar markets and the process of social climbing, we realize that motivation is greater when social climbing is in fact expected of an individual. This may happen because the social environment promotes social climbing or social adjustment upwards either through the continuous exposure to success stories or through the presence of social values that strengthen the process of taking greater levels of risk and, eventually, escapism. Traumatic feelings of absolute or relative deprivation support this process. The ability to climb socially depends also on the resources, either personal or financial, that an individual possesses and is willing to use.

Thus in general we can discern four groups or profiles of individuals, who according to their income and their behaviour differentiate their reaction with respect to the phenomenon of status markets. At the very high levels of income, the need to participate in superstar markets and to be in an advantageous position in status competition may seem natural and the ensuing effort can easily be financed. For middle-income individuals, to participate in superstar markets seems less feasible but nevertheless there is substantive motivation and some financial resources to pursue this goal. For lower middle-class individuals, the financial resources are much less and the risk of failure is much greater. Finally, low-income individuals and especially those coming from a working-class background are more likely to dissent from the values that are associated with status markets but, as mentioned before, there is high personal frustration and information noise from the exposure to superstar markets. Yet when there are experiences of absolute or relative deprivation in the lower social strata, the motive of social escapism through the participation in superstar markets becomes naturally stronger.

The policy implication of the differentiation of personal responses to the effect of status markets is that a greater portion of the resources that will be available from the progressive consumption taxation must be directed to those who are in disadvantage. This is a reasonable proposal when the issue is the level of debt that low-income individuals assume relative to their income for the purpose of excess positional consumption or for setting overambitious career objectives. However, low-income individuals who experience passively the various temptations of superstar markets need to be informed more. Therefore, resources must be allocated for their effective information. For them, it pays considerably if they are well informed and do not feel the pressure from the competition for relative position so that they are able to pursue their individual paradigms more aggressively.

An important aspect of the interventions that are required to curb the social problems that are associated with status markets refers to the choice of redistribution policies. In the past two decades, public spending was curtailed in both Europe and the USA with a few exceptions. Some of these measures included the removal of public programmes that were wasteful in the first instance, as was the case with subsidies that provided no clear benefits for the society as a whole. Yet there are still public programmes that benefit society. The finance of these programmes can take place from a slowdown of the expenditure rate on positional consumption and can be used to support useful public spending programmes. There are several examples of general public programmes including those to clean drinking water, to improve air quality standards, to enhance food inspection, to raise compensation for public school teachers and infrastructure maintenance, as well as to offer drug treatment and prevention assistance. There is no doubt that the improvement of these programmes, which may be financed by the curtailing of excess positional consumption and the working of status markets, will be beneficial to various groups of citizens. Yet this policy fails to deliver value to those who are at greater disadvantage because of the dynamics of status and superstar markets. As a consequence, there is a need for redistribution policies to correct the economic and social imbalances associated with those markets.

THE DESIGN OF DISTRIBUTION POLICIES AND CULTURE CHANGE

Status markets influence consumption activities with respect to goods and services associated with personal activities. As a consequence, they have an effect on the level of savings, financial investment and long-term welfare of individuals. In addition, superstar markets impact the labour choices of individuals. Thus in a microeconomic framework, positional interests pertain to aspects of the behaviour of labour as a factor of production in the labour market and of the behaviour of households in the demand of goods and services and in financial investment (through savings). To sustain excess consumption for the purpose of signalling relative social competence, individuals reduce their level of savings and portfolio investment and their long-term income welfare, and increase the level of debt that they undertake as well as their work load. To make occupational choices that may lead to a superstar status, individuals bypass more appropriate opportunities in the labour markets, work harder, miss opportunities to develop steady careers and often experience loss of income. On top of these difficulties, individuals both as consumers and as professionals internalize higher levels of anxiety, frustration and disappointment.

The design of redistribution policies has to take into account both the division of individuals among different income groups and the nature of the effect of superstar markets and relative position competition on these different groups. In addition, an important aspect of effective social and cultural policy orientation is to move beyond the mere recognition of the importance of cultural factors such as habits, norms and social influence in decision-making to include the role of strategic interplays that take place in different institutional areas in the targeting of specific groups in order to influence a certain attitude.[16] The analysis reveals a number of factors (or forces) that are relevant to the emergence of markets with a positional orientation. Some factors are more decisive while others are of secondary importance. These factors are presented in a structured manner in the appendix (Table A.1) with respect to their specificity. Thus there are five groups of relevant variables (Table A.1: subtables 1–5), that is, categories for economic, psychological, anthropological, sociological and political/philosophical factors. In these subtables, the most important variables that contribute to the strengthening of positional markets are presented in the first column. The possible objectives for policy-makers to correct the adverse impact of each one of these factors are presented in the second column. Finally, in the third column, the corresponding policy measures are described.

This detailed description has certain interesting implications. First, there are some causes of superstar markets, for which no correction through policy measures should be attempted because they are associated with technological progress, the subsequent growth of wealth as well as with human capital development. The only policy measures that are necessary are those that are designed to correct the impact of forces that are associated with endogenous preference formation. In this vein, the policies that are associated with redistribution are not characterized only by the provision of monetary value to those who are at disadvantage, but also by mitigating the impact of specific forces that cause endogenous preference formation in the context of superstar markets and positional activities. This principle operates as a safeguard for developing ad hoc policies for positional markets.

For example, factors that contribute to endogenous preference formation include the influence of television and information technologies in the formation of status markets for goods and services, and the behavioural process that generates individual signalling as a way of demonstrating social and professional competence. Another behavioural factor is the process of affective internalization of symbols and myths provided by pop-culture through the virtual exposure to television and the rest of the media as well as through advertisement exposure. Additionally, the use of positional symbols for social discrimination in a contented society and the influence of the thymotic motive in materializing a positional context in economic activity also contribute to similar behaviour. The rationale underlying the choice of policy objectives in the second column is straightforward because in essence it builds safeguarding policies against the specific forces that contribute to positional markets. For example, excess communication and exposure through the media can be mitigated by real interaction and the signal process by the emphasis on qualities such as observable talents or skills. In addition, the affective internalization of virtual myths and symbols can be replaced by real-life alternatives while the positional thymotic process underlying the behaviour of contented individuals can be substituted by a non-positional one. Finally, the unsuccessful quest for self-validation and the ensuing feelings of relative deprivation in the context of status markets can fade away by individual validation in the social process through the promotion of a social ascription system.

The real interaction of agents can take place through the financial support of organizations where people interact with each other in real terms. For example, community organizations in poorer neighbourhoods provide real-life experiences, effective mentoring and signal the ability to collaborate towards common goals. These activities reinforce the affective internalization of archetypes and values that are generated in the real tissue of the society rather than through the media. Another category of organizations are non-profit civic associations, which support the development of resources for the more disadvantaged in areas such as training, continuing education and quality of life through recreational and cultural activities. Since superstar markets often interface with pop-culture, a special category of non-profit civic organizations are youth organizations that help stimulate young people to be contented by being creative in terms of developing productive interests and skills and by being focused on social activities that relate to their individual or collective sensitivities.

While the promotion of the real over the virtual that was just described relates to the impact of the demand for goods and activities, there is another area that must also be considered, that is, the supply of labour. Thus considerable financial resources must be allocated to continuous occupational training with an emphasis on special skills that might appear less visible but are nevertheless valuable.

Another work-related policy measure is the financial support of the development of a visible social ascription programme regarding professional and social achievements in diverse areas from the medical field and the education system to the army, the arts and the civic society. Such a programme will eventually emphasize and highlight excellence and quality in a framework marked by social individualism rather than by self-centredness.

The support of heterogeneity with respect to positional aspirations plays an important role in policy formulation. In an equilibrium context, in which individuals have an incentive for dissonance reduction, status-conscious individuals benefit from the presence of agents with different status orientations. For example, in order to sustain positional consumption, people who prefer to acquire status eventually raise the average level of effort in the economy. Thus policies that tend to motivate individuals to be more recreation oriented also create benefits for consumption-oriented agents. This happens because they reduce their incentives to exert effort to sustain their positional consumption. It is obvious that the existence of behaviourally distinct classes of people is beneficial because it motivates each group to view their social standing positively.[17] From a policy perspective, leisure-oriented agents can improve social welfare and efficiency. This is especially true for those leisure activities or recreational activities that enhance the human capital and symbolic capital of individuals (that is, internalizing information from foreign cultures or developing creative and communication skills).

THE IMPLEMENTATION OF REDISTRIBUTION POLICIES

The policy measures that are generated by setting policy objectives, which reverse the impact of positional markets on endogenous taste formation, range from public programme development to social awareness campaigns. They appear in alternative forms such as finance, regulation, institutional building, training and education and other social programmes. This last category includes diverse programmes such as to raise social awareness, to build a social ascription system, to support communities as a facilitator of mentoring, to ensure the support of heterogeneity in certain policies and to develop major social initiatives such as Third World aid or climate change awareness. Another characteristic of this all-pervasive approach is that certain instruments appear many times as being effective in reversing the impact of positional markets. These instruments are continuing training to enhance human capital and the development of career choice centres; the support of heterogeneity; the support of recipients with a long-term outlook such as the community, the family and the youth; the support of real-life projects, as well as of recreational activities that enhance cultural capital, the development of proper regulation and independent regulation authorities; the set-up of a public awareness programme through an advertisement campaign; and the support of a major social initiatives programme. Of course, for the design of proper policies, allowance must be made for the different cultural qualities underlying the economic, business and social process of a country. For example, the mix of policies has to be different across northern European countries and Mediterranean countries such as Spain and Greece, or developing countries such as India and Brazil.

The diverse range of instruments, which contain the adverse impact of positional markets, can be applied in practice only if there is a strong sense of moral leadership among the politicians who are willing to adopt such policies. Moral leadership is crucial because in many situations the impact of positional markets appears powerful because of the impact of special interest groups and superstars. This is exacerbated by the fact that social policy-makers have been unable so far to understand properly and contain the diversity and the power of this phenomenon. For example, although the design of a diverse range of policy instruments is useful, their development requires efforts to overcome several obstacles and difficulties on various fronts. Thus there is a difficulty in building a diverse policy to correct the fragmented impact of positional markets especially in areas in which the difference between the real and the imaginary is distorted. It is because of the all-powerful and all-pervasive appearance of positional markets in various areas that the social process seems really caught by surprise, lacks commitment and ignores the means for developing the proper policies. This situation implies that additional ideological and institutional support for culture policy for positional markets and activities must be built. Ultimately, this leads to the conclusion that the policy intervention with its diverse measures to correct the excesses of positional markets can be effective only if it is backed by a strong sense of moral leadership and it is tied to a strong political commitment for redistribution. This may draw substantive know-how from international experience by using as a benchmark the social programmes followed in certain countries with an outstanding record, as in the Scandinavian countries. In short, the question of applying an effective culture policy with a redistributive character requires in essence the exercise of political commitment. This does not imply that all policy measures must be implemented by the state itself or that the state should replace the market especially when it is quite evident that in certain areas it does not have the appropriate know-how. Thus for example, certain programmes such as the development of social awareness or a social ascription system may require external consulting and will ultimately use the experience and know-how of symbolic analysts. However, some other programmes will be carried by communities and by expert consulting companies that operate at this level.

One may argue that policies for status markets in developing economies may be a luxury and of secondary importance. But, since the impact of endogenous taste formation is pervasive in essence no redistributive policy can be effective if it does not initiate some form of culture change that tackles positional markets.

BEHAVIOURAL MODELS OF CULTURE CHANGE AND THE CULTURAL CAPITAL FRAMEWORK

Interventions can be adequately situated within a model of culture change policy, which is based on behavioural assumptions. There is a growing use of behavioural models in the formulation and implementation of government policies. Behaviours explained by behavioural change models involve public interventions in diverse areas such as community participation, consumption, environment, health, transport, tax evasion and education retention. Some other approaches have been applied in the analysis of consumption and lifestyle change.[18] There are several multi-stage and multi-source policy approaches that are based on behavioural models and are utilized in important sectors such as health, education and environment. Among the most prominent approaches are social marketing, principles-based policies and intervention mapping. Some approaches like intervention mapping require the explicit selection and adoption of relevant models from behavioural theory. However, social marketing combines multiple types of engagement in an intervention mix. The idea of an intervention mix is central to another central model for policy-makers, the so-called 4E model, which is broadly used and stands for the four types of activities: enable, encourage, engage and exemplify. Each of these types is mapped against specific categories of intervention. Thus enabling relates to core infrastructure; encouraging to fiscal, legislative and regulatory measures; engaging to communication; and exemplifying to government demonstrating its commitment to the behaviour in question. Finally, a model which has expanded the boundaries of the 4Es framework by setting it in the wider context of culture change is the cultural capital framework that has produced a generic model, in which interventions address social and cultural norms as a catalyst. This culture change model is a long-term process model that resembles societal models of change because it incorporates the role of institutions and cultural norms such as in the needs, opportunities and abilities model. In this type of model, institutions and culture influence individual abilities and exercise behavioural control, which along with motivations influence intentions and consumer behaviour.[19]

CULTURE CHANGE POLICY AND STATUS

Examples of policy areas where the concept of culture change has been recognized as being relevant are the areas of education, health, prosperity, environment and community. With regard to the theme of prosperity, some issues that are relevant include social exclusion, social mobility, personal aspiration and entrepreneurialism. In Figures A.1 and A.2, there is a demonstration of the cultural change policy framework. In Figure A.1, a general culture change cycle framework in the form of a cultural capital model is presented, which was elaborated by the Strategy Unit of the Cabinet Office in the UK. Culture change is a cycle process that begins with society-wide policy influences. The origin of the behavioural cycle is the development of our attitudes, values, aspirations and sense of self-efficacy. These are influenced by the immediate world around us such as parents, peers and neighbours and broader society-wide variables such as technological, economic, political and media forces. Attitudes are affected by environmental factors such as mentoring and information through media. With values and aspirations, attitudes create a process that consolidates behavioural intentions. This process is filtered through people's reactions to incentives including financial ones, barriers, regulation, information and engagement practices to produce actual behaviour and transform it to norms. In Figure A.2, I demonstrate how this culture change cycle policy can be used in the case of status and superstar markets. The items, which are described in Table A.1, fit adequately within the four blocks of interventions towards the development of behavioural intentions and norms with respect to these markets. Thus culture change policy tied to distribution and policy signalling are essential parts of the first block while mentoring and development of a social ascription model fits within the second block of the cycle of culture change interventions. Finally, social marketing, that includes nudging, and measures such as the progressive consumption tax and regulation interventions fall within the third and fourth blocks respectively. Thus the implementation of culture change policy with regard to status markets is feasible within this model.[20]

The policy implementation requires a multi-stage process such as the one envisaged by the cultural capital framework that poses several challenges. First, policy-makers must filter information to determine if culture change is relevant, to clarify the objectives and rationale for government intervention, and to identify the relevant segments of the population. The next stages require evaluating the drivers of behaviour, determining the appropriateness of policy interventions, implementing them and developing systems for monitoring effectiveness. In each of these stages, policy-makers must address important challenges such as the identification of externalities to justify behavioural shifts, desired outcomes in terms of concrete costs and benefits and population segments, which are relevant to policy.

Designing comprehensive and coherent policies for culture change with respect to status markets is a challenge within the reach of contemporary policy-making. Judging from similar programmes in sectors such as education and health, certain practices can be adopted. These include the identification of targets which manifest a return to norms or an indication of visible improvement. Policies for social justice must evaluate inequalities, design interventions, prioritize the needs of disadvantaged groups and attempt to elevate groups to meet standards of average or representative population. The achievement of a number of culture change objectives depends clearly on individual attitudes and behaviour. For example, public service agreements that are in practice in areas such as education and health and require changes in attitudes may be designed to target changes in attitudes towards learning. In education, examples of these targets were the reduction of the proportion of young people not in education, employment or training (NEET) by 2 percentage points by 2010 and increasing the proportion of adults with effective skills for employability and advancement to more specialized levels of training. In health, examples of targets include tackling the underlying causes of ill health and health inequalities by policies aimed at reducing adult smoking rates and the under-18 conception rates.

Similar targets that relate to stated objectives of reform with regard to consumption and occupational excesses can be designed to correspond to increased opportunities that public investment creates. In particular, policy objectives may include actions such as substantially reducing credit exposure (loans and credit cards) and financial failure rates from overconsumption by a given date and percentage; mitigating the impact of financial deterioration and financial inequalities by reducing the annual growth of consumption of positional goods and services as a percentage of total spending; and reducing unemployment, which is caused by extensive involvement in sectors with highly risky tournament qualities by a given percentage for certain vulnerable target groups. In the area of education, policy actions may involve increasing the proportion of students at high school and university, who develop complementary skills that interface superstar activities towards win-win steady type of careers by setting certain percentages for those aged 18 to 30 and increasing the proportion of adults with effective skills for employability and advancement to more specialized levels of training.

With respect to clarifying objectives and the rationale for government intervention, culture change policy can be used to tackle the determinants of financial deterioration and health inequalities, in particular through promoting stable living, enhancing professional interests and increasing employment. One important stage of the process is to segment target populations and conduct profiling in order to design realistic and effective intervention packages for the achievement of economic and social objectives. An important step is to identify the relative role of attitudes in determining behaviour. These attitudes may vary between social groups with regard to a number of indicators. For example, one indicator may refer to the availability of rewarding occupational opportunities, which provide a sense of autonomy and self-control. Several target groups can be identified from stable self-reliant professionals, vulnerable individuals to resisters and those suffering from financial, professional and family instability. Depending on the exposure to the losses of positional activities, policy may range from intensive support to reinforce positive attitudes towards stable attitudes in consumption and occupational interests, to stronger intervention measures to break entrenched behavioural patterns. When the change in attitudes is supported by financial incentives and regulation they may transform to an active and productive behaviour.

Overall, for an effective culture change policy in the area of status and superstar markets to be developed, several types of activities are required. First, studies must produce quantitative evaluations of losses across different social groups because of possible involvement in positional activities. On the basis of these studies, financial plans can be developed to define sources of finance from taxation for distributive policies. These interventions may be designed, according to the cycle of cultural capital framework, in terms of measure roadmaps in connection to other types of policies such as fiscal policy and sectoral education, culture and sustainability policies. Moreover, policies for mitigating positional risks can be utilized as special chapters in sectoral policies such as in education. The process is complex with many interlinkages but contemporary policy can surely enhance its capacity through various programmes such as, for example, the European Union framework programmes to deliver the desired benefits.

CONCLUDING REMARKS

The rise of status markets activities produces various social costs. First, people tend to make wrong consumption, financial and occupational decisions. In order to catch up with the pressure of relative position competition they are exposed more to overworking hours, anxiety and the costs of undertaking the wrong risks with respect to occupational choices, savings and financial investment decisions. In this environment, people internalize unpleasant feelings that are associated with insecurity and social stereotypical discrimination. In addition, there is congestion for the best opportunities and an excessive consumption of positional goods and services that leads to social waste. Finally, superstar markets produce a tendency towards a greater income inequality, career inertia and wrong occupational choices. Interventions can be based on a model of culture change policy that utilizes behavioural assumptions. There is a growing use of behavioural models in the formulation and implementation of government. Culture change cycle policy on the basis of a cultural capital framework can be utilized in the case of status and superstar markets. As with other objectives in sectors such as education, health and sustainability, designing comprehensive and coherent policies for culture change with respect to status markets is a challenge within the reach of contemporary policy-making. More importantly, dealing with positional excesses in a culture change policy paves the way for developing political support for finance in the form of a progressive consumption tax.

There are two important considerations regarding the nature of the policy measures that have to be designed to curtail the social costs mentioned above. First, policies can take various forms. For example, measures can be designed to be motivational, cultural in nature, regulatory or fiscal. Individually motivating policies have a psychological connotation such as in the nudge approach, fiscal policies are economic in nature, regulation policies are influenced greatly by political factors, and cultural policies are determined by sociological, anthropological and philosophical considerations. Thus the design of appropriate policies for positional markets mirrors the interdisciplinary approach that was followed in this book. The second consideration is associated with the choice among general across-the-board policies and redistributive public programmes. The first type of policy is horizontal because the benefits are distributed equally among the members of the society and there is a general welfare benefit.[21] However, although status is desired by all, it matters more to the rich and the first comers than to the poor and the latecomers. The wealth of behavioural economic evidence and the insights provided by alternative social disciplines facilitate the connection of the analysis of status and superstar markets with the design and implementation of distributive culture change policies. While Galbraith's suggestions in *The Affluent Society* would have fared better with the support of ample contemporary empirical findings on the psychology of consumer behaviour, culture change policies on positional activities, which draw important insights from disciplines such as psychology and sociology, can certainly be effective today with the help of the empirical evidence provided by fields such as behavioural and evolutionary economics and social psychology.[22] Relating to the degree to which the less privileged are deprived more than the comfortable regarding the spread of positional activities, there is certainly scope for the imposition of redistributive policies. As it has been shown, the less comfortable are at a disadvantage when they participate in positional activities in various important ways. In the midst of the all-pervasive presence of positional activities in consumption and occupational choices, correcting these problems effectively and efficiently with suitable policies requires the political commitment to tie these problems with redistributive policies and moral leadership, and to acknowledge that culture change improves social welfare.

Appendix: table and figures

TABLE

Table A.1   Areas of alternative culture change policies across disciplines

Forces	Support	Tools
Subtable 1 – Economic forces		
Labour markets		
Relative performance rewards	NA – supply driven	
New technology and economies of scale	NA – supply driven	
Wealth growth	NA – supply driven	
High income inequality	Redistribution	Connection of culture policy with distribution policy
Human capital growth	Diversity	Diverse training programmes
Product and service markets		
Wealth growth	NA – supply driven	
Advertisement	Public awareness – regulation	Public messages – regulatory authority
Cultural capital growth	Diversity in cultural capital	Training – education programmes
Subtable 2 – Psychological forces		
Labour markets		
Territory signalling	Skills signalling	Training – skills enhancement
Lack of prediction	Information enhancement	Career guidance centres – nudging and social marketing
Visibility	Alternative visibility	Visible social ascription system
High stake incentives	Quality incentives	Training – education
Loss avoidance	Winning attitude	Training – education
Product and service markets		
Short-term satisfaction	Long-term satisfaction	Family and youth programmes
Cognitive concentration	Cognitive diversity	Cultural and recreational programmes

Forces	Support	Tools
Anchoring	Lower anchoring	Lower anchoring – develop mentoring
Self-worth validation	Skills worth – social worth	Skill enhancement – social awareness
Overexposure to media	Real-life exposure	Recreational programmes – community life
Diminished self-control	Social responsibility	Training – education enhancement
Status role affective identification	Identification of real models – rationality	Social ascription system
Stereotypical territorial thinking	Democratic awareness	Regulation and enforcement of access
Behavioural polarization shifts	Behavioural convergence	Lower anchoring – development of social institutions
Relative deprivation feelings	Relative satisfaction	Diverse social environment – lower-level mentoring
Lack of moral commitments	Social responsibility	Moral leadership – cultural strategy
Subtable 3 – Anthropological forces		
Labour markets		
Symbolic analysts capital	Diversity in symbolic capital	Professionalism set-up
Affective social identification	Real role models – rationality	Lower-level mentoring – approximation of real-life models – social institutions
Product and service markets		
Nostalgic excitement	Creativity	Diverse cultural programmes
Aesthetization and novelty	Heterogeneity	Diverse cultural programmes – awareness messages
Subculture marginalism	Across-the-board culture involvement	Major issues awareness and association with marginalism
Signal and myth projection	Mentor projection	Intelligent over aesthetic myths
Affective social identification	Rationality	Rational
Television desires and internalization	Real-life desires and internalization	Mentoring
Subtable 4 – Sociological forces		
Television influence	Real-life influence	Community and youth programmes – tax TV excesses
Popular culture influence	Heterogeneous art forms	Diverse cultural programmes

Forces	Support	Tools
Advertisement	Public awareness – regulation	Public messages – regulatory body – social marketing –nudging
Symbolic lifestyle	Real lifestyle – heterogeneity in symbolism	Creativity – recreational and learning programmes
Symbolic discrimination	Symbolic access	Social conscience
Ideological domination	Ideological plurality	Pluralism
Subtable 5 – Political and philosophical forces		
Contentment	Social awareness	Social regulation – enforcement
Political debate	Partisanship	Open discussion – consensus – moral leadership
Thymotic self	Superstar ascription	Social ascription system – skills
Decline of resentment	New solidarity	Programmes of social initiatives – development of social institutions
Lack of communicative reason	Social and communicative reason	Expansion of diversity in social forum

FIGURES

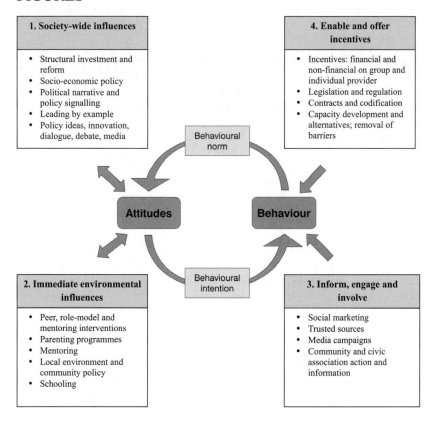

Source: Knott, Muyers and Aldridge (2008).

Figure A.1   Model of culture change policy

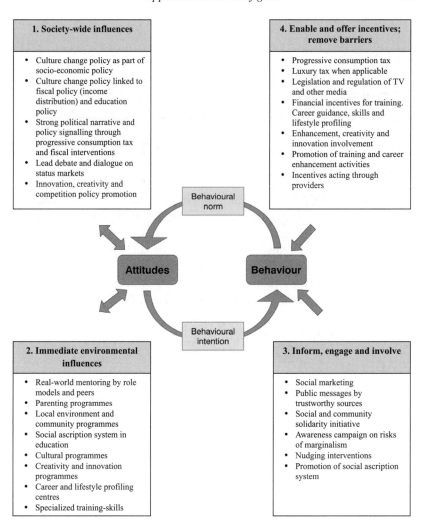

1. Society-wide influences

- Culture change policy as part of socio-economic policy
- Culture change policy linked to fiscal policy (income distribution) and education policy
- Strong political narrative and policy signalling through progressive consumption tax and fiscal interventions
- Lead debate and dialogue on status markets
- Innovation, creativity and competition policy promotion

4. Enable and offer incentives; remove barriers

- Progressive consumption tax
- Luxury tax when applicable
- Legislation and regulation of TV and other media
- Financial incentives for training. Career guidance, skills and lifestyle profiling
- Enhancement, creativity and innovation involvement
- Promotion of training and career enhancement activities
- Incentives acting through providers

Behavioural norm

Attitudes

Behaviour

Behavioural intention

2. Immediate environmental influences

- Real-world mentoring by role models and peers
- Parenting programmes
- Local environment and community programmes
- Social ascription system in education
- Cultural programmes
- Creativity and innovation programmes
- Career and lifestyle profiling centres
- Specialized training-skills

3. Inform, engage and involve

- Social marketing
- Public messages by trustworthy sources
- Social and community solidarity initiative
- Awareness campaign on risks of marginalism
- Nudging interventions
- Promotion of social ascription system

Figure A.2   Model of culture change policy relevant to status

Notes

CHAPTER 1   INTRODUCTION: STATUS, SUPERSTARS AND MARKETS

1. Veblen (1899: 74); for the modern interest in lifestyle and the impact of behavioural concerns on it, see Earl (1983; 1986) and Frank (1985; 1999).
2. Hirsch (1976); Frank (1985; 1999); for the difference between relative and absolute consumption, see Solnick and Hemenway (1998) and Oxoby (2004).
3. Rosen (1981); Adler (1985); MacDonald (1988); Frank and Cook (1995).
4. Frank (1999); Frey (2000).
5. Keynes (1936: 235).
6. Gamson (1994).
7. Rosen (1984; 1992).
8. Hartog (2002).
9. Pasinetti (1981); Lavoie (1992).
10. Trigg (2004).
11. Trigg (2001).
12. On the notion of socio-economics, see Etzioni (1991a); also Lawrence (1991); for a post-Keynesian notion of political economy, see Dow (1990).
13. Swedberg (1991).
14. On the history of socio-economics, see Swedberg (1991).
15. For new approaches and the development of cultural political economy, see Sum and Jessop (2013).

CHAPTER 2   THE ECONOMICS OF STATUS AND SUPERSTAR MARKETS

1. Rosen (1981: 845); as a credible alternative explanation of income disparity, see Krugman (2002); and earlier Krugman (1992b).

2. For an initial explanation of the notion of positional goods, see Hirsch (1976).
3. Rosen (1981).
4. Kingston and Smart (1990).
5. Huey (1993: 56); also, Merton (1968); Cole and Cole (1973); Merton (1988).
6. For examples from the media industry in Hollywood, see Faulkner (1983: 173).
7. Krugman (1992a).
8. Krugman (2002).
9. Piketty and Saez (2003).
10. Piketty and Saez (2003).
11. Marshall (1947), quoted by Rosen (1981: 857).
12. Piketty and Saez (2003); also, for the importance of income polarization, see Hacker (2006); in addition, Piketty (2014) argued that inequality is a natural symptom of capitalism arising from divergences between the rate of return on a special form of capital and the rate of economic growth.
13. For a first account of this hypothesis, see Kuttner (1983); for the relevance of neoliberal growth, see Palley (2013).
14. For an introduction to the puzzle, see Levy and Murnane (1992); for the possible relevance of rent compensation and luck rewards, see Garvey and Milbourn (2006).
15. Benjamin, Chinloy and Jud (2004).
16. Aizcorbe, Kennickell and Moore (2003).
17. Rosen (1981).
18. On the case of lawyers, see Buchanan, Tollison and Tullock (1980); Rosen (1992).
19. Farrell and Saloner (1985); Katz and Shapiro (1985).
20. On the impact of media and its tournament characteristics, see Weinraub (1994).
21. Rosen and Neal (1998).
22. Rosen and Sanderson (2000); Alesina, Di Tella and MacCulloch (2004).
23. Jacobs and Green (1998).
24. Atkinson (2004).
25. Ait-Sahalia, Parker and Yogo (2004).
26. Corneo and Jeanne (2001).
27. Brekke, Howarth and Nyborg (2003).
28. Wright and Dwyer (1990: 126).
29. Congleton (1980); Frank and Cook (1995).
30. Svenson (1981).

31. Brown and McIntosh (1998).
32. Ljungqvist and Uhlig (2000); Johansson-Stenman, Carlsson and Daruvala (2002); Pingle and Mitchell (2002); Alpizar, Carlsson and Johansson-Stenman (2005).
33. Van Long and Shimomura (2004).
34. Tatzel (2003).
35. Bloch, Rao and Desai (2004).
36. Rao (2001); Bloch, Rao and Desai (2004).
37. Johnson, Levine and Pesendorfer (2001).
38. Ruffle (1999).
39. Van Kempen (2003).
40. Van Kempen (2003).
41. Maxcy (2004).
42. Fisher (1930); Keynes (1936).
43. Keynes (1936).
44. Keynes (1936).
45. For the case of real estate with a premium for a view, see Benson et al. (1998).
46. For seminal work on the impact of advertisement on consumerism and industrial activity, see Galbraith (1979); for recent development of the ideas of Galbraith on the impact of marketing, see Sheehan (2010); for Keynes's views on social comparisons, see Keynes (1931).
47. Smith (1982 [1759]); Veblen (1899); Oxoby (2004).
48. Oxoby (2003).
49. Fehr and Gächter (2000); Goeree and Holt (2000); Bolton and Ockenfels (2000).
50. Nooteboom (2002b).
51. Oxoby (2004).
52. Oxoby (2003).
53. Benabou and Tirole (2000).
54. Canova, Manganelli-Rattazzi and Webley (2005).
55. Garnham (1987).
56. Singer and Singer (1980).
57. Toffler (1981: 165).
58. Bourdieu (1987).
59. Bourdieu (1984: 359).
60. Lokshin and Ravallion (2002).
61. Bourdieu (1987: 243).
62. Oxoby (2003).
63. Hopkins and Kornienko (2004).
64. Piketty (1998).

65. Jaramillo, Kempf and Moizeau (2003).
66. Cooper, Garcia-Penalosa and Funk (2001).
67. Piketty (1998).
68. Ackerman and Alstott (1999).
69. Oxoby (2003).
70. Schwartz (1991).
71. Wendner (2003).
72. Piketty (1998).
73. Ireland (1998).
74. Heffetz and Frank (2008).
75. Bruni and Stanca (2008).
76. Ellison and Fudenberg (1995); Bowden and McDonald (2008).
77. Clark and Horstmann (2005); Cashmore (2006).
78. Bikhchandani, Hirshleifer and Welch (1992; 1998); Banerjee (1992).
79. These approaches include the economics of superstars advanced by Rosen (1981); Adler (1985); and the microeconomic analysis of Pesendorfer (1995).
80. Bandura (1977).
81. Ho, Camerer and Weigelt (1998).
82. Fehr and Schmidt (1999).
83. Cowan, Cowan and Swann (2004).
84. Amaldoss and Jain (2005).
85. Campbell (1987).
86. Delre et al. (2007).
87. Dolfsma (2004).
88. Hopkins (2008).
89. Alpizar, Carlsson and Johansson-Stenman (2005).

CHAPTER 3   THE FUNDAMENTAL FORCES: TECHNOLOGY, TASTES AND VALUES

1. Naisbitt (1990: 3).
2. Naisbitt (1982).
3. Toffler (1981: 104–7).
4. Braverman (1974).
5. Rifkin (1996: 182).
6. Bell (1976).
7. Roediger and Foner (1989).
8. Kranzberg (1985: 50).
9. Naisbitt (1982: 22).

10. Negroponte (1970: 11–13); Masuda (1981: 49).
11. Bell (1980b: 529); Toffler (1981: 165).
12. For an early summary on information technology developments, see Forester (1987; 1988; 1989).
13. Castells (1996).
14. Dean, Yoon and Susman (1992).
15. Piore and Sabel (1984); Coriat (1990).
16. Coriat (1990: 165).
17. For a discussion of the relation between post-Fordism and post-modernity, see Kumar (1995).
18. Bettinger (1991).
19. Brusco (1982: 168).
20. On evidence of the growing importance of aide jobs in services that are cost-effective and quality enhancing, see Krugman (1997: 196).
21. Rees (1992).
22. On the idea of post-industrial era and its manifestations, see Toffler (1970).
23. Daniels (1993).
24. On the relation between information technology and organizational change, see Boyett and Conn (1991: 23); also, Amendola, Cohendet and Llerena (1989).
25. Naisbitt (1982: 4); for a sociological discussion of historical materialism, see Giddens (1987b).
26. Rorty (1989).
27. Epstein (2005).
28. Palley (2007); for a discussion of the downsizing of employment opportunities, see Palley (1998).
29. Storey and Dash (2009).

CHAPTER 4   PSYCHOLOGY AND BEHAVIOURAL FORCES

1. Hirsch (1976).
2. Empirical evidence shows that concerns about status also lead to an increase in wages as discussed by Frank (1984); Konrad and Pfeffer (1990); and Podolny (1993).
3. Brammer, Raleigh and McGuire (1994); Madsen (1994).
4. Mazur and Lamb (1980); Elias (1981); Mazur (1983).
5. For a theoretical framework that introduces a broad idea of utility or satisfaction derived from leisure activities, see Juster, Courant and Dow (1981).

6. For evidence that leisure activities such as childcare, house enter-
    tainment or outings with friends provide a very high level of
    satisfaction, see Juster, Courant and Dow (1985).
7. George (2001).
8. Bisin and Verdier (1998); Grüner (1995).
9. Miller (1956).
10. Goode (1978: 75).
11. Simon (1978).
12. Simon (1981: 139).
13. Simon (1981: 96); for the impact of cognitive limitations on
    decision-making and bounded rationality, see Simon (1979).
14. For seminal contributions of the Prospect School, see Kahneman
    and Tversky (1973); Tversky and Kahneman (1974); Nisbett and
    Ross (1980); Anderson, Lepper and Ross (1980).
15. For anchoring in a job market, see Tversky and Kahneman (1974).
16. Langer (1983).
17. Frank (1999).
18. Parker (1983).
19. Diener and Biswas-Diener (2002); Twenge and Campbell (2002).
20. Hanley and Wilhelm (1992).
21. Ahuvia and Wong (2002).
22. Tatzel (2003).
23. Festinger (1957).
24. Aronson (1969).
25. Aronson et al. (1974).
26. Aronson and Mills (1959); Aronson and Carlsmith (1963).
27. Ross et al. (1977).
28. Jones and Nisbett (1971).
29. Alloy and Abramson (1979).
30. Bem (1965).
31. Beauvois and Joule (1996); Aronson (2007).
32. Aronson (2007).
33. Oxoby (2003).
34. Benabou and Tirole (2000).
35. Bearden, Hardesty and Rose (2001).
36. Aronson, Willerman and Floyd (1966).
37. Moreland and Beach (1992).
38. Zajonc (1968).
39. Byrne (1961).
40. Petty and Cacioppo (1986).
41. Layard (1980: 741).
42. Nutt (1984: 446).

43. Dahlbäck (1990).
44. Festinger (1954).
45. On individual reports of well-being, see Myers and Diener (1995); Seidlitz and Diener (1993).
46. Diener and Lucas (1998).
47. Furnham and Cheng (2000); for basic references on positive psychology, see Seligman and Csikszentmihalyi (2000) and Seligman (2011).
48. Neumark and Postlewaite (1998).
49. Güth, Schmittberger and Schwarze (1982). This experiment is described extensively by Frank (1999).
50. Kahneman, Knetsch and Thaler (1986).
51. Kahn and Murnighan (1993).
52. Kahneman, Knetsch and Thaler (1986); Fehr, Kirchsteiger and Riedl (1993); Güth, Ockenfels and Wendel (1993); Rees (1993); Fehr and Kirchsteiger (1994); Frey and Bohnet (1995); Babcock, Wang and Lowenstein (1996).
53. For a summary of research in economics on relative position, see Zizzo (1997).
54. Torrance (1954); Holsti (1971).
55. Goffman (1951).
56. Feuer (1986).
57. Morley (1986).
58. Morley (1986: 72).
59. Crocker and Luhtanen (1990).
60. LeVine and Cambell (1972).
61. Oakes and Turner (1980).
62. Moscovici and Zavalloni (1969); Tajfel and Turner (1979).
63. Chapman and Chapman (1967).
64. Myers and Bishop (1971).
65. Dahlbäck (1990).
66. Strack, Martin and Stepper (1988).
67. For an explanation why relative deprivation can be a major cause of sudden social change, see Gurr (1970).
68. Newcomb (1961).
69. Heine, Kitayama and Lehman (2001); Snibbe et al. (2003).
70. Crosby (1976).
71. Kahneman and Varey (1990).
72. Kahneman and Tversky (1982).
73. Piketty (1998).
74. Stouffer et al. (1949).
75. Oxoby (2003).

76. Benabou and Tirole (2000).
77. Oxoby (2003; 2004).
78. Grüner (1995); Fernández and Gali (1999).
79. Oxoby (2003).
80. Maital and Maital (1984).
81. Nissel (1984).
82. Thaler and Shefrin (1981).
83. Etzioni (1975).
84. Alchian and Allen (1983: 555).
85. Alchian and Allen (1983: 99).
86. Hammond, McClelland and Mumpower (1980); Etzioni (1988) citing Mueller (1986: 18).
87. Etzioni (1975).
88. Maital and Maital (1984).
89. Hartfield, Walster and Berscheid (1978).
90. Becker (1981).
91. Kahneman, Knetsch and Thaler (1986).
92. Sabini and Silver (1982); Kahneman, Knetsch and Thaler (1986).
93. Frank (1999).
94. Frank (1999).
95. For an account of emotions playing a useful role in decision-making, see Cosmides and Tooby (1987); and Damasio (1994). For a review of the role of affect on consumer behaviour, see Pieters and van Raaij (1988).
96. Steiner (1980: 22); Berelson and Steiner (1964).
97. Zink et al. (2008).

CHAPTER 5 THE ANTHROPOLOGY OF POPULAR CULTURE AND IDENTITY FORMATION

1. Bukhtin (1968); Stalybrass and White (1986).
2. Elias (1978; 1982).
3. Mercer (1983); Shields (1990); Kennedy and Williams (2001).
4. Bailey (1986).
5. Williams (1982); Chaney (1983); Bennett (1988); Benjamin (2000).
6. Stephanson (1987); Urry (1988); Spigel (2001).
7. Dyer (2003).
8. Scott (2000).
9. Kellner (2002); Evans (2003).
10. Bourdieu (1984: 371); for an analysis of the creative class in terms of job function rather than income, see Florida (2002).

11. Bourdieu (1984: 370).
12. Foucault (1984).
13. Bell (1976).
14. Jameson (1984a).
15. Nye (1997).
16. Jameson (1984a: 78).
17. Jameson (1984c: xv).
18. Jameson (1979: 138).
19. Crane (1987).
20. DiMaggio (1987).
21. Jameson (1984a: 87).
22. Baudrillard (1983a: 148).
23. Eco (1986); Kellner (1987); Kellner and Homer (2004).
24. Kaplan (1986).
25. Kaplan (1986).
26. Lash (1988); and earlier Lyotard (1984).
27. Loch, Huberman and Stout (2000).
28. Bolton and Ockenfels (2000).
29. Jameson (1981: 134).
30. Benjamin (1982); Williams (1982); Chaney (1983).
31. On an account of a cyclical process in aesthetization and sensationalism, see Sztompka (1993: 144–54).
32. Sconce (2000).
33. Kroker (1985).
34. Baudrillard (1983a).
35. Simmel (1978); Frisby (1985).
36. Faurschou (1987: 72).
37. Frijters (1998).
38. Dolfsma (2004).
39. Bourdieu (1987: 243–4).
40. Bourdieu (1987: 246).
41. For a framework on the possibility of mapping diversification, see Harvey (1989: 116–26); also, for a critique of the mapping process, see Morris (1992).
42. Tagg (1985: 4).
43. Connor (1997: 228).
44. Haldrup and Larsen (2003); for a case-study, see Okamura (1998).
45. Halualani (2002); Bærenholdt et al. (2004); and earlier MacCannell (1989).
46. Urry (1995); Urry (2002).
47. MacCannell (2001); Bærenholdt and Haldrup (2004).
48. McLaren (2003).

49. O'Rourke (1997); Vivanco (2000); Sheller and Urry (2004).
50. Bærenholdt and Haldrup (2004).
51. Kirshenblatt-Gimblett (1998); Lippard (1999).
52. Garnham (2000).
53. Berland (2000).
54. Morley (1986).
55. Sabbah (1985) and Neuman (1991).
56. For Japan, see Kawashima (2006).
57. Schiller (1999).
58. Morley (1986).
59. Hobson (2003).
60. Tulloch (2000); Dyer (2004).
61. Davies (1984).
62. Hobson (1982: 133–5); Fiske (1987a: 125); Fiske (2004).
63. Katz, Peters and Liebes (2002).
64. Fiske (1987b).
65. Hartley (1982: 127).
66. Fiske and Hartley (1978).
67. Hartley (1983).
68. Barthes (1973).
69. Tulloch and Moran (1986: 247–8).
70. Ang (1985).
71. Seiter et al. (1987).
72. Katz and Liebes (1985).
73. Tulloch and Moran (1986).
74. Dyer (2004).
75. Brown (1987); Barkow (1989); De Waal (1996).
76. Davies (1984).
77. Modleski (1982).
78. Hobson (1980).
79. Katz and Liebes (1984: 32).
80. Barthes (1975b).
81. Jameson (1984b); Eco (1984).
82. Baudrillard (1983a).
83. Kroker and Cook (1987: 268).
84. Mandel, Petrova and Cialdini (2006).
85. Hoffner et al. (2006).
86. Hoffner et al. (2006); for a discussion of the relation between wishful identification, social identity and economic preferences, see Koutsobinas (2008).
87. Frazer and Brown (2002).
88. Nüesch (2007).

89. Ward (2002).
90. Stapel and Marx (2007); for an analysis of the affective impact of celebrities and superstars and their impact on endorsements, see Cashmore (2006).
91. For a summary of research findings, see Mussweiler et al. (2000).
92. Argo, White and Dahl (2006).
93. Debord (1995 [1967]).
94. Kellner (2003).
95. Debord (1995 [1967]: 42).

CHAPTER 6   THE SOCIOLOGY OF DISTINCTION, SUPERIORITY AND DEPRIVATION

1. Zukin (1988).
2. Elias (1978; 1982).
3. This argument is a basic tenet of the analysis of Galbraith (1967).
4. For an exposition of the neoclassical view of given preferences, see Becker (1976); Stigler and Becker (1977); for a summary of competing approaches in preference formation, see Blaug (1984).
5. For a framework that explains the study of preference formation and the moral dimension, see Etzioni (1988; 1991b). For discussions of the impact of advertisement, see Galbraith (1979; 1992) and Frank (1999).
6. Berlyne (1971: 193).
7. Oxoby (2003).
8. Tversky and Kahneman (1991).
9. Oxoby (2004).
10. Oxoby (2003).
11. Michaels (1998).
12. George (2001).
13. George (2001).
14. Baudrillard (1983a: 85).
15. Douglas and Isherwood (1980); Bourdieu (1984); Bourdieu and Passeron (1990).
16. Goffman (1951).
17. Bourdieu (1987: 242).
18. Baudrillard (1983a).
19. Baudrillard (1973 [1975]: 121).
20. Jameson (1979). On the depthless nature of post-modern social order, see Jameson (1991: 388).
21. Williams (1976: 68).

22. Barthes (1975a).
23. Barthes (1975a).
24. Trigg (2001).
25. Trigg (2001).
26. Bourdieu (1984); Bourdieu and Passeron (1990).
27. Bridge (2001).
28. Piketty (1998).
29. Merton (1953); Boudon (1973).
30. Piketty (1995).
31. For an account of post-modernism, see Featherstone (1991).
32. Jameson (1984b: 125).
33. Kohler (1977); Hassan (1985).
34. Huyssen (1984).
35. Lyotard (1971; 1984); Baudrillard (1983a).
36. Lyotard (1984).
37. Jameson (1994).
38. Jameson (1984b: 125).
39. An attempt in this direction was advanced by Habermas (1981).
40. Bell (1980a).
41. Bell (1973).
42. Bell (1976).
43. Lukacs (1971); Lefebvre (1978); Horkheimer and Adorno (1997). For a discussion of an expansion of sociology to incorporate diverse concerns, see Giddens (1987a).
44. Baudrillard (1983b); Jameson (1991).
45. Jameson (1991).
46. For the expansion of capital into uncommodified areas, see Jameson (1991: 36); for earlier Marxist accounts, see Mandell (1975).
47. Jameson (1991).
48. Jameson (1991: 87). Also, Jameson (1994).
49. Jameson (2005).
50. Jameson (1994).
51. Leiss (1978: 19); Bourdieu (1984).

CHAPTER 7   CONTENTMENT, POLITICS AND THE PHILOSOPHY OF SUPERIORITY

1. Veblen (1899). On political economy, see Ricardo (1891) and Marx (2004).
2. Baudrillard (1983a).
3. Bowles, Franzini and Pagano (1999: 2).

4. Loch, Huberman and Stout (2000).
5. Durham, Hirshleifer and Smith (1998).
6. Bowles, Franzini and Pagano (1999).
7. Galbraith (1992).
8. Galbraith (1992: 86).
9. Galbraith (1979).
10. Galbraith (1992).
11. Heilbronner (1995).
12. Hegel (1942).
13. For the relation between wealth-seeking and approbation, see Adam Smith (1982 [1759]: 50–51).
14. Schiller (1967: 124).
15. Didion (1968: 142–8).
16. For a discussion of the relation of aristocratic generosity and self-preservation in Hobbes, see Fukuyama (1992).
17. Hobbes (1958); for a contrast of the views between Hegel and Hobbes, see Strauss (1952; 1963).
18. For an account that explains how the thymotic quest provides satisfaction and how self-worth is related to utility, see Fukuyama (1992: 226).
19. For a detailed account of Plato's idea of thymos, see Zuckert (1988).
20. For the discussion of megalothymia in terms of Aristotle's mega-lopsychia, the desire for the greatest recognition for possessing the greatest virtue, see Aristotle (1998: II and IV).
21. References for the notion of thymos in Plato's *Republic* are found in Plato (1968).
22. For the relation between thymos with political commitment, see Rousseau (1964: 364–5).
23. For an analysis of the difference that exists between the desire for glory and the Christian notion of humility, see Hirschman (1977: 9–11).
24. For a justification of authority for the sake of the general good, see Machiavelli (1950: 226–7).
25. Nietzsche (1954).
26. Fukuyama (1992: 366).
27. Nietzsche (1967: 70); also, Nietzsche (1966).
28. Nietzsche (1968: 16).
29. For an account that discusses how businesspeople like Ford or Carnegie sought external confirmation of their self-worth in the economic process, see Fukuyama (1992: 326); for a comparison of this case with the behaviour of successful professionals such as

lawyers or MBA executives in the modern world, see Fukuyama (1992: 336).
30. Nietzsche (1954: 170–71).
31. Nietzsche (1968).
32. De Toqueville (2001).
33. Nietzsche (1966).
34. Laclan and Mouffe (1990).
35. Rorty (1989).
36. Rorty (1989).
37. Rorty (1999).
38. Habermas (1981).
39. Rorty (1999).
40. Habermas (1981).
41. Rorty (1999).

CHAPTER 8   ALTERNATIVE POLICIES FOR POSITIONAL ACTIVITIES

1. Chang and Tsai (2003).
2. Corneo and Jeanne (2001).
3. Gaspart and Seki (2003).
4. For an initial description of individuals who do not follow the context-dependent activities but nevertheless exhibit an attitude or feelings of disinterested envy, see Sztompka (1993: 248); also, Buchowski (2006); and Puchalska (1999).
5. Carroll (2000); Dynan, Skinner and Zeldes (2004). This evidence contrasts to traditional economic wisdom as expressed by Duesenberry (1949); Modigliani and Brumberg (1955); Friedman (1957); Kosicki (1987).
6. Business Wire (1997).
7. Even when individuals succeed, overworking seem the norm according to Wallich (1994: 77); also, Frank (1985).
8. Rifkin (1996: 234).
9. For evidence of overworking, see Schor (1991: 29); Roediger and Foner (1989).
10. On a framework that supports the role of the third sector and the community activities, see Rifkin (1996: 256); on maintenance of clean water, see Wuthnow (1996).
11. Brekke, Howarth and Nyborg (2003).
12. Martin and Kennedy (1993).
13. Krugman (1994: 38).

14. Tobin (1970: 263).
15. For an extended discussion of equity versus equal distribution, see Okun (1975).
16. Oxoby (2003); for the relevance of social indicators, see Rodolfo (2011).
17. Oxoby (2004).
18. Cooper, Garcia-Penalosa and Funk (2001).
19. Liebow (1967).
20. Oxoby (2003).
21. Piketty (1998).
22. Corneo and Jeanne (1998; 2001).
23. Ireland (1998).
24. Shi (2003).
25. Etzioni (2004).
26. Swisher (1999: B1).
27. Etzioni (2004).
28. For evidence that many low-paying jobs are likely to vanish, see Rifkin (1996: 168).
29. For an endorsement of an engineer's culture in the place of an entrepreneurial culture, see Veblen (1899).
30. Frank (1999; 2007). For an overview of the arguments of the advocates of a progressive consumption tax, see Seidman (1997).
31. On early supporters of cuts on excessive positional consumption, see Hobbes (1958), quoted by Seidman (1997: 12); and Fisher and Fisher (1942: 3–6), quoted by Seidman (1997: 14).
32. Seidman and Lewis (1996; 1997).
33. Mason (2000).
34. Van Kempen (2003).
35. On the incentive effect, see Gale, Engen and Scholz (1996).
36. For views of the advocates of a progressive consumption tax, see Slemrod (1990); Hubbard and Skinner (1996); Poterba, Venti and Wise (1996); Auerbach and Slemrod (1997). For Frank's analysis of a progressive consumption tax, see Frank (1999; 2007).
37. For a review of the support for a progressive consumption tax, see Seidman (1997).
38. Bowles, Franzini and Pagano (1999).
39. Oxoby (2003).
40. Oxoby (2004).
41. Keynes (1936). For a discussion of the formation of conventional expectations and its relation to social influence, see Koutsobinas (2004).

42. Alesina and Rodrik (1992).
43. Decker, Stiehler and Strobel (2003).
44. Michaels (1998).
45. On the relation between techno-economic institutions, political party policies and ideology, see Castells (1996).
46. Sztompka (1993: 114); for further discussion of the relation of a possible imposition of progressive consumption tax with regulation and new social norms, see Koutsobinas (2005).
47. Thaler and Sunstein (2008).

CHAPTER 9   THE POLITICAL ECONOMY OF STATUS AND CULTURE CHANGE POLICY

1. Casson (2002); Nooteboom (2002b).
2. Mant (1983).
3. Nooteboom (2002a).
4. Casson (2002).
5. Nooteboom (2002b).
6. Shackle (1968).
7. Nooteboom (2002b).
8. Gambetta (1988); Castelfranchi and Falcone (2000).
9. Uchida, Norasakkunkit and Kitayama (2004).
10. Snibbe et al. (2003); Heine, Kitayama and Lehman (2001).
11. Oishi and Diener (2001).
12. Seyfang (2004).
13. An example is the fuel duty in the UK for Knott, Muyers and Aldridge (2008).
14. Knott, Muyers and Aldridge (2008).
15. Giddens (1984; 1987b).
16. Knott, Muyers and Aldridge (2008).
17. Heine, Kitayama and Lehman (2001); Snibbe et al. (2003).
18. See Bagozzi, Gürnao-Canli and Priester (2002); Maio et al. (2007).
19. For an extensive review of behavioural change models and their uses in policy, see Darnton (2008). For specific approaches such as the needs, opportunities and abilities model, see Gatersleben and Vlek (1998); for intervention mapping, see Bartholomew, Parcel and Kok (1998); for 4E model, see Defra (2008); for principles-based models, see Gardner and Stern (1996); for the cultural capital framework, see Knott, Muyers and Aldridge (2008).
20. Knott, Muyers and Aldridge (2008).

21. The public policies proposed by Frank (1999; 2007) are horizontal in nature.
22. Galbraith (2007). For an assessment of the influence of Galbraith's work, see Earl (2005).

References

Ackerman, B. and A. Alstott (1999), *The Stakeholder Society*, New Haven, CT: Yale University Press.

Adler, M. (1985), 'Stardom and talent', *American Economic Review*, **75** (1), 208–12.

Ahuvia, A.C. and N.Y. Wong (2002), 'Personality and values based materialism: their relationship and origins', *Journal of Consumer Psychology*, **12** (4), 389–402.

Ait-Sahalia, Y., J.A. Parker and M. Yogo (2004), 'Luxury goods and the equity premium', *Journal of Finance*, **59** (6), 2959–3004.

Aizcorbe, A.M., A.B. Kennickell and K.B. Moore (2003), 'Recent changes in U.S. family finances: evidence from the 1998 and 2001 Survey of Consumer Finances', *Federal Reserve Bulletin*, **89**, 1–32.

Alchian, A.A. and W.R. Allen (1983), *Exchange and Production: Competition, Coordination, and Control*, 3rd edn, Belmont, CA: Wadsworth.

Alesina, A. and D. Rodrik (1992), 'Distribution, political conflict, and economic growth: a simple theory and some empirical evidence', in A. Cuckierman, Z. Hercowitz and L. Leiderman (eds), *Political Economy, Growth, and Business Cycles*, Cambridge, MA: MIT Press, pp. 23–50.

Alesina, A., R. di Tella and R. MacCulloch (2004), 'Happiness and inequality: are Europeans and Americans different', *Journal of Public Economics*, **88** (9), 2009–42.

Alloy, L.B. and L.Y. Abramson (1979), 'Judgment of contingency in depressed and non-depressed students: sadder but wiser?', *Journal of Experimental Psychology*, **108** (4), 441–85.

Alpizar, F., F. Carlsson and O. Johansson-Stenman (2005), 'How much do we care about absolute versus relative income and consumption', *Journal of Economic Behavior and Organization*, **56** (3), 405–21.

Amaldoss, W. and J. Jain (2005), 'Conspicuous consumption and sophisticated thinking', *Management Science*, **51** (10), 1449–66.

Amendola, M.P., P. Cohendet and P. Llerena (1989), *Flexibilite, Information et Decision*, Paris: Editions Economica.

Anderson, C.A., M.R. Lepper and L. Ross (1980), 'Perseverance of social theories: the role of explanation in the persistence of discredited information', *Journal of Personality and Social Psychology*, **39** (6), 1037–49.

Ang, I. (1985), *Watching Dallas: Soap Opera and the Melodramatic Imagination*, London: Methuen.

Argo, J.J., K. White and D.W. Dahl (2006), 'Social comparison theory and deception in the interpersonal exchange of consumption information', *Journal of Consumer Research*, **33** (1), 99–108.

Aristotle (1998), *The Nicomachean Ethics*, trans. D. Ross (revised by J.L. Ackrill and J.O. Urmson), Oxford: Oxford University Press.

Aronson, E. (1969), 'The theory of cognitive dissonance: a current perspective', *Advances in Experimental Social Psychology*, **4**, 1–34.

Aronson, E. (2007), *The Social Animal*, 10th edn, London: Palgrave Macmillan.

Aronson, E. and J.M. Carlsmith (1963), 'Effect of the severity of threat on the devaluation of a forbidden behavior', *Journal of Abnormal and Social Psychology*, **66** (6), 584–8.

Aronson, E. and J. Mills (1959), 'The effect of severity of initiation on liking for a group', *Journal of Abnormal and Social Psychology*, **59** (2), 177–81.

Aronson, E., B. Willerman and J. Floyd (1966), 'The effect of a pratfall on increasing interpersonal attractiveness', *Psychonomic Science*, **4** (6), 227–8.

Aronson, E., T. Chase, R. Helmreich and R. Ruhnke (1974), 'Feeling stupid and feeling guilty – two aspects of the self-concept which mediate dissonance arousal in a communication situation', *International Journal of Communication Research*, **3**, 340–52.

Atkinson, A.B. (2004), 'Income tax and top income over the twentieth century', *Revista de Economia Publica*, **168** (1), 123–41.

Auerbach, A.J. and J. Slemrod (1997), 'The economic effects of the tax reform act of 1986', *Journal of Economic Literature*, **35** (2), 589–632.

Babcock, L., X. Wang and G. Lowenstein (1996), 'Choosing the wrong pond: social comparisons in negotiations that reflect a self-serving bias', *Quarterly Journal of Economics*, **111** (1), 1–19.

Bagozzi, R., Z. Gürnao-Canli and J. Priester (2002), *The Social Psychology of Consumer Behaviour*, Buckingham: Open University Press.

Bailey, P. (1986), *Music Hall: The Business of Pleasure*, Milton Keynes: Open University Press.

Bandura, A. (1977), 'Towards a unifying theory of behavioural change', *Psychological Review*, **84** (2), 191–215.

Banerjee, A. (1992), 'A simple model of herd behaviour', *Quarterly Journal of Economics*, **107**, 797–817.

Barkow, J.H. (1989), 'The transition from primate dominance to human self-esteem', *Darwin, Sex, and Status: Biological Approaches to Mind and Culture*, Toronto: University of Toronto Press, pp. 185–95.

Barthes, R. (1973), *Mythologies*, London: Paladin.

Barthes, R. (1975a), *S/Z*, trans. R. Miller, London: Cape.

Barthes, R. (1975b), *The Pleasure of the Text*, New York: Hill and Wang.

Bartholomew, K., G. Parcel and G. Kok (1998), 'Intervention mapping: a process for developing theory and evidence-based health education programs', *Health Education and Behavior*, **25**, 545–63.

Baudrillard, J. (1973 [1975]), *Le Miroir de la Production: ou l' Illusion Critique du Materialisme Historique*, Tournai: Casterman, reprinted in trans. M. Poster (1975), *The Mirror of Production*, St. Louis, MO: Telos Press.

Baudrillard, J. (1983a), *Simulations*, New York: Semiotext(e).

Baudrillard, J. (1983b), *In the Shadow of the Silent Majorities*, New York: Semiotext(e).

Bærenholdt, J.O. and M. Haldrup (2004), 'On the track of the Vikings', in M. Sheller and J. Urry (eds), *Tourism Mobilities: Places to Play, Places in Play*, London: Routledge, pp. 78–89.

Bærenholdt, J.O., M. Haldrup, J. Larsen and J. Urry (2004), *Performing Tourist Places*, Aldershot: Ashgate.

Bearden, W.O., D.M. Hardesty and R.L. Rose (2001), 'Consumer self-confidence: refinements in conceptualization and measurement', *Journal of Consumer Research*, **28** (1), 121–34.

Beauvois, J.L. and R.V. Joule (1996), *A Radical Theory of Dissonance*, London: Taylor and Francis.

Becker, G. (1976), *The Economic Approach to Human Behavior*, Chicago, IL: University of Chicago Press.

Becker, G.A. (1981), *A Treatise on the Family*, Cambridge, MA: Harvard University Press.

Bell, D. (1973), *The Coming of Post-Industrial Society*, New York: Basic Books.

Bell, D. (1976), *The Cultural Contradictions of Capitalism*, New York: Basic Books.

Bell, D. (1980a), 'Beyond modernism, beyond self', in D. Bell, *Winding Passage: Essays and Sociological Journeys, 1960–1980*, New York: Basic Books, pp. 275–302.

Bell, D. (1980b), 'The social framework of the information society', in T. Forester (ed.), *The Microelectronics Revolution*, Oxford: Blackwell, pp. 500–549.

Bem, D. (1965), 'An experimental analysis of self-persuasion', *Journal of Experimental Social Psychology*, **1** (3), 199–218.

Benabou, R. and J. Tirole (2000), 'Self-confidence: intrapersonal strategies', *Woodrow Wilson School Working Paper*, 209.

Benjamin J.D., P. Chinloy and G.D. Jud (2004), 'Real estate versus financial wealth in consumption', *The Journal of Real Estate Finance and Economics*, **29** (3), 341–54.

Benjamin, W. (1982), *Das Passagen-Werk*, R. Tiedermann (ed.), Frankfurt: Suhrkamp.

Benjamin, W. (2000), *The Arcades Project*, Cambridge, MA: Harvard University Press.

Bennett, T. (1988), 'The exhibitionary complex', *Culture/Power/History: A Reader in Contemporary Social Theory*, Oxford: Oxford University Press, pp. 127–40.

Benson, E.D., J.L. Hansen, A.L. Schwartz Jr and G.T. Smersh (1998), 'Pricing residential amenities: the value of a view', *The Journal of Real Estate Finance and Economics*, **16** (1), 55–73.

Berelson, B. and G.A. Steiner (1964), *Human Behaviour: An Inventory of Scientific Findings*, New York: Harcourt, Brace and World.

Berland, J. (2000), 'Cultural technologies and the "evolution" of technological cultures', in T. Swiss and A. Herman (eds), *The World Wide Web and Contemporary Cultural Theory*, New York: Routledge, pp. 235–58.

Berlyne, D.E. (1971), *Aesthetics and Psychology*, New York: Appleton-Century-Crofts.

Best, S. and D. Kellner (2001), *The Postmodern Adventure. Science Technology, and Cultural Studies at the Third Millennium*, New York and London: Guilford and Routledge.

Bettinger, C. (1991), *High Performance in the 1990's: Leading the Strategic and Cultural Revolution in Banking*, Homewood, IL: Business One Irwin.

Bikhchandani, S., D. Hirshleifer and I. Welch (1992), 'A theory of fads, fashion, custom, and cultural change as informational cascades', *Journal of Political Economy*, **100**, 992–1026.

Bikhchandani, S., D. Hirshleifer and I. Welch (1998), 'Learning from the behaviour of others: conformity, fads, and informational cascades', *Journal of Economic Perspectives*, **12** (3), 151–70.

Bisin, A. and T. Verdier (1998), 'On the cultural transmission of preferences for social status', *Journal of Public Economics*, **70** (1), 75–97.

Blaug, M. (1984), *The Methodology of Economics: or How Economists Explain*, New York: Cambridge University Press.

Bloch, F., V. Rao and S. Desai (2004), 'Wedding celebrations as conspicuous consumption signaling social status in rural India', *Journal of Human Resources*, **39** (3), 675–95.

Bolton, G.E. and A. Ockenfels (2000), 'ERC – a theory of equity, reciprocity and competition', *American Economic Review*, **90**, 166–93.

Boudon, R. (1973), *L'Inégalité des Chances, la mobilité sociale dans les sociétés industrielles,* Paris: Armand Colin.

Bourdieu, P. (1984), *Distinction: A Social Critique of the Judgment of Taste*, Cambridge, MA: Harvard University Press.

Bourdieu, P. (1987), 'The forms of capital', in J.G. Richardson (ed.), *Handbook of Theory and Research for the Sociology of Education*, New York: Greenwood Press, pp. 241–58.

Bourdieu, P. and J.C. Passeron (1990), *Reproduction in Education, Society and Culture*, 2nd edn, London: Sage.

Bowden, M. and S. McDonald (2008), 'The impact of interaction and social learning in aggregate expectations', *Computational Economics*, **31** (3), 289–306.

Bowles, S., M. Franzini and U. Pagano (1999), *The Politics and Economics of Power*, London: Routledge.

Boyett, J.H. and H.P. Conn (1991), *Workplace 2000: The Revolution Reshaping American Business*, New York: Dutton.

Brammer, G.I., M.J. Raleigh and M.T. McGuire (1994), 'Neurotransmitters and social status', in L. Ellis (ed.), *Social Stratification and Socioeconomic Inequality*, **2**, Westport, CT: Greenwood, pp. 75–91.

Braverman, H. (1974), *Labor and Monopoly Capital: The Degradation of Work in the Twentieth Century*, New York: New York Press.

Brekke, K.A., R.B. Howarth and K. Nyborg (2003), 'Status-seeking and material affluence: evaluating the Hirsch hypothesis', *Ecological Economics*, **45** (1), 29–39.

Bridge, G. (2001), 'Estate agents as interpreters of economic and cultural capital: the gentrification premium in the Sydney housing market', *International Journal of Urban and Regional Research*, **25** (1), 87–101.

Brown, D. and S. McIntosh (1998), 'If you're happy and you know it … job satisfaction in the low wage service sector', CEPDP 0405, Centre for Economic Performance, London School of Economics and Political Science.

Brown, M.E. (1987), 'The politics of soaps: pleasure and feminine empowerment', *Australian Journal of Cultural Studies*, **4** (2), 1–25.

Bruni, L. and L. Stanca (2008), 'Watching alone: relational goods, television and happiness', *Journal of Economic Behavior and Organization*, **65** (3), 506–28.

Brusco, S. (1982), 'The Emilian model: productive decentralisation and social integration', *Cambridge Journal of Economics*, **6** (2), 167–84.

Buchanan, J.M., R.D. Tollison and G. Tullock (eds) (1980), *Toward a Theory of the Rent-Seeking Society*, College Station, TX: Texas A&M University Press.

Buchowski, M. (2006), 'The specter of Orientalism in Europe: from exotic other to stigmatized brother', *Anthropological Quarterly*, **79** (3), 463–82.

Bukhtin, M.M. (1968), *Rabelais and His World*, Cambridge, MA: MIT Press.

Business Wire (1997), 'Credit card debt reaches all-time high among lower-income Americans', *Business Wire, Inc.*, 24 March.

Byrne, D. (1961), 'Interpersonal attraction and attitude similarity', *Journal of Abnormal and Social Psychology*, **62** (3), 713–15.

Campbell, C. (1987), *The Romantic Ethic and the Spirit of Modern Consumerism*, Oxford: Blackwell.

Canova, L., A.M. Manganelli Rattazzi and P. Webley (2005), 'The hierarchical structure of saving motive', *Journal of Economic Psychology*, **26** (1), 21–34.

Carroll, C.D. (2000), 'Why do the rich save so much', in J. Slemrod (ed.), *Does Atlas Shrug: The Economic Consequences of Taxing the Rich*, Cambridge, MA: Harvard University Press, pp. 467–84.

Cashmore, E. (2006), *Celebrity Culture*, New York: Routledge.

Casson, M. (2002), 'Leadership and cultural change: an economic analysis', *De Economist*, **150** (4), 409–38.

Castelfranchi, C. and R. Falcone (2000), 'Trust is much more than subjective probability: mental components and sources of trust', in *System Sciences, Proceedings of the 33rd Annual Hawaii International Conference on IEEE*, pp. 1–10.

Castells, M. (1996), *The Rise of Network Society*, Boston, MA: Blackwell.

Chaney, D. (1983), 'The department store as a cultural form', *Theory, Culture and Society*, **1** (3), 22–31.

Chang, W.Y. and H.F. Tsai (2003), 'Money, social status, and capital accumulation in a cash-in-advance model: a comment', *Journal of Money, Credit and Banking*, **35** (4), 657–61.

Chapman, I.J. and J.P. Chapman (1967), 'Genesis of popular but erroneous psychodiagnostic observations', *Journal of Abnormal Psychology*, **72** (3), 193–204.

Clark, R.C. and I.J. Horstmann (2005), 'Advertising and coordination in markets with consumption scale effects', *Journal of Economics and Management Strategy*, **14** (2), 377–401.

Cole, J.R. and S. Cole (1973), *Social Stratification in Science*, Chicago, IL: University of Chicago Press.

Congleton, R. (1980), 'Competitive process, competitive waste, and institutions', in J.M. Buchanan, R.D. Tollison and G. Tullock (eds), *Toward a Theory of the Rent-Seeking Society*, College Station, TX: Texas A&M Press, pp. 153–79.

Connor, S. (1997), *Postmodernist Culture: An Introduction to Theories of Contemporary*, Oxford: Blackwell.

Cooper, B., C. Garcia-Penalosa and P. Funk (2001), 'Status effects and negative utility growth', *Economic Journal*, **111** (473), 642–65.

Coriat, B. (1990), *L'Atelier et le Robot*, Paris: Christian Bourgois.

Corneo, G. and O. Jeanne (1998), 'Social organization, status, and savings behaviour', *Journal of Public Economics*, **70** (1), 37–51.

Corneo, G. and O. Jeanne (2001), 'Status, the distribution of wealth, and growth', *Scandinavian Journal of Economics*, **103** (2), 283–93.

Cosmides, L. and J. Tooby (1987), 'From the evolution to behavior: evolutionary psychology as the missing link', in J. Dupre (ed.), *The Latest on the Best: Essays on Evolution and Optimality*, Cambridge, MA: MIT Press, pp. 207–306.

Cowan, R., W. Cowan and P. Swann (2004), 'Waves in consumption with interdependence among consumers', *Canadian Journal of Economics*, **37** (1), 149–77.

Crane, D. (1987), *The Transformation of the Avant-Garde: The New York Art World 1940–1985*, Chicago, IL: University of Chicago Press.

Crocker, J. and R. Luhtanen (1990), 'Collective self-esteem and ingroup bias', *Journal of Personality and Social Psychology*, **58** (1), 60–67.

Crosby, F. (1976), 'A model of egoistical relative deprivation', *Psychological Review*, **83** (2), 85–113.

Dahlbäck, O. (1990), 'The social value of risk-taking', *European Journal of Social Psychology*, **20** (6), 531–5.

Damasio, A. (1994), *Desccartes' Error: Emotion, Reason, and the Human Brain*, New York: G.P. Putnam and Sons.

Daniels, P.W. (1993), *Service Industries in the World Economy*, Oxford: Blackwell.

Darnton, A. (2008), *GSR Behaviour Change Knowledge Review: Reference Report: An Overview of Behaviour Change Models and their Uses*, London, Centre for Sustainable Development, University of Westminster.

Davies, J. (1984), 'The Television Audience Revisited', paper presented at the Australian Screen Studies Association Conference, Brisbane.

De Tocqueville, A. (2001), *The Old Regime and the Revolution, Volume II: Notes on the French Revolution and Napoleon*, Chicago, IL: University of Chicago Press.

De Waal, F.B. (1996), *Good Natured: The Origins of Right and Wrong in Humans and Other Animals*, Cambridge, MA: Harvard University Press.

Dean, J.W., S.J. Yoon and G.I. Susman (1992), 'Advanced manufacturing technology and organization structure: empowerment or subordination?', *Organization Science*, **3** (2), 203–29.

Debord, G. (1995 [1967]), *The Society of the Spectacle*, trans. D. Nicholson-Smith, New York: Zone Press.

Decker, T., A. Stiehler and M. Strobel (2003), 'A comparison of punishment rules in repeated public good games: an experimental study', *Journal of Conflict Resolution*, **47** (6), 751–72.

Defra (2008), *A Framework for Pro-Environmental Behaviours: Annexes*, London: Defra.

Delre, S.A., W. Jager, T.H.A. Bijmolt and M.A. Janssen (2007), 'Targeting and timing promotional activities: an agent-based model for the takeoff of new products', *Journal of Business Research*, **60** (8), 826–35.

Didion, J. (1968), *Slouching Towards Bethlehem*, New York: Dell.

Diener, E. and R. Biswas-Diener (2002), 'Will money increase subjective well-being? A literature review and guide to needed research', *Social Indicators Research*, **57** (2), 119–69.

Diener, E. and R.E. Lucas (1998), 'Personality and subjective well-being', in D. Kahneman, E. Diener and N. Schwartz (eds), *Understanding Well-Being: Scientific Perspectives on Enjoyment and Suffering*, New York: Russell Sage.

DiMaggio, P. (1987), 'Classification in art', *American Sociological Review*, **52** (4), 440–55.

Dolfsma, W. (2004), 'Paradoxes of modernist consumption – reading fashions', *Review of Social Economy*, **62** (3), 351–64.

Douglas, M. and B. Isherwood (1980), *The World of Goods: Towards an Anthropology of Consumption*, Harmondsworth, UK: Penguin.

Dow, S.C. (1990), 'Post-Keynesianism as political economy: a methodological discussion', *Review of Political Economy*, **2** (3), 345–58.

Duesenberry, J.S. (1949), *Income, Saving, and the Theory of Consumer Behavior*, Cambridge: Harvard University Press.

Durham, Y., J. Hirshleifer and V. L. Smith (1998), 'Do the rich get richer and the poor poorer? Experimental tests of a model of power', *American Economic Review*, **88** (4), 970–83.

Dyer, R. (1985), 'Male sexuality in the media', in A. Metcalf and M. Humphries (eds), *The Sexuality of Men*, London: Pluto, pp. 28–43.

Dyer, R. (2004), *Heavenly Bodies: Film Stars and Society*, 2nd edn, London: Routledge.

Dyer, S. (2003), 'Markets in the meadows: department stores and shopping centres in decentralization of Philadelphia, 1920–1980', *Enterprise and Society*, **3** (4), 606–12.

Dynan, K.E., J. Skinner and S.P. Zeldes (2004), 'Do the rich save more', *Journal of Political Economy*, **112** (2), 397–444.

Earl, P.E. (1983), *The Economic Imagination: Towards a Behavioural Analysis of Choice*, Brighton, UK: Wheatsheaf Books.

Earl, P.E. (1986), *Lifestyle Economics: Consumer Behaviour in a Turbulent World*, New York: St. Martin's Press.

Earl, P.E. (2005), 'Economics and Psychology in the Twenty-First Century', *Cambridge Journal of Economics*, **29** (6), 909–26.

Eco, U. (1984), 'A Guide in the Neo Television of the 1980s', *Framework*, **25**, 18–25.

Eco, U. (1986), *Travels in Hyperreality*, trans. W. Weaver, San Diego, New York and London: Harcourt, Brace and Company.

Elias, M. (1981), 'Serum cortisol, testosterone, and testosterone-binding globulin responses to competitive fighting in human males', *Aggressive Behavior*, **7** (3), 215–24.

Elias, N. (1978), *The Civilizing Process, Vol. 1, The History of Manners*, Oxford: Basil Blackwell.

Elias, N. (1982), *The Civilizing Process, Vol. 2, State Formation and Civilization*, Oxford: Basil Blackwell.

Ellison, G. and D. Fudenberg (1995), 'Word-of-mouth communication and social learning', *Quarterly Journal of Economics*, **110** (1), 93–125.

Epstein, G.A. (ed.) (2005), *Financialization and the World Economy*, Cheltenham, UK and Northampton, MA, USA: Edward Elgar.

Etzioni, A. (1975), *A Comparative Analysis of Complex Organizations: On Power, Involvement, and their Correlates*, New York: The Free Press.

Etzioni, A. (1988), *The Moral Dimension: Toward a New Economics*, New York: The Free Press.

Etzioni, A. (1991a), 'Socio-economics: the next steps', in A. Etzioni and P.R. Lawrence (eds), *Socio-Economics Toward a New Synthesis*, New York: M.E. Sharpe, pp. 347–52.

Etzioni, A. (1991b), 'Contemporary liberals, communitarians and individual choices', in A. Etzioni and P.R. Lawrence (eds), *Socio-Economics Toward a New Synthesis*, New York: M.E. Sharpe, pp. 59–73.

Etzioni, A. (2004), 'The post affluent society', *Review of Social Economy*, **62** (3), 407–20.

Evans, G. (2003), 'Hard branding the cultural city – from Prado to Prada', *International Journal of Urban and Regional Research*, **27** (2), 417–40.

Farrell, J. and G. Saloner (1985), 'Standardization, compatibility, and innovation', *RAND Journal of Economics*, **16**, 70–83.

Faulkner, R.R. (1983), *Music on Demand: Composers and Careers in the Hollywood Film Industry*, New Brunswick, NJ: Transaction Books.

Faurschou, G. (1987), 'Fashion and the cultural logic of postmodernity', *Canadian Journal of Political and Social Theory*, **11** (1–2), 68–82.

Featherstone, M. (1991), *Consumer Culture and Postmodernism*, London: Sage.

Fehr, E. and S. Gächter (2000), 'Fairness and retaliation: the economics of reciprocity', *Journal of Economic Perspectives*, **14** (3), 159–81.

Fehr, E. and G. Kirchsteiger (1994), 'Insider power, wage discrimination, and fairness', *Economic Journal*, **104** (424), 571–83.

Fehr, E. and K.M. Schmidt (1999), 'A theory of fairness, competition, and cooperation', *Quarterly Journal of Economics*, **114** (3), 817–68.

Fehr, E., G. Kirchsteiger and A. Riedl (1993), 'Does fairness prevent market clearing? An experimental investigation', *Quarterly Journal of Economics*, **108** (2), 439–59.

Fernández, R. and J. Gali (1999), 'To each according to ...? Markets, tournaments and the matching problem with borrowing constraints', *Review of Economic Studies*, **66** (4), 799–824.

Festinger, L. (1954), 'A Theory of Social Comparison Processes', *Human Relations*, **7**, 117–40.

Festinger, L. (1957), *A Theory of Cognitive Dissonance*, Stanford, CA: Stanford University Press.

Feuer, J. (1986), 'Dynasty', paper presented to the International Television Studies Conference, London.

Fisher, I. (1930), *The Theory of Interest*, New York: Macmillan.

Fisher, I. and H.W. Fisher (1942), *Constructive Income Taxation: A Proposal for Reform*, New York: Harper and Brothers.

Fiske, J. (1987a), *Television Culture*, London and New York: Methuen.

Fiske, J. (1987b), 'British cultural studies', in R. Allen (ed.), *Channels of Discourse: Television and Contemporary Criticism*, Chapel Hill: University of North Carolina Press, pp. 254–89.

Fiske, J. (2004), *Reading Television*, London: Routledge.

Fiske, J. and J. Hartley (1978), *Reading Television*, London: Routledge.

Florida, R.L. (2002), *The Rise of the Creative Class: and How it's Transforming Work, Leisure, Community and Everyday Life*, New York: Basic Books.

Forester, T. (1987), *High-Tech Society: The Story of the Information Technology Revolution*, Oxford: Blackwell.

Forester, T. (1988), *The Materials Revolution*, Oxford: Blackwell.

Forester, T. (1989), *Computers in the Human Context*, Oxford: Blackwell.

Foucault, M. (1984), 'What is Enlightenment', in P. Rabinow (ed.), *The Foucault Reader*, Harmondsworth, UK: Penguin, pp. 32–50.

Frank, R.H. (1984), 'Interdependent preferences and the competitive wage structure', *RAND Journal of Economics*, **15** (4), 510–20.

Frank, R.H. (1985), *Choosing the Right Pond*, New York: Oxford University Press.

Frank, R.H. (1999), *Luxury Fever: Why Money Fails to Satisfy in an Era of Excess*, New York: Free Press.

Frank, R.H. (2007), *Falling Behind: How Rising Inequality Harms the Middle Class*, Berkeley, Los Angeles and London: University of California Press.

Frank, R.H. and P.J. Cook (1995), *The Winner-Take-All Society*, New York: The Free Press.

Frazer, B.S. and W.J. Brown (2002), 'Media, celebrities, and social influence: identification with Elvis Presley', *Mass Communication and Society*, **5** (2), 183–206.

Frey, B.S. (2000), 'Luxury is fun – but should be taxed', *Journal of Economic Methodology*, **7** (3), 447–8.

Frey, B.S. and I. Bohnet (1995), 'Institutions affect fairness: experimental investigations', *Journal of Institutional and Theoretical Economics*, **151**, 286–303.

Friedman, M. (1957), *A Theory of the Consumption Function*, Princeton, NJ: Princeton University Press.

Frijters, P. (1998), 'A model of fashions and status', *Economic Modelling*, **15** (4), 501–17.

Frisby, D. (1985), 'Georg Simmel, first sociologist of modernity', *Theory, Culture and Society*, **2** (3), 49–67.

Fukuyama, F. (1992), *The End of History and the Last Man*, London: Penguin Books.

Furnham, A. and H. Cheng (2000), 'Lay theories of happiness', *Journal of Happiness Studies*, **1** (2), 227–46.

Galbraith, J.K. (1967), *The New Industrial State*, Boston, MA: Houghton Mifflin.

Galbraith, J.K. (1979), *The Affluent Society*, 3rd edn, London: Penguin.

Galbraith, J.K. (1992), *The Culture of Contentment*, London: Penguin.

Gale, W., E. Engen and J. Scholz (1996), 'The illusory effects of saving incentives on savings', *Journal of Economic Perspectives*, **10** (4), 113–38.

Gambetta, D. (1988), 'Can we trust trust?', in P. Dasgupta and D. Gambetta (eds), *Trust: Making and Breaking Cooperative Relations*, Oxford: Blackwell, pp. 213–37.

Gamson, J. (1994), *Claims to Fame. Celebrity in Contemporary America*, Berkeley, Los Angeles and London: University of California Press.

Gardner, G.T. and P.C. Stern (1996), *Environmental Problems and Human Behavior*, Boston, MA: Allyn and Bacon.

Garnham, N. (1987), 'Concepts of culture: public policy and the cultural industries', *Cultural Studies*, **1** (1), 23–37.

Garnham, N. (2000), '"Information society" as theory or ideology', *Information, Communication and Society*, **3** (2), 139–52.

Garvey, G.T. and T.T. Milbourn (2006), 'Asymmetric benchmarking in compensation: executives are rewarded for good luck but not penalized for bad', *Journal of Financial Economics*, **82** (1), 197–225.

Gaspart, F. and E. Seki (2003), 'Cooperation, status seeking and competitive behaviour: theory and evidence', *Journal of Economic Behavior and Organization*, **51** (1), 51–77.

Gatersleben, B. and C. Vlek (1998), 'Household consumption, quality of life and environmental impacts', in K.J. Noorman and A.J.M. Schoot-Uiterkamp (eds), *Green Households? Domestic Consumers, Environment and Sustainability*, London: Earthscan, pp. 141–83.

George, D. (2001), *Preference Pollution: How Markets Create the Desires we Dislike*, Ann Arbor, MI: University of Michigan Press.

Giddens, A. (1984), *The Constitution of Society: Outline of the Theory of Structuration*, Berkeley, CA: University of California Press.

Giddens, A. (1987a), 'Nine theses on the future of sociology', in A. Giddens, *Social Theory and Modern Sociology*, Cambridge: Polity Press, pp. 22–51.

Giddens, A. (1987b), *A Contemporary Critique of Historical Materialism: The Nation-State and Violence*, **2**, Berkeley, CA: University of California Press.

Goeree, J.K. and C.A. Holt (2000), 'Asymmetric inequality aversion and noisy behaviour in alternating offer bargaining games', *European Economic Review*, **44** (4), 1079–89.

Goffman, E. (1951), 'Symbols of class status', *British Journal of Sociology*, **2** (4), 294–304.

Goode, W.J. (1978), *The Celebration of Heroes*, Berkeley, CA: University of California Press.

Grüner, H.P. (1995), 'Evolutionary stability of social norms in a socio-economic equilibrium model', *Constitutional Political Economy*, **6** (3), 233–45.

Gurr, T. (1970), *Why Men Rebel*, Princeton: Princeton University Press.

Güth, W., P. Ockenfels and M. Wendel (1993), 'Efficiency by trust in fairness? Multiperiod ultimatum bargaining experiments with an increasing cake', *International Journal of Game Theory*, **22** (1), 51–73.

Güth, W., R. Schmittberger and B. Schwarze (1982), 'An experimental analysis of ultimatum bargaining', *Journal of Economic Behavior and Organization*, **3** (4), 367–88.

Habermas, J. (1981), 'Modernity versus postmodernity', *New German Critique: An Interdisciplinary Journal of German Studies*, **22**, 3–14.

Hacker, J.S. (2006), *The Great Risk Shift: The Assault on American Jobs, Families, Health Care, and Retirement and How You Can Fight Back*, New York: Oxford University Press.

Haldrup, M. and J. Larsen (2003), 'The family gaze', *Tourist Studies*, **3** (1), 23–46.

Halualani, R.T. (2002), *In the Name of Hawaiians: Native Identities and Cultural Politics*, Minneapolis, MN: University of Minnesota Press.

Hammond, K.R., G.H. McClelland and J. Mumpower (1980), *Human Judgment and Decision Making: Theories, Methods, and Procedures*, New York: Praeger.

Hanley, A. and M.S. Wilhelm (1992), 'Compulsive buying: an exploration into self-esteem and money attitudes', *Journal of Economic Psychology*, **13** (1), 5–18.

Hartfield, E., G.W. Walster and E. Berscheid (1978), *Equity: Theory and Research*, Boston, MA: Allyn and Bacon.

Hartley, J. (1982), *Understanding News*, London: Methuen.

Hartley, J. (1983), 'Television and the power of dirt', *Australian Journal of Cultural Studies*, **1** (2), 62–82.

Hartog, J. (2002), 'Desperately seeking structure: Sherwin Rosen (1938–2001)', *Economic Journal*, **112** (483), 519–31.

Harvey, D. (1989), *The Condition of Postmodernity: An Enquiry Into the Origins of Social Change*, Oxford: Blackwell.

Hassan, I. (1985), 'The culture of postmodernism', *Theory, Culture and Society*, **2** (3), 119–31.

Heffetz, O. and R.H. Frank (2008), 'Preferences for status: evidence and economic implications', *Handbook of Social Economics*, **1**, 69–91.

Hegel, G.W.F. (1942), *Hegel's Philosophy of Right*, trans. with notes by T.M. Knox (ed.), Oxford: Clarendon.

Hegel, G.W.F. (1967), *The Phenomenology of Mind*, trans. J.B. Baillie, New York: Harper and Row.

Heilbroner, R. (1995), *Visions of the Future: The Distant Past, Yesterday, Today, Tomorrow*, New York: Oxford University Press.

Heine, S.J., S. Kitayama and D.R. Lehman (2001), 'Cultural differences in self-evaluation: Japanese readily accept negative self-relevant information', *Journal of Cross-Cultural Psychology*, **32** (4), 434–43.

Hirsch, F. (1976), *The Social Limits to Growth*, Cambridge, MA: Harvard University Press.

Hirschman, A.O. (1977), *The Passions and the Interests: Political Arguments for Capitalism Before its Triumph*, Princeton, NJ: Princeton University Press.

Ho, T.H., C. Camerer and K. Weigelt (1998), 'Iterated dominance and iterated best response in experimental "P-beauty contests"', *American Economic Review*, **88** (4), 947–69.

Hobbes, T. (1958), *Leviathan, Parts I and II*, Indianapolis, IN: Bobbs-Merrill.

Hobson, D. (1980), 'Housewives and the mass media', in S. Hall, D. Hobson, A. Lowe and P. Willis (eds), *Culture, Media, Language*, London: Hutchinson, pp. 105–14.

Hobson, D. (1982), *Crossroads: The Drama of a Soap Opera*, London: Methuen.

Hobson, D. (2003), *Soap Opera*, Cambridge: Polity Press.

Hoffner, C.A., K.J. Levine, Q.E. Sullivan, D. Crowell, L. Pedrick and P. Berndt (2006), 'TV Characters at work: television as role in the occupational aspirations of economically disadvantaged youths', *Journal of Career Development*, **33** (1), 3–18.

Holsti, O.R. (1971), 'Crisis, stress, and decision-making', *International Social Science Journal*, **23**, 53–67.

Hopkins, E. (2008), 'Inequality, happiness and relative concerns: what actually is their relationship?', *Journal of Economic Inequality*, **6** (4), 351–72.

Hopkins, E. and T. Kornienko (2004), 'Running to keep in the same place: consumer choice as a game of status', *American Economic Review*, **94** (4), 1085–107.

Horkheimer, M. and T. Adorno (1997), *Dialectic of Enlightenment*, New York: Verso.

Hubbard, R.G. and J.S. Skinner (1996), 'Assessing the effectiveness of savings incentives', *Journal of Economic Perspectives*, **10** (4), 73–90.

Huey, J. (1993), 'How McKinsey does it', *Fortune*, **128** (11), 56–81.

Huyssen, A. (1984), 'Mapping the postmodern', *New German Critique*, **33**, 5–52.

Ireland, N.J. (1998), 'Status-seeking, income taxation, and efficiency', *Journal of Public Economics,* **70** (1), 99–113.

Jacobs, J.A. and K. Green (1998), 'Who are the overworked Americans', *Review of Social Economy*, **56** (4), 442–59.

Jameson, F. (1979), 'Reification and utopia in mass culture', *Social Text*, **1**, 130–48.

Jameson, F. (1981), *The Political Unconscious: Narrative as a Socially Symbolic Act*, Ithaca, NY: Cornell University Press.

Jameson, F. (1984a), 'Postmodernism: or the cultural logic of late capitalism', *New Left Review*, **146**, 53–92.

Jameson, F. (1984b), 'Postmodernism and the consumer society', in H. Foster (ed.), *Postmodern Culture*, London: Pluto Press, pp. 111–25.

Jameson, F. (1984c), 'Foreword', in J.F. Lyotard (ed.), *The Postmodern Condition: A Report on Knowledge*, trans. G. Bennington and B. Massumi, Minneapolis, MN: University of Minnesota Press and Manchester, UK: University of Manchester Press, pp. vii–xxi.

Jameson, F. (1991), *Postmodernism, or, The Cultural Logic of Late Capitalism*, Durham, NC: Duke University Press.

Jameson, F. (1994), *The Seeds of Time*, New York: Columbia University Press.

Jameson, F. (2005), *Archaeologies of the Future: The Desire Called Utopia and Other Science Fictions*, London and New York: Verso.

Jaramillo, F., H. Kempf and F. Moizeau (2003), 'Inequality and club formation', *Journal of Public Economics*, **87** (5), 931–55.

Johansson-Stenman, O., F. Carlsson and D. Daruvala (2002), 'Measuring future grandparents preferences for equality and relative standing', *Economic Journal*, **112** (479), 362–83.

Johnson, P., D. Levine and W. Pesendorfer (2001), 'Evolution and information in a gift-giving game', *Journal of Economic Theory*, **100** (1), 1–21.

Jones, E.E. and R.E. Nisbett (1971), 'The actor and the observer: divergent perceptions of the causes of behavior', in E.E. Jones, D. Kanouse, H.H. Kelley, R.E. Nisbett, S. Valins and B. Weiner (eds), *Attribution: Perceiving the Causes of Behavior*, Morristown, NJ: General Learning Press, pp. 79–94.

Juster, F.T., P.N. Courant and G.K. Dow (1981), 'A theoretical framework for the measurement of well-being', *Review of Income and Wealth*, **27** (1), 1–31.

Juster, F.T., P.N. Courant and G.K. Dow (1985), 'A conceptual framework for the analysis of time-allocation data', in F.T. Juster and F.P. Stafford, *Time, Goods and Well-Being*, Ann Arbor, MI: Survey Research Center, Institute for Social Research, University of Michigan, pp. 113–31.

Kahn, L.M. and J.K. Murnighan (1993), 'A general experiment on bargaining in demand games with outside options', *American Economic Review*, **83**, 1260–80.

Kahneman, D. and A. Tversky (1973), 'On the psychology of prediction', *Psychological Review*, **80** (4) 237–51.

Kahneman, D. and A. Tversky (1982), 'The simulation heuristic', in D. Kahneman, P. Slovic and A. Tversky (eds), *Judgment Under Uncertainty: Heuristics and Biases*, New York: Cambridge University Press, pp. 201–8.

Kahneman, D. and C.A. Varey (1990), 'Propensities and counterfactuals: the loser that almost won', *Journal of Personality and Social Psychology*, **59** (6), 1101–10.

Kahneman, D., J. Knetsch and R. Thaler (1986), 'Perceptions of unfairness: constraints on wealth-seeking', *American Economic Review*, **76**, 728–41.

Kaplan, E.A. (1986), 'History, spectator and gender address in music television', *Journal of Communication Inquiry*, **10** (1), 3–14.

Katz, E. and T. Liebes (1984), 'Once upon a time in Dallas', *Intermedia*, **12** (3), 28–32.

Katz, E. and T. Liebes (1985), 'Mutual aid in the decoding of Dallas: Preliminary notes from a cross-cultural study', in P. Drummond and R. Paterson (eds), *Television in Transition*, London: British Film Institute, pp. 187–98.

Katz, E., J.D. Peters and T. Liebes (2002), *Canonic Texts in Media Research: Are there Any? Should There Be? How about These*, Cambridge, UK: Polity Press.

Katz, M.L. and C. Shapiro (1985), 'Network Externalities, competition and compatibility', *American Economic Review*, **75** (3), 424–40.

Kawashima, N. (2006), 'Advertising agencies, media and consumer market: the changing quality of TV advertising in Japan', *Media, Culture and Society*, **28** (3), 393–410.

Kellner, D. (1987), 'Baudrillard, semiurgy and death', *Theory, Culture and Society*, **4** (1), 125–46.

Kellner, D. (2002), 'Theorizing globalization', *Sociological Theory*, **20** (3), 285–305.

Kellner, D. (2003), *Media Spectacle*, London and New York: Routledge.

Kellner, D. and S. Homer (2004), *Fredric Jameson: A Critical Reader*, Basingstoke, UK: Palgrave.

Kennedy, L.B. and M.R. Williams (2001), 'The past without the pain: the manufacture of nostalgia in Vietnam's tourist industry', in H.T. Hue-Tam (ed.), *The Country of Memory: Remaking the Past in Late Socialist Vietnam*, Berkeley, CA: University of California Press, pp. 135–63.

Keynes, J.M. (1931), 'Economic possibilities for our grandchildren', in J.M. Keynes, *Essays in Persuasion*, London: Macmillan, pp. 358–73.

Keynes, J.M. (1936), *The General Theory of Employment, Interest and Money*, New York: Harcourt and Brace and World, reprinted in D.E. Moggridge (ed.) (1973), *Collected Writings of J.M. Keynes*, VII, London: Macmillan.

Kingston, P.W. and J.C. Smart (1990), 'The economic pay-off of prestigious colleges', in P.W. Kingston and L.S. Lewis (eds), *The High-Status Track: Studies of Elite Schools and Stratification*, Albany, NY: State University of New York, pp. 147–74.

Kirshenblatt-Gimblett, B. (1998), *Destination Culture: Tourism, Museums, and Heritage*, Berkeley, CA: University of California Press.

Knott, D., S. Muyers and S. Aldridge (2008), *Achieving Culture Change: A Policy Framework*, A discussion paper by the Strategy Unit, London: Cabinet Office, Crown Copyright.

Kohler, M. (1977), 'Postmodernismus: ein begriffsgeschichichter überblick', *America Studies*, **22** (1), 8–18.

Konrad, A.M. and J. Pfeffer (1990), 'Do you get what you deserve? Factors affecting the relationship between productivity and pay', *Administrative Science Quarterly*, **35**, 258–85.

Kosicki, G. (1987), 'A test of the relative income hypothesis', *Southern Economic Journal*, **54** (2), 422–34.

Koutsobinas, T. (2004), 'The formation of conventional expectations in Keynesian fundamental uncertainty', *International Journal of Social Economics*, **31** (11/12), 1108–19.

Koutsobinas, T. (2005), 'The design of new policies in the global economy and society: the case of star markets and cultural change', *International Journal of Humanities*, **1**, 1567–79.

Koutsobinas, T. (2008), 'Cultural identification and economic preferences', *Journal of Interdisciplinary Social Sciences*, **3** (6), 115–20.

Kranzberg, M. (1985), 'The information age: evolution or revolution', in B.R. Guile (ed.), *Information Technologies and Social Transformation*, Washington, DC: National Academy of Engineering.

Kroker, A. (1985), 'Baudrillard's Marx', *Theory, Culture and Society*, **2** (3), 69–83.

Kroker, A. and D. Cook (1987), *The Postmodern Scene: Excremental Culture and Hyper-Aesthetics*, New York: St. Martin's Press.

Krugman, P. (1992a), 'The right, the rich, and the facts', *The American Prospect*, **3** (11), 19–31.

Krugman, P. (1992b), 'Disparity and despair', *U.S. News and World Report*, 23 March, pp. 54–5.

Krugman, P. (1994), *Peddling Prosperity*, New York: W.W. Norton.

Krugman, P. (1997), *Pop Internationalism*, Cambridge, MA: MIT Press.

Krugman, P. (2002), 'For richer', *New York Times Magazine*, 20 October.

Kumar, K. (1995), *From Post-Industrial to Post-Modern Society*, Oxford, UK and Cambridge, USA: Blackwell.

Kuttner, R. (1983), 'The declining middle', *The Atlantic*, 60–72.

Laclan, E. and C. Mouffe (1990), *Hegemony and Socialist Strategy: Towards a Radical Democratic Politics*, London and New York: Verso.

Langer, E. (1983), *The Psychology of Control*, Beverly Hills, CA: Sage.

Lash, S. (1988), 'Discourse or figure? Postmodernism as a regime of signification', *Theory, Culture and Society*, **5** (2–3), 311–36.

Lavoie, M. (1992), *Foundations of Post-Keynesian Economic Analysis*, Aldershot, UK and Brookfield, VT, USA: Edward Elgar.

Lawrence, P. (1991), 'Socioeconomics: A Grounded Perspective', in A. Etzioni and P. Lawrence (eds), *Socio-Economics Toward a New Synthesis*, New York: M.E. Sharpe.

Layard, R. (1980), 'Human satisfaction and public policy', *Economic Journal*, **90**, 737–50.

Lefebvre, H. (1978), *Einfuhrung in die Modernita*, Frankfurt: Suhrkamp.

Leiss, W. (1978), *The Limits to Satisfaction*, London: Marion Boyars.

LeVine, R.A. and D.T. Campbell (1972), *Ethnocentrism: Theories of Conflict, Ethnic Attitudes, and Group Behavior*, New York: Wiley and Sons.

Levy, F. and R.J. Murnane (1992), 'U.S. earnings levels and earnings inequality: a review or recent trends and proposed explanations', *Journal of Economic Literature*, **30** (3), 1333–81.

Liebow, E. (1967), *Tally's Corner*, Boston, MA: Little Brown.

Lippard, L.R. (1999), *On the Beaten Track: Tourism, Art and Place*, New York: The New Press.

Ljungqvist, L. and H. Uhlig (2000), 'Tax policy and aggregate demand management under catching up with the Joneses', *American Economic Review*, **90** (3), 356–66.

Loch, C.H., B.A. Huberman and S. Stout (2000), 'Status competition and performance in work groups', *Journal of Economic Behavior and Organization*, **43** (1), 35–55.

Lokshin, M. and M. Ravallion (2002), 'Rich and powerful?: Subjective power and welfare in Russia', *Journal of Economic Behavior and Organization*, **56** (2), 141–72.

Lukacs, G. (1971), *History and Class Consciousness*, trans. R. Livingstone, London: Merlin Press.

Lyotard, J.F. (1971), *Discours, Figure*, Paris: Klincksieck.

Lyotard, J.F. (1984), *The Postmodern Condition: A Report on Knowledge*, trans. G. Bennington and B. Massumi, Minneapolis, MN: University of Minnesota Press and Manchester, UK: University of Manchester Press.

MacCannell, D. (1989), *The Tourist: A New Theory of the Leisure Class*, New York: Schocken Books.

MacCannell, D. (2001), 'Remarks on the commodification of cultures', in V.L. Smith and M. Brent (eds), *Tourism Issues of the 21st Century*, New York: Cognizant Communication Corp., pp. 380–90.

MacDonald, G.M. (1988), 'The economics of rising stars', *American Economic Review*, **78** (1), 155–66.

Machiavelli, N. (1950), *The Prince and Discourses*, New York: Modern Library.

Madsen, D. (1994), 'Serotonin and social rank among human males', in R.D. Masters and M.T. McGuire (eds), *The Neurotransmitter Revolution: Serotonin, Social Behavior, and the Law*, Carbondale, IL: Southern Illinois University Press, pp. 146–58.

Maio, G., B. Verplanken, A. Manstead, W. Stroebe, C. Abraham, P. Sheeran and M. Conner (2007), 'Social psychological factors in lifestyle change and their relevance to policy', *Journal of Social Issues and Policy Review*, **1** (1), 99–137.

Maital, S. and S.L. Maital (1984), *Economic Games People Play*, New York: Basic Books.

Mandel, N., P.K. Petrova and R.B. Cialdini (2006), 'Images of success and the preference for luxury brands', *Journal of Consumer Psychology*, **16** (1), 57–69.

Mandell, E. (1975), *Late Capitalism*, London: Verso.

Mant, A. (1983), *Leaders We Deserve*, Oxford: M. Robertson and Company.

Marshall, A. (1947), *Principles of Economics*, 8th edn, London: Macmillan.

Martin, M.C. and P.E. Kennedy (1993), 'Advertising and social comparison: consequences for female preadolescents and adolescents', *Psychology and Marketing*, **10** (6), 513–30.

Marx, K. (2004), *Capital: A Critique of Political Economy*, Digireads. com Publishing.

Mason, R. (2000), 'Conspicuous consumption and the positional economy: policy and prescription since 1970', *Managerial and Decision Economics*, **21** (3–4), 123–32.

Masuda, Y. (1981), *The Information Society as Post-Industrial Society*, Bethesda, MD: World Future Society.

Maxcy, J. (2004), 'Motivating long-term employment contracts: risk management in major league baseball', *Managerial and Decision Economics*, **25** (2), 109–20.

Mazur, A. (1983), 'Physiology, dominance, and aggression in humans', in A.P. Goldstein (ed.), *Prevention and Control of Aggression*, New York: Pergamon Press, pp. 145–55.

Mazur, A. and T.A. Lamb (1980), 'Testosterone, status, and mood in human males', *Hormones and Behavior*, **14** (3), 236–46.

McGuire, M.T., M.J. Raleigh and G.L. Brammer (1982), 'Sociopharmacology', *Annual Review of Pharmacology and Toxicology*, **22** (1), 643–61.

McLaren, D. (2003), *Rethinking Tourism and Ecotravel*, Bloomfield, CT: Kumarian Press.

Mercer, C. (1983), 'A poverty of desire: pleasure and popular politics', in T. Bennett and J. Burin (eds), *Formations of Pleasure*, London: Routledge and Kegan Paul, pp. 84–100.

Merton, R. (1953), 'Reference group theory and social mobility', in R. Bendix and S.M. Lipset (eds), *Class, Status and Power*, New York: The Free Press, pp. 403–10.

Merton, R. (1968), 'The Matthew effect in science', *Science*, **159** (3810), 56–63.

Merton, R.K. (1988), 'The Matthew effect in science, II: cumulative advantage and the symbolism of intellectual property', *Isis*, **79** (4), 606–23.

Michaels, R.J. (1998), 'Addiction, compulsion, and the technology of consumption', *Economic Inquiry*, **26** (1), 75–88.

Miller, G.A. (1956), 'The magical number seven, plus or minus two: Some limits on our capacity for processing information', *Psychological Review*, **63** (2), 81–97.

Modigliani, F. and R. Brumberg (1955), 'Utility analysis and the consumption function: an interpretation of cross-section data', in K. Kurihara (ed.), *Post-Keynesian Economics*, London: Allen and Unwin, pp. 128–97.

Modleski, T. (1982), *Loving With a Vengeance: Mass Produced Fantasies for Women*, London: Methuen.

Moreland, R.L. and S.R. Beach (1992), 'Exposure effects in the classroom: the development of affinity among students', *Journal of Experimental Social Psychology*, **28** (3), 255–76.

Morley, D. (1986), *Family Television: Cultural Power and Domestic Leisure*, London: Comedia.

Morris, M. (1992), 'The man in the mirror: David Harvey's "Condition of Postmodernity"', *Theory, Culture and Society*, **9** (1), 253–79.

Moscovici, S. and M. Zavalloni (1969), 'The group as a polarizer of attitudes', *Journal of Personality and Social Psychology*, **12** (2), 125–35.

Mueller, D.C. (1986), 'Rational egoism versus adaptive egoism as fundamental postulate for a descriptive theory of human behavior', *Public Choice*, **51** (1), 3–23.

Mussweiler, T., S. Gabriel and G.V. Bodenhausen (2000), 'Shifting social identities as a strategy for deflecting threatening social comparisons', *Journal of Personality and Social Psychology*, **79** (3), 398–409.

Myers, D.G. and G.D. Bishop (1971), 'Enhancement of dominant attitudes in group discussion', *Journal of Personality and Social Psychology*, **20** (3), 386–96.

Myers, D.G. and E. Diener (1995), 'Who is happy', *Psychological Science*, **6** (1), 10–19.

Naisbitt, J. (1982), *Megatrends: Ten New Directions Transforming Our Lives*, New York: Warner Books.

Naisbitt, J. (1990), *Megatrends, 2000*, New York: Warner Books.

Negroponte, N. (1970), *The Architecture Machine: Towards a More Human Environment*, Cambridge, MA: MIT Press.

Neuman, W.R. (1991), *The Future of Mass Audience*, New York: Cambridge University Press.

Neumark, D. and A. Postlewaite (1998), 'Relative income concerns and the rise in married women's employment', *Journal of Public Economics*, **70** (1), 157–83.

Newcomb, T. (1961), *The Acquaintance Process*, New York: Holt, Rinehart and Winston.

Nietzsche, F. (1954), *The Portable Nietzche*, trans. W. Kaufmann, New York: Viking Press.

Nietzsche, F. (1966), *Beyond Good and Evil: Prelude of Philosophy of the Future*, trans. W. Kaufmann, New York: Vintage Books.

Nietzsche, F. (1967), *On the Genealogy of Morals and Ecce Homo*, trans. W. Kaufmann and R.J. Hollingdale, New York: Vintage Books.

Nietzsche, F. (1968), *The Will to Power*, trans. W. Kaufmann and R.J. Hollingdale, New York: Vintage Books.

Nisbett, R. and L. Ross (1980), *Human Inference: Strategies and Shortcomings of Social Judgment*, Englewood Cliffs, NJ: Prentice-Hall.

Nissel, M. (1984), 'Indicators of Human Betterment', in K.E. Boulding (ed.), *The Economics of Human Betterment*, London: Macmillan, pp. 15–35.

Nooteboom, B. (2002a), *Trust: Forms, Foundations, Functions, Failures, and Figures*, Cheltenham, UK and Northampton, MA, USA: Edward Elgar.

Nooteboom, B. (2002b), 'Discussion of leadership and cultural change: an economic analysis', *De Economist*, **150** (4), 439–52.

Nüesch, S. (2007), *The Economics of Superstars and Celebrities*, München: Gabler.

Nutt, P.C. (1984), 'Types of organizational decision processes', *Administrative Science Quarterly*, **29** (3), 414–50.

Nye, D. (1997), *Narratives and Spaces: Technology and the Construction of American Culture*, New York: Columbia University Press.

Oakes, P.J. and J.C. Turner (1980), 'Social categorization and intergroup behaviour: does minimal intergroup discrimination make social identity more positive?', *European Journal of Social Psychology*, **10** (3), 295–301.

Oishi, S. and E. Diener (2001), 'Goals, culture, and subjective well-being', *Personality and Social Psychology Bulletin*, **27** (12), 1674–82.

Okamura, J.Y. (1998), 'The illusion of paradise', in D.C. Gladney (ed.), *Making Majorities*, Palo Alto, CA: Stanford University Press, pp. 264–339.

Okun, A.M. (1975), *Equality and Efficiency: The Big Tradeoff*, Washington, DC: Brookings Institution Press.

O'Rourke, D. (1997), 'Beyond cannibal tours: tourists, modernity, and the other', in S. Yamahita, J.S. Eades and K. Din (eds), *Tourism and*

Cultural Development in Asia and Oceania, Bangi, Malaysia: Penerbit Univesity, pp. 32–47.

Oxoby, R.J. (2003), 'Attitudes and allocations: status, cognitive dissonance and the manipulation of attitudes', *Journal of Economic Behavior and Organization*, **52** (3), 365–85.

Oxoby, R.J. (2004), 'Cognitive dissonance, status and growth of the underclass', *Economic Journal*, **114** (498), 727–49.

Palley, T.I. (1998), *Plenty of Nothing: The Downsizing of the American Dream and the Case for Structural Keynesianism*, Princeton, NJ: Princeton University Press.

Palley, T.I. (2007), 'Financialization: what it is and why it matters', No. 525, Working Papers, The Levy Economics Institute.

Palley, T.I. (2013), 'Europe's crisis without end: the consequences of neoliberalism run amok', (No. 111-2013), IMK at the Hans Boeckler Foundation, Macroeconomic Policy Institute.

Parker, T. (1983), *Rules of Thumb*, Boston, MA: Houghton and Mifflin.

Pasinetti, L.L. (1981), *Structural Change and Economic Growth*, Cambridge, UK: Cambridge University Press.

Pesendorfer, W. (1995), 'Design innovations and fashion cycles', *American Economic Review*, **85** (4), 771–92.

Petty, R.E. and J.T. Cacioppo (1986), 'The elaboration likelihood model of persuasion', in L. Berkowitz (ed.), *Advances in Experimental Social Psychology*, **19**, New York: Academic Press, pp. 123–205.

Pieters, R.G.M. and W.F. van Raaij (1988), 'The role of affect in economic behaviour', in W.F. van Raaij, G.M. van Veldhoven and K.E. Warneryd (eds), *Handbook of Economic Psychology*, Netherlands: Springer, pp. 108–42.

Piketty, T. (1995), 'Social mobility and redistributive politics', *Quarterly Journal of Economics*, **110** (3), 551–85.

Piketty, T. (1998), 'Self-fulfilling beliefs about social status', *Journal of Public Economics*, **70** (1), 115–32.

Piketty, T. (2014), *Capital in the Twenty-first Century*, Cambridge, MA: Harvard University Press.

Piketty, T. and E. Saez (2003), 'Income inequality in the United States, 1913–1998', *Quarterly Journal of Economics*, **118** (1), 1–39.

Pingle, M. and M. Mitchell (2002), 'What motivates positional concerns for income', *Journal of Economic Psychology*, **23** (1), 127–48.

Piore, M.J. and Sabel, C.F. (1984), *The Second Industrial Divide: Possibilities for Prosperity*, New York: Basic Books.

Plato (1968), *The Republic of Plato*, trans. A. Bloom, New York: Basic Books.

Podolny, J. (1993), 'A status-based model of market competition', *American Journal of Sociology*, **98**, 829–72.

Poterba, J.M., S. Venti and D. Wise (1996), 'How retirement saving programs increase savings', *Journal of Economic Perspectives*, **10** (4), 91–112.

Puchalska, B. (1999), 'Structuring of identities in relation to material possessions in Poland of the 1990s: issues of policy, culture, and individual life-worlds', *Journal of Law and Society*, **26** (4), 449–69.

Rao, V. (2001), 'Celebrations as social investments: festival expenditures, unit price variation and social status in rural India', *Journal of Development Studies*, **38** (1), 71–97.

Rees, A. (1993), 'The role of fairness in wage determination', *Journal of Labor Economics*, **11** (1), 243–52.

Rees, T. (1992), *Skill Shortages, Women, and the New Information Technologies*, Luxembourg: Office for Official Publications of the European Communities.

Ricardo, D. (1891), *Principles of Political Economy and Taxation*, London: G. Bell and Sons.

Rifkin, J. (1996), *The End of Work: The Decline of the Global Labor Force and the Dawn of the Post-Market Era*, New York: Putnam.

Rodolfo, G.Z. (2011), *Society at a Glance-OECD Social Indicators*, Paris: OECD Publishing.

Roediger, D. and P. Foner (1989), *Our Own Time: A History of American Labor and the Working Day*, Westport, CT: Greenwood Press.

Rorty, R. (1989), *Contingency, Irony and Solidarity*, Cambridge, UK: Cambridge University Press.

Rorty, R. (1999), *Philosophy and Social Hope*, New York: Penguin.

Rosen, S. (1981), 'The economics of superstars', *American Economic Review*, **71** (5), 845–58.

Rosen, S. (1982), 'Authority, control and the distribution of earnings', *Bell Journal of Economics*, **13** (2), 311–23.

Rosen, S. (1984), 'The distribution of prizes in a match-play tournament with single eliminations', NBER Working Papers 1516, National Bureau of Economic Research, Inc.

Rosen, S. (1992), 'The market for lawyers', *Journal of Law and Economics*, **35** (2), 215–46.

Rosen, S. and D. Neal (1998), 'Theories of distribution of labor earnings', NBER Working Papers 6378, National Bureau of Economic Research, Inc.

Rosen, S. and A. Sanderson (2000), 'Labour markets in professional sports', NBER Working Papers 7573, National Bureau of Economic Research, Inc.

Ross, L., D. Green and P. House (1977), 'The "false-consensus" effect: an egocentric bias in social perception and attribution processes', *Journal of Experimental Social Psychology*, **13** (3), 279–301.

Rousseau, J.J. (1964), *Oeuvres Completes*, **4**, Paris: Editions Gallimard.
Ruffle, B.J. (1999), 'Gift giving with emotions', *Journal of Economic Behavior and Organization*, **39** (4), 399–420.
Sabbah, F. (1985), 'The new media', in M. Castells (ed.), *High Technology, Space, and Society*, Beverly Hills, CA: Sage, pp. 10–25.
Sabini, J. and M. Silver (1982), *Moralities of Everyday Life*, New York: Oxford University Press.
Schiller, D. (1999), 'Introduction' and 'The neoliberal networking drive originates in the United States', in D. Schiller (1999), *Digital Capitalism: Networking the Global Market System*, Cambridge: MIT Press, pp. xiii–xvii and 1–36.
Schiller, F. (1967), 'Letters on the aesthetic education of man', in M. De Montaigne and C.A. Sainte-Beuve (eds), *Literary and Philosophical Essays: French, German, and Italian*, New York, NY: Cosimo, Inc., pp. 221–322.
Schlesinger, A.M. (1958), *The Age of Roosevelt, The Coming of the New Deal*, **2**, Boston, MA: Houghton Mifflin.
Schor, J. (1991), *The Overworked American: The Unexpected Decline of Leisure*, New York: Basic Books.
Schwartz, J. (1991), 'The moral environment of the poor', *The Public Interest*, **103**, 21–37.
Sconce, J. (2000), *Haunted Media: Electronic Presence From Telegraphy to Television*, Durham, NC: Duke University Press.
Scott, A.I. (2000), *The Cultural Economy of Cities: Essays on the Geography of Image-Producing Industries*, London: Sage.
Seidlitz, L. and E. Diener (1993), 'Memory for positive versus negative life events: theories for the differences between happy and unhappy persons', *Journal of Personality and Social Psychology*, **64** (4), 654–64.
Seidman, L. (1997), *The USA Tax: A Progressive Consumption Tax*, Cambridge, MA: MIT Press.
Seidman, L.S. and K.A. Lewis (1996), *Transition Protections During Conversion to a Personal Consumption Tax*, University of Delaware, Department of Economics Working Paper.
Seidman, L.S. and K.A. Lewis (1997), 'The design of a tax rule for housing under a personal consumption tax', *Public Finance Quarterly*, **25** (1), 5–24.
Seiter, E., H. Borchers, G. Kreutzner and E.M. Warth (1987), 'Don't treat us like we're so stupid and naïve: towards an ethnography of soap opera viewers', in E. Seiter, H. Borchers, G. Kreutzner and E.M. Warth (eds), *Remote Control: Television, Audiences, and Cultural Power*, London: Routledge, pp. 223–47.

Seligman, M.E. (2011), *Learned Optimism: How to Change Your Mind and Your Life*, New York: Random House LLC.

Seligman, M.E. and M. Csikszentmihalyi (2000), 'Positive psychology: an introduction', *American Psychological Association*, **55** (1), 5–14.

Seyfang, G. (2004), 'Consuming values and contested cultures: a critical analysis of the UK Strategy for sustainable consumption and production', *Review of Social Economy*, **62** (3), 323–38.

Shackle, G.L.S. (1968), *Uncertainty in Economics and Other Reflections*, Cambridge: Cambridge University Press.

Sheehan, B. (2010), *The Economics of Abundance: Affluent Consumption and the Global Economy*, Cheltenham, UK and Northampton, MA, USA: Edward Elgar.

Sheller, M. and J. Urry (eds) (2004), *Tourism Motilities: Places to Play, Places in Play*, London: Routledge.

Shi, D. (2003), 'Early American simplicity: the Quaker ethic', in A. Etzioni (ed.), *Voluntary Simplicity: Responding to Consumer Culture*, Lanham, MD: Rowman and Littlefield Publishers.

Shields, R. (1990), '"The system of pleasure": Liminality and the carnivalesque in Brighton', *Theory, Culture and Society*, **7** (1), 39–72.

Simmel, G. (1978), *The Philosophy of Money*, trans. T. Bottomore and D. Frisby, London: Routledge and Kegan Paul.

Simon, H. (1978), 'Rationality as process and as product of thought', *American Economic Review*, **68** (2), 1–16.

Simon, H. (1979), 'Rational decision making in business organizations', *American Economic Review*, **69** (4), 493–513.

Simon, H. (1981), *The Sciences of the Artificial*, 2nd edn, Cambridge, MA: MIT Press.

Singer, J.L. and D.G. Singer (1980), 'Imaginative play in preschoolers. Some research and theoretical implications', in *Symposium on The Role of Pretend in Cognitive-Emotional Development*, American Psychological Association Annual Convention, Montreal.

Slemrod, J. (1990), 'The economic impact of the tax reform act of 1986', in J. Slemrod (ed.), *Do Taxes Matter? The Impact of the Tax Reform Act of 1986*, Cambridge, MA: MIT Press, pp. 1–12.

Smith, A. (1982 [1759]), *The Theory of Moral Sentiments*, Indianapolis, IN: Liberty Classics.

Snibbe, A.C., S. Kitayama, H.R. Markus and T. Suzuki (2003), 'They saw a game: a Japanese and American field study', *Journal of Cross-Cultural Psychology*, **34** (5), 581–95.

Solnick, S.J. and D. Hemenway (1998), 'Is more always better? A survey on positional concerns', *Journal of Economic Behavior and Organization*, **37** (3), 373–83.

Spigel, L. (2001), 'Outer space and inner cities: African American responses to NASA', in L. Spigel, *Welcome to the Dreamhouse: Popular Media and Postwar Suburbs*, Durham, NC: Duke University Press, pp. 141–82.

Stalybrass, P. and A. White (1986), *The Politics and Poetics of Transgression*, London: Methuen.

Stapel, D.A. and D.M. Marx (2007), 'Distinctiveness is key: how different types of self-other similarity moderate social comparison', *Personality and Social Psychology Bulletin*, **33** (3), 439–48.

Steiner, I.D. (1980), 'Attribution of choice', in M. Fishbein (ed.), *Progress of Social Psychology*, Hillsdale, NJ: Lawrence Erlbaum Associates.

Stephanson, A. (1987), 'Regarding postmodernism: a conversation with Fredric Jameson', *Social Text*, **17**, 29–54.

Stigler, G.J. and G.S. Becker (1977), 'De gustibus non est duspitandum', *American Economic Review*, **67** (2), 76–90.

Storey, L. and E. Dash (2009), 'Bankers reaped lavish bonuses during bailouts', *New York Times*, 31 July.

Stouffer, S.A., E.A. Suchman, L.C. DeVinney, S.A. Star and R.M. Williams (1949), *The American Soldier: Adjustments During Army Life*, **1**, Princeton, NJ: Princeton University Press.

Strack, F., L.L. Martin and S. Stepper (1988), 'Inhibiting and facilitating conditions of the human smile: a nonobtrusive test of the facial feedback hypothesis', *Journal of Personality and Social Psychology*, **54** (5), 768–77.

Strauss, L. (1952), *The Political Philosophy of Hobbes: Its Basis and Genesis*, trans. E. Sinclair, Chicago, IL: University of Chicago Press.

Strauss, L. (1963), *On Tyranny*, Ithaca, NY: Cornell University Press.

Sum, N.L. and B. Jessop (2013), *Towards a Cultural Political Economy*, Cheltenham, UK and Northampton, MA, USA: Edward Elgar.

Svenson, O. (1981), 'Are we all less risky and more skillful than our fellow drivers', *Acta Psychologica*, **47**, 143–8.

Swedberg, R. (1991), 'The new "battle of methods"', in A. Etzioni and P. Lawrence (eds), *Socio-Economics Toward a New Synthesis*, New York: M.E. Sharpe, pp. 13–33.

Swisher, K. (1999), 'Families: a couple with online connections', *The Wall Street Journal*, 6 January, B1.

Sztompka, P. (1993), *The Sociology of Social Change*, Oxford: Blackwell.

Tagg, J. (1985), 'Postmodernism and the born-again avant-garde', *Block II*, **2**, 3–7.

Tajfel, H. and J.C. Turner (1979), 'An integrative theory of inter-group conflict', in S. Worchel and W.G. Austin (eds), *The Social Psychology of Intergroup Relations*, Monterey, CA: Brooks-Cole, pp. 94–109.

Tatzel, M. (2003), 'The art of buying: coming to terms with money and materialism', *Journal of Happiness Studies*, **4** (4), 405–35.

Thaler, R. and H. Shefrin (1981), 'An economic theory of self-control', *Journal of Political Economy*, **89**, 392–405.

Thaler, R. and C.R. Sunstein (2008), *Nudge: Improving Decisions about Health, Wealth, and Happiness*, New Haven, CT: Yale University Press.

Tobin, J. (1970), 'On limiting the domain of inequality', *Journal of Law and Economics*, **13**, 263–77.

Toffler, A. (1970), *Future Shock*, New York: Random House.

Toffler, A. (1981), *The Third Wave*, New York: Bantam Books.

Torrance, E.P. (1954), 'The behavior of small groups under the stress conditions of "survival"', *American Sociological Review*, **19** (6), 751–5.

Trigg, A.B. (2001), 'Veblen, Bourdieu and conspicuous consumption', *Journal of Economic Issues*, **35** (1), 99–115.

Trigg, A.B. (2004), 'Deriving the Engel curve: Pierre Bourdieu and the social critique of Maslow's hierarchy of needs', *Review of Social Economy*, **62** (3), 393–406.

Tulloch, J. (2000), *Watching Television Audiences: Cultural Theories and Methods*, New York: Oxford University Press.

Tulloch, J. and A. Moran (1986), *A Country Practice: 'Quality Soap'*, Sydney: Currency Press.

Tversky, A. and D. Kahneman (1974), 'Judgment under uncertainty: heuristics and biases', *Science*, **185** (4157), 1124–31.

Tversky, A. and D. Kahneman (1991), 'Loss aversion and riskless choice', *Quarterly Journal of Economics*, **106** (4), 1039–61.

Twenge, J.M. and W.K. Campbell (2002), 'Self-esteem and socioeconomic status: a meta-analytic review', *Personality and Social Psychology Review*, **6** (1), 59–71.

Uchida, Y., V. Norasakkunkit and S. Kitayama (2004), 'Cultural constructions of happiness theory and empirical evidence', *Journal of Happiness Studies*, **5** (3), 223–39.

Urry, J. (1988), 'Cultural change and contemporary holiday-making', *Theory, Culture and Society*, **5** (1), 35–55.

Urry, J. (1995), *Consuming Places*, London: Routledge.

Urry, J. (2002), *The Tourist Gaze: Leisure and Travel in Contemporary Societies*, London: Sage.

Van Kempen, L. (2003), 'Fooling the eye of the beholder: deceptive status signaling among the poor in developing countries', *Journal of International Development*, **15**, 157–77.

Van Long, N. and K. Shimomura (2004), 'Relative wealth, status-seeking, and catching-up', *Journal of Economic Behavior and Organization*, **53** (4), 529–42.

Veblen, T. (1899), *The Theory of the Leisure Class*, New York: Macmillan.

Vivanco, L. (2000), 'Encountering the otherness of community and nature in a Costa Rican cloud forest reserve', in K. Hollinshead and C. de Burlo (eds), *Journeys into Otherness: The Representation of Difference and Identity in Tourism*, 27, Clevedon, UK: Channel View Publications, pp. 79–92.

Wallich, P. (1994), 'The workaholic economy', *Scientific American*, August, p. 77.

Ward, M. (2002), 'Does television exposure affect emerging adults' attitudes and assumptions about sexual relationships? Correlational and experimental confirmation', *Journal of Youth and Adolescence*, **31** (1), 1–15.

Weinraub, B. (1994), 'How a movie satire turned into reality', *New York Times*, 16 August, C15.

Wendner, R. (2003), 'Status, environmental externality, and optimal tax programs', *Economics Bulletin*, **8** (5), 1–10.

Williams, R.H. (1976), *Keywords*, London: Fontana.

Williams, R.H. (1982), *Dream Worlds: Mass Consumption in Late Nineteenth Century France*, Berkeley, CA: University of California Press.

Wright, J.W. and E.J. Dwyer (1990), *The American Almanac of Jobs and Salaries*, New York: Avon Books.

Wriston, W.B. (1992), *The Twilight of Sovereignty: How the Information Revolution Is Transforming Our World*, New York: Scribner's Sons.

Wuthnow, R. (1996), *Poor Richard's Principle: Rediscovering the American Dream Through the Moral Dimension of Work, Business, and Money*, Princeton, NJ: Princeton University Press.

Zajonc, R.B. (1968), 'Attitudinal effects of mere exposures', *Journal of Personality and Social Psychology*, **9** (2), 1–27.

Zink, C., Y. Tong, Q. Chen, D. Bassett, J. Stein and A. Meyer-Lindenberg (2008), 'Know your place: neural processing of social hierarchy in humans', *Neuron*, **58** (2), 273–83.

Zizzo, D.J. (1997), *Relativity-Sensitive Behavior in Economics: An Overview with New Experimental Evidence*, Doctoral Dissertation, University of Oxford.

Zuckert, C.H. (1988), 'On the role of spiritedness in politics', in C.H. Zuckert (ed.), *Understanding the Political Spirit: Philososophical Investigations From Socrates to Nietzsche*, New Haven, CT: Yale University Press.

Zukin, S. (1988), *Loft Living: Culture and Capital in Urban Change*, 2nd edn, London: Radius/Hutchinson.

Index

Abercrombie and Fitch 1
abuse 81
academics 16
accounting 160
accumulation 47
action 66
activities 36, 60–61, 67–8, 158
  context-dependent 60, 61, 65, 67–8
  leisure 68, 158
  positional 36, 81
  recreational 158
adaptation 3
  cognitive 80
addiction 104
adjustment 39
Adler, Moshe 10
advantage 37, 73
  competitive 37
  relative 3
advertisement 3, 27, 29 44, 89, 96,
    109–10
  messages 110
  political 107
Aegean islands 88
aesthetics 90
affect 59, 71, 169
affluence 17, 127
Affluent Society, The 185
agents 40–41
  dominant 40
  lower-class 78
aggressiveness 77
alcohol 74
alienation 104
allocation 82
ambition 89, 96, 107
ambivalence 82
analyst
  software 21

symbolic 21, 50, 51, 89
  system 11
anchoring 13
anomie 110, 169
antagonism 152
anthropology 10
antinomy 122
antithesis 141
apathy 132
applause 60
appreciation 69
arcade 88
archetype 110
architect 21, 164
architecture of social choice 164
aristocracy 153
art 88
art directors 21
art, high 89
artist 88
aspirations 40, 41, 71, 177
  feel-good 55
  want-it-all 55
asset demand 27
assistant 17
associations symbolic 7
ataraxia 72
Athens 114
athletes 40, 108
athletics 61
atruism 74
attention 53, 64
attitude change 150
attraction 94
attribute 98
attribution 66–7
attributional inference 66
audience 20, 33, 97
Austrian school 7

author 108
autonomy 31, 73, 90, 82
avant-garde 140
avenger 99
award 73

banker 17
   investment 17
barrier 89
Barthes, Roland 114
basketball player 20
Baudrilllard, Jean 8, 116, 117–19
bay 88
beach 61, 92
beauty 88
   contest 159
behaviour 4
   deviant 170
   and forces 4
   irrational 68
   low-class 149
   positional 63–5
   rational 3
behavioural economics 13, 124
beliefs 38, 76
   cultural 45
   manipulation 68
   self-fulfilling 37, 116
   traditional 52
   universal 53–6
believability 98
Bell, Daniel 117
benchmark 29
benefits 18, 167
Benetton 1
bet 159
betterment 148
bias 13, 58
   cognitive 13, 63, 64, 83
   subjective 58
biotechnology 21, 48
body 112
Bold and Beautiful 97
Bono, U2 39
bonus 56
books 4, 108
booms 55

boots 151
Boudon, Raymond 116
boundary 10, 90
Bourdieu, Pierre 8, 116, 177
brand clothing 1
branding 167
Branson, Richard 75
Brazil 180
broadness 89
bubbles 8
   financial 8
   speculative 39
Buffet, Warren 39

Cabinet office, 182
café 94
Canal Plus 32
capacity, cognitive 62
capital 18, 20
   educational 92
   industrial 18, 54
   physical 20, 50
capitalism 27, 126
   fragility 126
   late 27, 117–18, 121
   market 121
   monopoly 121
Capri 114
career 4, 16, 159
   choice 179
   corporate 151
   overambitious 79
Caribbean islands 1
cars 31, 148
cascades model 40
catwalk 114
cause, social 46
CBS 32
celebrations 24, 70
celebrities 4, 6, 101–2, 109, 51
CEO compensation 19
ceremonies 100
certainty 108
change 39, 53
   behavioural 39
   post-modern 122, 152
   social 53, 91

channel-jumping 100
channels, television 100
characters 98
  feminine 98, 102
choice, impulsive 157
choices occupational 101, 178
Chrysler 32
cigarette smoking 74
costs 7, 13, 32
Citibank 54
cities, inner 132
city 88, 134
class 1, 13, 53
  affluent 43
  bottom-tier 34
  conflict 34, 112
  creative 50, 89, 92
  leisure 126
  lower 35–7, 38
  managerial 20
  middle 43, 115, 129, 150, 160
  second 29
  upper 34–5, 37,1 29
  working 49, 92
classification schemes 113
classifier 114
clients 17
clothes 27
coach 108
Coca-Cola 32
cognition 66
cognitive dissonance 38, 66
cognitive limitations 62–3
collective action 147
comedians 108
comfortable 120, 151
comfortable, less 120
commentators 128
commercialism 47
commitments 81–2, 84
  moral 81
commodification 118–20
commodity fetishism 123
commodity-sign 120
common sense 98
communication 69, 113
communication ecstasy 113
communicative reason 133

comparison 5, 14, 103
  relative position 65, 72–3
  social 5, 29, 78–9
  see also relative position competition
compensation 18, 19, 43
competency 69
competition, relative position
  see also relative position competition
competition, social 6, 38
competitiveness 60
complacency 143
complaints 125
complexity 9, 25,48, 52,70
concerns positional 5, 85
concerts 61
conflict theory 76
congestion 146–7
  and inequality 146
connectedness 168
consumerism 27, 96, 113
consumers 13, 31
  bottom-tier 13, 42
  dissatisfied 27
  top-tier 3, 13, 42, 43
consumption 2–3, 19, 153–4, 170
  conspicuous 2, 19, 153
  luxury 3, 21, 91, 100, 145, 153
  of positional goods 41, 153–4, 170
  sustainable 147, 170
contented 148
contented majority 128
contentment 72, 136
contestants 159
contingency 140
conventions 97
conversations, 62–3
Cook, Philip 3
Cook, Scott 151
cosmopolitanism 116
credit 2, 150
crime 126
crisis 17, 46
  environmental 46
  financial 17, 54
Cross, Marcia 20
cues 40–42
cultural 12, 13, 119–20, 152
  differences 169

domination 119–20
  engineering 167
  events 108
  intermediaries 92
  logic 119
  norms 152
cultural capital 8, 34–5, 36, 115–16,
    181–4
Cultural capital framework 182–3
culturalization 12
cultural political economy 10–12
cultural theory 13
culture change 9, 11, 13, 121–2, 162–4,
    166
  behavioural models 181–4
  engineering 157
  and fiscal policy 184
  leadership 167–9
  policy 173–6, 182–3, 185–6
culture 12, 51
  corporate 130
  high 34, 90
  pop 88
  popular 33, 36, 47, 51, 89, 108
  post-modern 52, 117, 120
  pulsar 109
  of signification 100
  signifying 91, 119
  simulational 90
  societal 80
  symbolic 89–90
cybernetics 112
cyclicality 131

Dallas 98
  J.R. 98
daydreaming 33
De Onis, Federico 117
debt 83, 146
deception 24
decisions 17
  investment 7
default 164
demand, 10, 18
demarcation 27, 122
democracy 82, 107
democratization 51

demonstration 130
depression 127
deprivation 78–9, 149–50
  financial 145
  relative 7, 13, 58, 78–9, 81, 85,
    149–50, 169
derivatives 54
Derrida, Jacques 117
desire 29, 33, 67
destination 94
deterioration 148
dialectics 125
dialogue 99
differences, cross-cultural 78
disadvantaged 110
discomfort 38, 79, 80
discrimination 5, 38, 51, 58, 115, 133
  social 9, 27, 106, 111–14
  stereotypical 185
discussions 75
Disney 88
Disneyland 88
disorder 88
disposition 92
dissonance 66, 79, 83, 149
  reduction 110
distinction 5, 10, 15, 34, 41, 44, 92, 115
  cultural 34
  social 34–5
distress 3, 138
distribution 7, 15, 36, 38, 149–50,
    173–6
  of earnings 20
  equitable 160, 176–8
  of human capital 148–9
  of income 17, 49
  unequal 148
distributors 32
diversification 33
diversity 34, 49, 52
doctors 17
doers 81
domination
  cultural form of 129
  ideological 36
  social 42
down-shifters 151
dream worlds 88

drive 66
  aversive 66
  primal 108
drugs 79
Dynasty 107

earnings 18
  dispersion 20
  growth in 2, 17
  inequality 19
  polarization 18
  relative 22
eclectic approaches 14
ecological dangers 26–7
ecological destruction 25
ecological economics 147
ecology 26
economic man 80
economic micro-foundations 124
economies of scale 9, 16, 43
Economy 9, 11, 27, 121–2, 132
  culture 11
  ecstasy 8, 111
  editor 21
  positional 151
  of signs 112
education 18, 61, 178–83
  continuing 178
  and culture change, 178, 183
  system 35
  university 35
edutainment 88
effort 23, 37, 95
ego 91
  massaging 96
egoism 82–3
elections 96
electoral majority 131, 163
Ellen, Sue 98
employer 22, 24
employment 18, 55
emulation 15, 36
  status 42, 173
  strategy 79
  of superstars 39
endorsements 97
  celebrity 39

enforcement of law 152
England 157
Enlightenment 133
entitlement 78–9
entrepreneur 21, 119
entrepreneurialism 47
environment 26, 78
  human 56
  moral 38
envy 145, 170
equilibrium 7
equity 54, 83, 173
Equity theory 78
escapism 33, 36
esteem 80, 149
ethical totality 133
ethnicity 25
ethnography 94
Etzioni, Amitai 9
eudaimonia 72
Europe 95, 152
European social model 7, 174
European Union 163
Eurozone 130
Eurozone crisis 130, 132
excitement 87–8
exclusivity 41
executive 16, 20
executive room 69
exercise 73
exhibition 88
exotic place 1
expenditures 119
  military 120
exposure 61, 88
externality 81

Facebook 111
failure 1, 78
fame 59
family 95, 98
  lower-income 146
  obligations 146
famous 108
fans 102
fascination 91, 108
fashion 50, 87

cycle 40, 92
  emulation 145
  novelty 87, 91, 100
fashion leader 39, 42
fast food 74
fear 99
feedback 78
feel-good 33
feelings 78, 83, 87, 89
feminism 98, 120
film producers 32
films 108
finance 54
  equity 54
financial accumulation 135
financial crisis 131
financial instability 127
financialization 54–5
financier 17, 108
firms 70
  blue-chip 70
Fisher, Irving 26, 155
Florida 1, 114
fortune 170
Foucault, Michel 117
fractions 4
fragmentation 52, 111
France 17
Frank, Robert 3, 7, 13, 110, 153, 155,
    160
freedom 72
freedom of choice 132
freelance 49
free time 110
French revolution 133
frenzy 145
Freudian analysis 84
friends 6, 110
Friends 97, 98
frustration 27, 68, 73, 175
frustration-aggression theory 76
fusion 92

Galbraith, John Kenneth 7, 12, 13, 27,
    110, 129, 185
gambling 71
game theory 40–41

behavioural 40
  evolutionary 41
Gates, Bill 151
gender 75
  differences 76
generational escape 131
genetic messages 122
Geneva 130
genre 90
getaway 59
gift 24, 70
gift-giving 24
glitz 92
globalization 52, 54, 112, 130
God 136
goods
  brand-name 25
  counterfeit 25
  cultural 33, 107
  industrial 31
  luxury 153
  positional 15, 27, 59, 74
  public 29, 81–2, 159–60
  symbolic 31, 89
gossip 75
Gothenburg 130
gourmet 1
government 128
  intervention 128
  programmes 128
  regulation 130
graduates 16
gratification 116
Great Depression 131
Great Moderation 126
Great Recession 17, 126, 129, 132
Greece 134, 180
greed 136
Green book, HM Treasury 173
groups 154
  bottom-tier 150, 174
  dominant 5
  reference of 39
  social 39
  top-tier 6, 150
guilt 66–88
gym 69

Habermas, Jürgen 117
habit 12, 64, 74, 111
habituation 111
Habitus 8, 115–16
Hamptons 114
Hanks, Tom 75
happiness 71–2, 169
Harrods 91
Harvard 16, 25
health 25
Hegel, Georg Wilhelm Friedrich 132–3
Heidegger, Martin 137–41
Heilbroner, Robert 9
herding 40
hero 97
heroine 97
heterogeneity 122
heuristics 63–4
    adjustment 54
    anchoring 54
    availability 63
    theory of 78
hierarchy 19, 31, 35, 48, 115
hint 164
Hirsch, Fred 59
historicism 141
history 90
holiday 44, 59
holiday package 59
homogenization 33
house 31
Housewives 107
housing 19, 44
    low-cost 129
HSBC 54
human capital theory 19
human race 99
humanism 120
hyperreality 8, 90, 111–13, 126
    and popular culture 111–12
    signs of 90

icons 88
idealism 137–40
    German 137–8
identification 13, 74, 101–2, 108
    affective 13

automatic 13
    with celebrities 101–2
    party 82
    social 108
    with superstars 101–2
    of status role 74–5
    wishful 101
Identity 31, 45, 69, 86, 89, 92, 94
    imaginative 36
    post-modern 45
    social 36, 39, 94, 96–7, 104–5, 106
    and television 96–7
    virtual 105
identity signalling 44
ideological opposition 163
ideological struggle 121, 125
ideology 36
idol 41
idolization 145
illness 31
illusions 94
image 31, 75, 89, 91
    symbolic 85
imagery 88
imaginary 113, 118
imitation 40
immigration 127
impersonators 102
implication 97–8
incentives 19, 22, 23, 157
    financial 37
    non-monetary 71
    traditional 80
income 15, 18
    distribution of 126–8
    growth of 17, 160
    inequality 18, 107–8
    redistribution 36, 173–8
    relative 71
    transfer 160
India 180
individualism 27, 38, 48, 56, 132
individuality 38, 167
individuals 24, 92, 159
    high–status 92
    marginalized 104
    poor 24, 25
    post-modern 50

successful 97
young 159
industrial dispute 98
industry 16
inefficiency 36
inequality 7, 13, 18, 19, 34–5, 37,
    116–17, 146–7, 170–72, 182–3
inertia 4
inference 66
inflation 56, 127
infrastructure maintenance 161
injuries 148
innovation 41, 48, 167
instability 126
Instagram 111
instincts 99–100
    basic 99
institutions 14, 43
institutional reform 13
institutionalists 13
institutionalization 98
insurance 26, 162
interdisciplinary research 13, 27
interest rate 18
Internal Revenue Service 3
internalization 4, 6, 58, 81, 96–9, 120
internalization of discrimination 37
Internet 63, 91, 95
intersubjectivity 132–3
Interventions
    across-the-board 146
intimacy 99
investment funds 155
investors 6
ironism 140–41
ironist culture 141
irony 141

jacket 151
Jameson, Fredric 8, 113, 117–19
Japan 95
jeans 151
Job search 162
jobs 18
    blue-collar 18, 101
Joneses 4, 6, 13, 73, 97, 111
journalist 89

journals 95
joy 85
judgement 4, 64
    discriminatory 111
    self-reference 78

Kahneman, Daniel 9
Keynes, Maynard 6, 26, 29,
    159
Keynesians 7
    Post Keynesians 7, 8, 13
Kidman, Nicole 75
kings 135
Kristeva, Julia 117

labour theory of value 20
laissez-faire 130, 157–8, 162
lake 61
late capitalism 27, 117–18, 121
    see also late market economy
latecomers 41, 92, 147
law 153
lawyer 17, 20
lay theory 72
Le Monde 95
leader 98
leadership 11, 40, 180
    moral 11, 167–8
learning 37
legitimacy 34
leisure 24, 61, 63, 79, 84
leisure time 47
liberals 156
libertarian paternalism 173
life 48, 134, 148, 151
    economization of 112
    expressive 92
    good 134
    length of 148
    material 48
    simple 151
lifestyle 62, 89
    artistic 51
    contemporary 52
    ethnic 46
    feel-good 167
    individual 113–14

materialistic 46, 170
  positional 38, 99–100, 110, 150
litigation 153
lobbying 129
localism 112
locality 89
locomotive 104
London 70, 88, 91
loss 3, 84
loss aversion 73, 173
lottery 20, 23
love 83
Lowe, Adolf 9
lure 146
luxury 40, 101
Lyotard, Jean-François 8, 117–18, 120

Macy's 91
magazines 4
management 20
management consulting 21
Mandell, Ernest 27
manufacturing 18, 99
mapping 164
marginalism 93–4
market economy 121–2, 132
  fragility 131
  late 120
market fair 88
market position 34
marketing 24, 32, 89
  specialists 21
  studies 42
markets 12,15, 26, 54, 109
  capital 54, 157
  credit 54
  cultural 32, 109
  financial 26, 54
  investment 26
  labour 12, 99
  mass 15
marriage 83
  adviser 89
married 20
Marx, Karl 9, 33, 126
Marxism 12, 27, 91, 120
Marxist culture theory 118

Marxist social theory 121
Maslow, Abraham 8
mate 99
MBA 16
meaning 32
media 12, 13, 20, 42, 100–104, 118,
  121, 150, 170, 178, 182
Mediterranean countries 180
megalothymia 134–5
memory 63
mentoring 179
Mercedes SLK 59
merchant 16
merit 35
meta-narrative 52
meta-preferences 9, 10, 110, 123
middle class 1–3, 13, 18–21, 35, 46, 51,
  89, 97, 115, 125, 143–5, 151, 161
  decline of 20
mid-twenties 89
Milan 113, 114
mimetics 107
misallocation 61
misery 134
mistakes 145
mobility upward 116
model 4E, 181
modernism 91
modernity 52
Modigliani–Miller theorem 54
money 7
mono-utility 81
morality 66, 81, 89
motivation 31
  intrinsic 23
motorist 146
movies 4,51
MTV 90
murder rates 96
museum 88
music 16, 51
myth 97, 99
mythology 6

narratives 52
  radical 98
nationality 46

need 29
negligence 26
neighbourhood 5
    poor 178
neighbours 5, 6, 39, 61
neoclassical economics 84, 80, 128, 156
neoliberal growth model 18, 127
network 17, 94
    social 24
networking 70
net-worth 157–8
neural system 109
neuro-economics 85
neuroscience 60
New York 96
New York Times 95
newcomer 154
news programme 100
news story 98
niche 51
Nietzsche, Friedrich 135, 136, 137, 141,
        143
    miserable man 135
    modern man 135
    last men 137
    wise men 137
nihilism 135
nominalism 141
norms 167
    social 12, 167
nostalgia 87–8
novelty 62, 68, 98
nudge 164–6, 173
nudity 108
nutrition 25

obligations 7
occasion 24
    special 24–5
occupational choices 7, 146, 174, 185
odds 73
OECD 148
old money 152
Opel 32
opportunism 167
opportunity 88
opposition ideological 113

optimality 23
organization 19
orthodox economics 14, 163
output 91
overconfidence 23, 79
overconsumption 1
overcrowding 159
overexposure 68, 95
    effect 69
ownership 54

paradox of power 127
paralegals 22
Pareto optimality 150
Paris 91, 114
parliament 53
path-dependency 16
payoffs 40–41
pepsico 32
performance 15
performance absolute 2–3, 15, 44
performance relative 15, 16, 44, 156
performer, footloose 88
persistent inequality theory 116
persuasion 62
    central and peripheral routes 69
persuasive argument theory
Pesendorfer, Wolfgang 10
photographs 94
planners 21, 81
Plato 134
pleasure 33, 84
pluralism 9, 11
poets 140
polarization 13, 20, 76
polarization shifts 76
policies 10, 56, 173–85
    cultural 167–8
    horizontal 156, 166
    neoliberal 143, 170
    principles-based 181
    public 13, 160
    redistributive 38, 146, 166,
        173–81,185
    social 13
policy signalling 154, 164–5, 182
political commitment 139, 180

political debate 156–7
political dispute 154
political economy 9
political economy of culture change 27
political economy of post-modern
  culture 112–13
political economy of status 11
political leaders 167
politician 108, 134
politics 53
pollution 146
poor 36, 38, 131, 161
Porsche Cayenne 60
portfolio 158
poses 10, 89
position, relative 62, 65, 67, 78
positional benefits 144–5
positional costs 145–6, 173–4
positional markets 144–5, 164, 168–9
Positionality 5, 15, 43, 59, 72
  top 72
positivism 137
possessions 127
post-modern society 107–8
post-modernism 8, 91, 120
post-modernist condition 121
poverty 131
power 35, 53, 127–8
pragmatism 8, 137–40
  American 137
prejudice 167
premium 19, 27
  economic 124
  gentrification 116
  liquidity 27
  for novelty 92
Presley, Elvis 102
prestige 59–60, 67
prices 37
  demand 28
pride 135
primary process 91
priniciples-based approach, 181
privilege, social 35
probability 28, 63
proclivities 111
product 40
  cultural 113

recall 40
production, cultural 12
programme 161–2
  cultural 33
  public 161–2, 179–81
progressive consumption tax, 153–62
  see also taxation
progressives 162
proletariat 136
promiscuity 87
prospect theory 63
prosperity 22
Protestantism 133
prototype 102
proximity 5
psychological evidence 78
psychological motives 44
psychological research 27
psychologists 89
psychology 26, 40, 58, 74, 83, 124, 140
  social 40, 74
pub 153
public choice 82, 164
public economics 157
public relations 21, 89

racism 114
radicals 162
radio 108
ranking, narrow 40
rationality 84
  bounded 13
  hypothesis 62
  rational choice 61, 111
rationalization 26
Reagan, Ronald 127
reality 87, 91
  distortion 95
  shows 99
  virtual 91, 105
recognition 134
redistributive policies 10, 12, 14,
    149–50, 175–9, 183–5
  and cultural factors 177
  and endogernous preference
    formation 177–9

and internalization 77
referencc group theory 78, 115
references 83, 85, 110
  benchmarks 109
  frame of 96, 107
  permanent 124
  social 108
reflexiveness 26, 119
Reformation 133
reformism 137
regret 70
regulation 13, 64, 152–4, 164
relations social 12
relationships 115
relative deprivation theory 78
relative position competition 14,
    109–10, 123, 147, 170
relativism 140–41
religion 75
repertoire 33
representations 93–4
reputation 17
resentment 78, 80, 127, 136
resistance 129, 136
restaurant 70, 94
retirement 31
returns to scale 13
revolution 19
  sexual 19
rewards 13, 17, 24, 59
  emotional 167
  financial 17
  intrinsic 24, 84
  monetary 13, 17, 19, 59
  personal 35
  psychological 59
  tangible 24
Ricardo, David 126
rich 17, 36, 37
  new 20, 12, 112
Rihanna 97
risk 25–6, 185
risk-averse 71
risk-neutral 71
risk shifts 71–2
risk-taker 71
risk-taking 25
role model projection 99

Rome 146
Rosen, Sherwin 3, 7, 10, 15
Rousevelt, Franklin 131
routine 87, 109
rules 13
rules of thumb 64

safety 148
salaries 17–19
savings 3, 55
Scandinavian countries 152
scarcity 34
scepticism 132
schemes classificatory 92, 112
schizophrenia 120
Schmidt, Eric 151
schools, business 35
Schumpeter, Joseph 9
science 52–3
scripts 94
Seattle 130
security 27, 65
seduction 97, 99
segmentation social 21–2, 99
Seinfield, Jerry 21
self 66
self-actualization 72
self-confidence 30–31, 51, 68, 79
self-consciousness 119
self-control 74
self-deception 68, 103
self-determination 119
self-esteem 14, 30–31, 51, 65, 102, 127,
    134
self-evaluation 105
self-governance 145
self-gratification 31
self-handicapping 79
self-image 68
self-interest 167
self-other 102
self-projection 99
self-protection 102
self-reference 109
self-respect 134
self-space 63
self-worth 4, 27, 58, 65–6, 86, 135–6

semiology 114–20
Sen, Amartya 9
sensationalism 106–8
services 17, 49
  cultural 107
  public 81
  symbolic 89
sexiness 98
sexism 114
sex scandals 108
sexual conquest 133
sexuality 88, 99
shopping 47
shopping mall 111
short termism 13
sightseeing 94
signifiers 120
signs 75, 85, 91, 95, 114, 117–18, 119,
    154
  domination 117
  post-modern 122
  saturation 121
similarity 9, 102
Simon, Herbert 9
simplicity movement 151
simplifiers 51
simulations 88, 91, 118
singers 20
skills enhancement 20
snob strategy 79
snobs 41
social ascription system 180
social awareness 179
social choice 164–5
social choice planning 166
social comparison theory 77
social democracy 12
social democracy institutions 129, 136,
    138
social engineering 53, 139–40
social forces 80
social greetings 128
socialization 73
social marketing 166, 181
social media 100
social sciences 3, 10
social standing 37
social tensions 152

social tranquillity 130
social waste 150, 185
Society 18, 53, 91
  civic 18
  consumer 91–2
  feel-good 108
  industrial 50
  multi-cultural 53
  post-industrial 20
  rich 70
  self-gratified 130
  values 74
Society of the Spectacle 103–4
sociology, economic 124
Socrates 134
Soviet 12
Spain 114, 180
Spears, Britney 77
spectacle 100, 105
spectator 53, 91
spenders 65
spending 73
spiritedness 134
Springsteen, Bruce 151
St. Lucia 88
standardization 122
Stanford 16
status 2, 4, 9, 58–9, 145, 154, 182–3
  differentiation 67
  game 67, 79
  goods 2, 9, 58–9
  image 60
  local 39
  markets 2, 4, 36, 145
  seekers 23
  services 58–9
  signalling 25, 37, 41, 95, 114, 154
  social 24, 38–9, 48, 147
  socio-economic 65
stereotypes 75–6, 86, 100
  classification of 75
stereotypes, sexual 102
stock exchange 26
stock options 56
stores 88
  department 91
strategic process 42
stratification 31, 39, 116

stress 26, 73
strolling 94
structuration theory 173
sub-culture 97
subjectivity 75, 132–3
substitutes, imperfect 22
suburbs 88, 94
superiority 136
superiority complex 132
superiority, positional 59
superrich 1
superstar markets 3, 4, 13, 15–16, 18,
    21, 22–3, 159, 174–5
superstars 2, 6, 9, 15, 85, 101, 145
    endorsements 28
    hypothesis 15, 19
    lifestyles 39
    and media 39
superstructure 91
supply 9, 16
SUVs 1
Sweden 157
swimming 61
symbolism 8, 113–15
symbols 77
    saturation of 122

tactics 91
talent 16
talk shows 75
tartiness 97
tastes 4, 50
taxation 11, 13, 37, 129, 155
    and political debate 156–8
    Progressive consumption tax 153,
        155–62, 163, 175, 185
tax deductions 155
tax luxury 155
tax rates 38
teachers 22
Teatro alla Scala 113
technological change 18
technological progress 14, 18, 43, 48
technology 6, 9, 13, 95
    information 47, 48, 50, 95
television 20, 33–4, 95–100
    advertisements 110

channels 32
culture 74–5
messages 100
programmes 35, 74, 100
shows 20, 107
sitcoms 96–7
soap-operas 96–7, 98–9
world 103–4
territorial control 86
territory 78, 86
Thatcher, Margaret 127
Theory of the Leisure Class 126
therapists 22
Third world 131
thrill 99
thymos 133–4
thymotic anger 134
Thymotic morality 132–3
time-inconsistency 79
tolerance 53
tourism 94–5
tourist places 94
tournament 1, 15, 16, 20
township 21
traders 17
traditional wisdom 128
transaction costs 83
transfers, rent 19
travel 73, 94
    exotic trips 59
    time 149
trends 45
    cultural 121
    social 56
t-shirts 115
twentieth-century 89
Twitter 111

UK 153
ultimatum bargaining game 72
uncertainty 17, 25, 43, 99, 168–9
uncertainty and state of confidence 25
uncertainty strong 169
underclass 22
underprivileged 3, 13, 80, 129, 147
unemployment 18, 132, 142, 162, 183
unions 18

labour 49, 98
United Nations 170
universal truths 138
urbanism 88
USA 18, 95, 96, 128, 129, 151, 156, 175
utility 36, 44, 149
utopia 91
utopian pragmatism 54, 142
utopian politics 136

vacuum 104
value 31, 81, 92
  exchange 4, 33
  human 95
  second-order 43
  social 98
  use 32
VAT 155
Veblen, Thornstein 2, 7, 12, 13, 126
Versace 60
video 94, 108
Vietnam 88
viewers 107
villain 97
violence 109
visibility 2, 12, 39–40, 43, 61–3
  and media 4, 6
vision 139
vitality 73
vocabulary 141
voice 112

Wall Street 70
warrior 134
watch 60

wealth 17, 24
  and real estate 19
wealth effects 19
Weber, Max 9
wedding 24
weight of argument 26
welfare 161
well-being 71
will for power 135
wine 33, 115
women 75
work 46–47
  blue collar 46
  Taylorized 46
workers 21–2
  blue-collar 21
  education 22
  human services 22
  knowledge 21
  manual 21
work ethic 109
workforce 18
working hours 148
world 104, 119–20
  aesthetic 120
  hyperreal 111
  simulational 91, 119, 120
  social 104
World War II 91
worthiness
writers 89

young people 77
Young and Restless 98
YouTube 95